Teenage Wasteland

About the Author

Donna Gaines is a journalist and sociologist. After spending most of her high school years playing pinball and hanging around candy stores, she earned a master's degree in social work and a Ph.D. in sociology. She is a New York State certified social worker, and has worked on a suicide hot line, as a parent advocate, and with teenagers on the streets of suburbia. In addition to writing for magazines like *Rolling Stone*, *SPIN*, and *The Village Voice*, Gaines contributes to scholarly collections, conferences, and underground 'zines. She teaches sociology at Barnard College of Columbia University and lives in New York City.

Teenage Wasteland

Suburbia's Dead End Kids

With a new Afterword

Donna Gaines

The University of Chicago Press
Chicago and London

The University of Chicago Press, Chicago 60637
The University of Chicago Press, Ltd., London
Copyright © 1990, 1991 by Donna Gaines
Afterword © 1998 by Donna Gaines
All rights reserved. Originally published 1991 by Pantheon Books.
An earlier version appeared in 1990 as a doctoral dissertation at
State University of New York, Stony Brook.
University of Chicago Press Edition 1998
Printed in the United States of America
03 02 01 00   6 5 4
ISBN: 0-226-27872-7

Library of Congress Cataloging-in-Publication Data

Gaines, Donna, date.
    Teenage wasteland : suburbia's dead end kids : with a new
afterword / Donna Gaines. — University of Chicago Press ed.
        p.   cm.
    Originally presented as the author's thesis (Ph.D.)—State
University of New York at Stony Brook, 1990.
    Originally published: New York : Pantheon Books, c1991.
    ISBN 0-226-27872-7 (alk. paper)
    1. Teenagers—New Jersey—Bergenfield—Case studies.   2. Suburban
life—New Jersey—Bergenfield—Case studies.   3. Teenagers—New Jersey—
Bergenfield—Social life and customs—Case studies.
4. Alienation (Social psychology)—New Jersey—Bergenfield—Case
studies.   5. Teenagers—Suicidal behavior—New Jersey—Bergenfield—
Case studies.   I. Title.
HQ796.G25   1998
305.235′09749′21—dc21   97-43544
                                                            CIP

♾ The paper used in this publication meets the minimum requirements of the American National Standard for Information Sciences—Permanence of Paper for Printed Library Materials, ANSI Z39.48-1992.

Contents

This book is dedicated to the memory of my parents,
Betty, Herbie, and Artie.

And to every kid who died in teenage wasteland.

Acknowledgments

Lou Reed once said, "Between thought and expression lies a lifetime." To Ellen Willis, my dear friend and former editor at *The Village Voice*, thanks for showing me how to get there a little sooner.

I am indebted to all the people who sent me material, or otherwise supported and enhanced this work: John Atwood, Steve Bonge, Peter Breggin, Paul Cangialosi, Iain Chambers, Lynn Chancer, Robert Christgau, Lee Clarke, Bob Cloud, Carole DeSanti, Liegia DiFazio, Bill DiFazio, Paul DiMaggio, Chuck Eddy, Barbara Ehrenreich, Deborah Frost, Andrew Goldberg, Lyle Hallowell, Andrew Herman, Dave Herndon, Philip Leggiere, Jean Malone, Evelyn McDonnell, Kevin McHale, Mark Melendez, Barbara O'Dair, Diane Pacom, Ann Powers, Jon Rieder, Andrew Ross, Ann Rotchford, John C. Russell, Danny Schecter, Vinny Segarra, Bryan Shaffer, Susan Walker. To my wonderful editors at *Rolling Stone*, *SPIN* and *The Village Voice*, thanks for letting me be myself again and again.

Special thanks to Doug Mitchell and Maggie Hivnor of the University of Chicago Press for their enthusiasm, editorial grace, and guidance.

I am grateful to my teachers: to my esteemed professor Lewis Coser, who dragged me up from the gutters of positivism. To Stanley Aronowitz, David Halle, Dick Howard, Frank Romo, Michael Schwartz, and the late Arthur Liebman. You gave an unbridled sociological imagination form and substance. You supported, defended, and encouraged me at every turn. I can never repay you for your gift—for passing sociology on to me.

It was my parents who taught me that book smarts were useless without street smarts. Murray first came into my life as a stepfather, in 1965, when he married my mother. But I always call him my father because he set a curfew for me, made me go to school, gave me driving lessons, and bailed me out of jail. He empowered me to become independent, to be proud of myself, to say what I think and not back down. For that, I owe him into the next life.

Before she was my mother, Betty Bradley was a singer, a big band vocalist. Halfway into the writing of this book my beautiful mother became ill, and eventually she died. Betty taught me to love words, music, and people. She is gone. I love her and I miss her every day.

Ever-present in their absence, always alive in my heart, are my cherished friends, the late Paul Feldman, Joanne Taxter Liebl, and Jeffrey Klein. Sam Strang, Sara-Ann, Coco, Lila, and the immortal Johnny Thunders, I can't put my arms around your memory.

To the rest of my family and friends, including some people I've already mentioned: my life is sweeter because of you. To the Jalberts, Langs, Slugs, CorpseGrinders, Joey Ramone, Pyrexia, NutJob, Los Gusanos, Sea Monster, Blackfire, the Jones Benally Family, Reckless Fortune, the Goads, Adontis, Teru, Tommy Hot, Skank Rosenblum, FNMOC, Norma Coates, Ms. Gail Lerner, the Charlenes, Linda "Binky" Henley, Mr. Ace, and Anthony James Mixon III: in the words of the Holy Zep, all of my love to you.

All of my love plus my heart & soul belong to The Great Dark Man, my muse, Raymond Jalbert.

To all the people formally interviewed and named in this book— the time you gave me is deeply appreciated. And of course without the help of "the kids," the young people known here only by pseudonyms, this book could not have been written.

Moreover, without them I would have had no passion to write it. You know who you are: you offered hospitality when I was a stranger, patience when I was ignorant, faith when I had lost it. You showed me that goodness is alive and kicking in the U.S.A. To you and to all the other people acknowledged here, I am grateful.

I am grateful too, to my Sociology of Youth students at Barnard College of Columbia University. Thanks for showing me the 1990s.

Walk tall, hang loose, stay free.

Introduction

When I heard about the suicide pact it grabbed me in the solar plexus. I looked at the pictures of the kids and their friends. I read what the reporters said. I was sitting in my garden apartment looking out on Long Island's Jericho Turnpike thinking maybe this is how the world ends, with the last generation bowing out first.

In Bergenfield, New Jersey, on the morning of March 11, 1987, the bodies of four teenagers were discovered inside a 1977 rust-colored Chevrolet Camaro. The car, which belonged to Thomas Olton, was parked in an unused garage in the Foster Village garden apartment complex, behind the Foster Village Shopping Center. Two sisters, Lisa and Cheryl Burress, and their friends, Thomas Rizzo and Thomas Olton, had died of carbon monoxide poisoning.

Lisa was sixteen, Cheryl was seventeen, and the boys were nineteen—they were suburban teens, turnpike kids like the ones in the town I live in. And thinking about them made me remember how it felt being a teenager too. I was horrified that it had come to this. I believed I understood why they did it, although it wasn't a feeling I could have put into words.

You could tell from the newspapers that they were rock and roll kids. The police had found a cassette tape cover of AC/DC's *If You Want Blood, You've Got It* near the bodies. Their friends were described as kids who listened to thrash metal, had shaggy haircuts, wore lots of black and leather. "Dropouts," "druggies," the papers called them. Teenage suburban rockers whose lives revolved around their favorite bands and their friends. Youths who barely got by in school and at home and who did not impress authority figures in any remarkable way. Except as fuck-ups.

My friends, most of whom were born in the 1950s, felt the same way about the kids everyone called "burnouts." On the weekend following the suicides, a friend's band, the Grinders, were playing at My Father's Place, a Long Island club. That night the guys dedicated a song, "The Kids in the Basement," to the four teens from Bergenfield—"This is for the suicide kids." In the weeks following the suicide pact, a number of bands in the tri-state area also dedicated songs to them. Their deaths had hit close to home.

Long Island is a lot like New Jersey. City people make fun of suburbia, but I have lived here for most of my life and I like it. My social life has always revolved around music. The Grinders have played around in various incarnations since the middle 1970s. The guys have good union jobs in shipping, sanitation, and one owns an automotive repair business. As wives and girlfriends, we have jobs in glamour trades, careers in software engineering, and one of us is a guitarist with a band of her own.

We all grew up hanging out, but now, some fifteen years after high school, most of us are involved in our jobs, married, having children, and saving up to buy homes. We still dress with big rock and roll hair and full black leather regalia. For years, we have looked forward to band practice or to seeing shows at downtown New York clubs and on the Island. For a long time after high school, some of us drank, others got high, then went into detox, stayed on methadone maintenance, or joined A.A. programs. Basically, we still consider ourselves rockers.

Sometimes, in the passionate pursuit of pleasure and danger, our friends died in car crashes or from drug overdoses. Only rarely did anyone commit suicide intentionally. We, too, were known as "fucked-up kids."

Like many of my peers, I spent a lot of my early adulthood recovering from a personal history of substance abuse, family trauma, school failure, and arrests. With most of that behind me, I wanted to help "troubled" teenagers. First I was a big sister with junior high school kids in Brooklyn. Then I worked on a suicide-prevention hotline. Eventually I became a New York State certified social worker, employed mainly in child welfare, investigating allegations of abuse and neglect, later organizing self-advocacy groups for parents. I also worked in special adoptions and youth services.

For a while I had an interesting job as a street worker in the nearby community of Levittown. Some of my colleagues also had outlaw "pasts" that helped to prepare them for this work. Our earlier careers as identified outcasts in our families, at school, and in the neighborhoods we grew up in enriched what we now thought of as "social work practice skills."

More like 1950s gang workers than agency-based outreach workers, street workers were to provide "positive role modeling" and concrete services for "alienated youth at risk." We did this exclusively on the kids' turf, and on their terms. We were there as a resource, to help negotiate with police, parents, schools, employers. We were there for the kids—like an older friend to walk them through the wasted years. I think we wanted to make "growing up" easier for them, less painful than it had been for us.

My office was the parking lot of a small shopping center known commonly as a village green. "Therapeutic interventions" took place in cars, in the laundromat, spontaneously—on the streets, as needed. The kids could seek us out for emotional support or quick advice, hit us up for rides, small cash loans, whatever. Sometimes we arranged baseball games, "rap groups," small trips. Since many of the kids' parents had moved out to Long Island hoping to protect their children from urban life, some kids were a little phobic about "the city." So once I took the girls to Little Italy for one of the feasts.

Eventually I got too old to do street work. It's hard on the body, especially during the winter. Besides, the pay isn't very good. Child welfare workers have a heavy burnout rate to begin with, but by the end of the 1970s, many of the more innovative programs were phased out—defunded or devoured by larger, more conventional social service organizations.

By the beginning of the 1980s, like many of my colleagues, I had moved into indirect services: research and program evaluation. I began picking up consulting jobs. Hoping to compete for bigger contracts, I wanted to become computer literate, and to learn advanced statistics. So I went back to school.

I spent the next few years working on a doctorate in sociology, commuting a few days a week from my neighborhood to the State University of New York at Stony Brook, teaching, doing consulting work, and freelancing as a journalist. In my free time I stayed involved with the Grinders, but was now also interested in the West Coast–based hardcore bands like Black Flag, MDC, and Flipper. By 1987, the young people in my life were either my students, my neighbors, or people I met at shows.

A week or two after the suicide pact, *The Village Voice* assigned me to go to Bergenfield. Now this was not a story I would've volunteered for. Usually I write about things I enjoy: computers, guns, pornography, tattoos, rock and roll, cars. I don't like the idea of "research subjects" or getting vulnerable people to trust me with their secrets so I can go back and tell about them. Generally, I prefer leaving people alone.

But one day my editor at the *Voice* called to ask if I wanted to go to Bergenfield. She knew my background—that I knew suburbia, that I could talk to kids. By now I fully embraced the sociologist's ethical commitment to the "rights of the researched," and the social worker's vow of client confidentiality. As far as suicidal teenagers were concerned, I felt that if I couldn't help them, I didn't want to bother them.

But I was really pissed off at what I kept reading. How people in Bergenfield openly referred to the four kids as "troubled losers." Even after they were dead, nobody cut them any slack. "Burnouts," "druggies," "dropouts." Something was wrong. So I took the opportunity.

From the beginning, I believed that the Bergenfield suicides symbolized a tragic defeat for young people. Something was happening in the larger society that was not yet comprehended. Scholars spoke ominously of "the postmodern condition," "societal upheaval," "decay," "anomie." Meanwhile, American kids kept losing ground, showing all the symptoms of societal neglect. Many were left to fend for themselves, often with little success. The news got worse. Teenage suicides continued, and still nobody seemed to be getting the point.

Now, in trying to understand this event, I might have continued working within the established discourse on teenage suicide. I might have carried on the tradition of obscuring the bigger picture, psychologizing the Bergenfield suicide pact, interviewing the parents of the four youths, hounding their friends for the gory details. I might have spent my time probing school records, tracking down their teachers and shrinks for insights, focusing on their personal histories and intimate relationships. I might have searched out the individual motivations behind the words left in the note written and signed by each youth on the brown paper bag found with their bodies on March 11. But I did not.

Because the world has changed for today's kids. We also engaged in activities that adults called self-destructive. But for my generation, "doing it" meant having sex; for them, it means committing suicide.

"Teenage suicide" was a virtually nonexistent category prior to 1960. But between 1950 and 1980 it nearly tripled, and at the time of the Bergenfield suicide pact it was described as the second leading cause of death among America's young people; "accidents" were the first. The actual suicide rate among people aged fifteen to twenty-four—the statistical category for teenage suicide—is estimated to be even higher, underreported because of social stigma. Then there are the murky numbers derived from drug overdoses and car crashes, recorded as accidents. To date, there are more than 5,000 teen suicides annually, accounting for 12 percent of youth mortalities. An estimated 400,000 adolescents attempt suicide each year. While youth suicide rates leveled off by 1980, by mid-decade they began to increase again. Although they remained lower than adult suicide rates, the acceleration at which youth suicide rates increased was alarming. By 1987, we had books and articles detailing "copycat" and "cluster" suicides. Teenage suicide was now described as an epidemic.

Authors, experts, and scholars compiled the lists of kids' names, ages, dates, and possible motives. They generated predictive models: Rural and suburban white kids do it more often. Black kids in America's urban teenage wastelands are more likely to kill each other. Increasingly, alcohol and drugs are involved. In some cases adults have tried to identify the instigating factor as a lyric or a song —Judas Priest, Ozzy Osbourne. Or else a popular film about the subject—the suicide of a celebrity; too much media attention or not enough.

Some kids do it violently: drowning, hanging, slashing, jumping, or crashing. Firearms are still the most popular. Others prefer to go out more peacefully, by gas or drug overdose. Boys do it more than girls, though girls try it more often than boys. And it does not seem to matter if kids are rich or poor.

Throughout the 1980s, teenage suicide clusters appeared across the country—six or seven deaths, sometimes more, in a short period of time in a single community. In the boomtown of Plano, Texas. The fading factory town of Leominster, Massachusetts. At Bryan High School in a white, working-class suburb of Omaha, Nebraska.

A series of domino suicides among Arapaho Indian youths at the Wind River Reservation in Wyoming. Six youth suicides in the county of Westchester, New York, in 1984; five in 1985 and seven in 1986.

Sometimes they were close friends who died together in pacts of two. In other cases, one followed shortly after the other, unable to survive apart. Then there were strangers who died alone, in separate incidents timed closely together.

The Bergenfield suicide pact of March 11 was alternately termed a "multiple-death pact," a "quadruple suicide," or simply a "pact," depending on where you read about it. Some people actually called it a *mass* suicide because the Bergenfield case reminded them of Jonestown, Guyana, in 1978, where over nine hundred followers of Jim Jones poisoned themselves, fearing their community would be destroyed.

As experts speculated over the deaths in Bergenfield, none could recall a teenage suicide pact involving four people dying together; *it was historically unique.*

I wondered, did the "burnouts" see themselves as a community under siege? Like Jim Jones's people, or the 960 Jews at Masada who jumped to their deaths rather than face defeat at the hands of the Romans? Were the "burnouts" of Bergenfield choosing death over surrender? Surrender to what? Were they martyrs? If so, what was their common cause?

Because the suicide pact was a *collective act*, it warrants a social explanation—a portrait of the "burnouts" in Bergenfield as actors within a particular social landscape.

For a long time now, the discourse of teenage suicide has been dominated by atomizing psychological and medical models. And so the larger picture of American youth as members of a distinctive generation with a unique collective biography, emerging at a particular moment in history, has been lost.

The starting-off point for this book, then, is a teenage suicide pact in an "upper-poor" white ethnic suburb in northern New Jersey. But, of course, the story did not begin and will not end in Bergenfield.

Yes, there were specific sociocultural patterns operating in Bergenfield through which a teenage suicide pact became objectively possible. Yes, there were particular conditions which influenced how the town reacted to the event. Yes, there were reasons—that unique constellation of circumstances congealed in the lives of the four youths in the years, weeks, and days prior to March 11—that made suicide seem like their best alternative.

Given the four youths' personal histories, their losses, their failures, their shattered dreams, the motivation to die in this way seems transparent. Yet, after the suicide pact, in towns across the country, on television and in the press, people asked, "Why did they do it?" But I went to Bergenfield with other questions.

This was a suicide pact that involved close friends who were by no accounts obsessed, star-crossed lovers. What would make four people want to die together? Why would they ask, in their collective suicide note, to be waked and buried together? Were they part of a suicide cult?

If not, what was the nature of the *social* bond that tied them so closely? What could be so intimately binding that in the early morning hours of March 11 not one of them could stop, step back from the pact they had made to say, "Wait, I can't do this"? Who were these kids that everybody called "burnouts"?

"Greasers," "hoods," "beats," "freaks," "hippies," "punks." From the 1950s onward, these groups have signified young people's refusal to cooperate. In the social order of the American high school, teens are expected to do what they are told—make the grade, win the prize, play the game. Kids who refuse have always found something else to do. Sometimes it kills them; sometimes it sets them free.

In the eighties, as before, high school kids at the top were the "preps," "jocks," or "brains," depending on the region. In white suburban high schools in towns like Bergenfield, the "burnouts" are often the kids near the bottom—academically, economically, and socially.

To outsiders, they look tough, scruffy, poor, wild. Uninvolved in and unimpressed by convention, they create an alternative world, a retreat, a refuge. Some burnouts are proud; they "wave their freak flags high." They call themselves burnouts to flaunt their break with the existing order, as a form of resistance, a statement of refusal.

But the meaning changes when "burnout" is hurled by an outsider. Then it hurts. It's an insult. Everyone knows you don't call somebody a burnout to their face unless you are looking for a fight. At that point, the word becomes synonymous with "troubled loser," "druggie"—all the things the press and some residents of the town called the four kids who died together in Tommy Olton's Camaro.

How did kids in Bergenfield *become* "burnouts," I wondered. At what point were they identified as outcasts? Was this a labeling process or one of self-selection? What kinds of lives did they have? What resources were available for them? What choices did they have? What ties did these kids have to the world outside Bergenfield? Where did their particular subculture come from? Why in the 1980s, the Reagan years, in white, suburban America?

What were their hopes and fears? What did heavy metal, Satan, suicide, and long hair mean to them? Who were their heroes, their gods? What saved them and what betrayed them in the long, cold night?

And what was this "something evil in the air" that people spoke about? Were the kids in Bergenfield "possessed"? Was the suicide pact an act of cowardice by four "losers," or the final refuge of kids helplessly and hopelessly trapped? How different was Bergenfield from other towns?

Could kids be labeled to death? How much power did these labels have? I wanted to meet other kids in Bergenfield who were identified as "burnouts" to find out what it felt like to carry these labels. I wanted to understand the existential situation they operated in—not simply as hapless losers, helpless victims, or tragic martyrs, but also as *historical actors* determined in their choices, resistant, defiant.

Because the suicide pact in Bergenfield seemed to be a symptom of something larger, a metaphor for something more universal, I moved on from there to other towns. For almost two years I spent my time reading thrash magazines, seeing shows, and hanging out with "burnouts" and "dirtbags" as well as kids who slip through such labels.

Since I had lived in turnpike suburbia for a long time, the lines between my life and "the field" were already fluid. I had always been aware of the kids in my neighborhood. I'd see them where they worked, or catch-as-catch-can on the pike, casual, just shooting the shit. In the beginning the young people I knew informally appeared as friendly fixtures in my environment. I saw them every day in their appointed places and they saw me in mine. They were invisible, a simple, unacknowledged part of everyday life.

But after I started going to Bergenfield I began to examine my existing ties with the young people in my town. I began talking to my neighbor Scott. He was staying with his father across the yard, sleeping in an alcove in the living room. Meanwhile his parents continued a long, horrible divorce. His father traveled a lot, and Scott was always just hanging around. Sometimes his sister came by, and he had a lot of friends. The neighbors complained about the noise and loud parties. Periodically Scott would lose his keys and have to break into the apartment. Who was he?

I found another scene a few miles down the road at a convenience store. This was a totally different clique of kids from another high school. Late at night I'd find the small store full of proud-to-be-dirtbags, friends and lovers of Cliff and Eddie, two metalheads who got through their tedious graveyard shift by blasting Metallica tunes off this huge boom box from midnight to 9:00 A.M.

Then there were my friends' teenage kids, kids I'd watched growing up, and then all the kids I knew from the clubs, from the train, from shows, stores, and the beach.

I started thinking critically about these people, about where I lived and where I came from. At some point in Bergenfield, I had gotten a strong sense of a new and different generation in a very changed world. Even though I had counseled and advocated for teenage clients, taught college students, and had young friends from the hardcore scene, before the Bergenfield suicide pact I hadn't really considered these people as a generation—in a collective, historical sense. Apparently, I wasn't the only one guilty of ignoring them in this way.

While the shelves of university libraries were glutted with sociological and historical works on youth, only a few dated much beyond 1974. American scholars stopped studying American youth in collective terms once all the flurry from Woodstock Nation had died down. In contrast, British social critics were extremely concerned with the collective cultural activities of young people during the 1970s and 1980s. The punk, the skinhead, the "rude boy" and the less exotic working-class "lad" Paul Willis wrote about were understood in broader terms: cultural, socioeconomic, and political.

From the beginning, I decided I didn't want to dwell too much on the negatives. I wanted to understand how alienated kids survived, as well as how they were defeated. How did they maintain their humanity against what I now felt were impossible odds? I wondered. What keeps young people together when the world they are told to trust no longer seems to work? What motivates them to be decent human beings when nobody seems to respect them or take them seriously?

History is always written by those who survive, rarely by those silenced in it. The radical pedagogue Paulo Freire has said about the United States, "This is one of the most alienated of all countries, people know they are exploited and dominated, but they feel incapable of breaking down the dehumanized wall."

The radical educator begins by validating the dominated person's local, intuitive knowledge of the world. Likewise, the therapeutic intervention must reinforce this knowledge, acknowledge it, constitute it as a truth. That means—to borrow my neighbor Scott's words —"calling out the bullshit" when and how you see it coming down.

I wanted to do that for every kid who survived "the decade of greed," and for all the ones who didn't.

Before I went to Bergenfield for the first time, my mother called me up and said, "Please, don't cause any more pain." Given the moral constraints imposed by two humanistically oriented disciplines—social work and sociology—and a deeply religious mother, I have tried to stay righteous, *and* to answer some of the questions the Bergenfield suicide pact has posed.

Where real names of young people appear, it is because they are already known to us as part of the public record, through media accounts. Real names of police, school officials, and other public figures also appear, either from media accounts or because I met them in the course of performing their duties. Celebrities' real names are also used, as is the name of my friend Anthony.

As I promised the kids I met hanging out on the streets of Bergen County and on Long Island, "No names, no pictures." Names such as "Joe," "Eddie," and "Doreen" are fictitious, changed to protect their privacy. To further disguise their true identities, numerous details have been changed: appearance, age, residence, and some elements of personal history. Such information has been either omitted, or switched, or smudged.

In my efforts to ensure the "rights of the researched" and honor the confidence of people who trusted me, I hope I haven't transformed vibrant human lives into bland, homogenized milk. Above all, I hope that I have kept my promise to my mother, and to the real people whose real lives are portrayed here.

The Kids in the Basement

Kids in the Basement

Down in the cellar there's a boy
   who's trying to live his life in private.
But someday he'll have to join the world upstairs
   and he never will survive it.
Eyes glued to the T.V. ears glued to the headphones,
   left to his devices, a stranger in his own home.

And the boy in the basement has given up on everyone
   And the boy in the basement's even given up on the Son
And the boy in the basement picks up his daddy's gun

Her head beneath the pillow,
   she can still hear the screaming.
And she wishes she could wake up to discover
   that she's only been dreaming.
Her underground prison isn't much of a sanctuary.
   And the fear aint gonna go away until she's dead and buried.

And the girl in the basement can't let her feelings show
   And the girl in the basement's got no place else to go.
And the girl in the basement is the saddest girl I know.

Brutalized or brainwashed, no identity and no recognition,
   Threatened, bribed, intimidated or terrorized into submission

Turn them into robots so they won't present a problem.
   When they're not being abused
they're being totally forgotten.

And the kids in the basement will carry on
   the family name.
And the kids in the basement will turn out
   just the same
And the kids in the basement will have more
   kids to blame

—Raymond Jalbert

n most nights they just hung around the Circle at the end of Georgian Court, in the Foster Village garden apartment complex behind the shopping center. They did that for years, partied hard night after night. For a special occasion, they'd head out to the Palisades, to the cliffs overlooking the Hudson River. It was one of the great views. By day the signs here inform you that the cliffs are steep, dangerous. That the park closes after dark. State troopers will be there to back up that claim. But if you come here at night, and you're cool about it, you can have some privacy.

On the night of September 2, 1986, a group of close friends arranged to have a going-away party for a friend who was moving upstate. Lisa Burress's boyfriend, Joe Major, dropped by the house to ask her to drive out to the cliffs with him. They had been seeing each other for about six months. From all reports, Joe was a hero, a guy with personality and substance. People adored Joe Major. He was someone they could talk to, confide in about anything. His friendship was something people cherished. He was a leader, a good person.

Joe was also a little reckless; he was a drinker, and that sometimes worried his parents. School wasn't his thing either. He got in trouble, cut classes, and eventually he just dropped out. But he had gotten his equivalency and he was working in his father's welding business. Joe loved fishing, he was full of life. He was the center of Lisa's world. But that night Lisa's mother and stepfather insisted she stay home. It was her sixteenth birthday and they had other plans for her.

Joe left and headed out to the cliffs with a couple of cases of beer. Everybody was having a good time. Tommy Olton had to miss the party; he was away in an alcohol rehab program at Fair Oaks in Summit.

Something horrible happened on the cliffs that night. Joe Major was joking around, he was high, he walked out on a ledge. He was much too close to the edge. Joe's best friend, Tommy Rizzo, cautioned him to get back. A moment later Joe slipped and fell two hundred feet to his death as Tommy Rizzo looked on. After that, Tommy Rizzo had trouble sleeping at night.

Lisa said she would never enjoy her birthday again because that was the day Joe died. She didn't talk about it much, but she and her sister, Cheryl, kept Joe alive. He was always part of their day. They visited his grave in Paramus regularly, telling friends they were "going to see Joe." They left little presents for him, flowers, notes. Other people left him things too—crosses, fishhooks.

Lisa and Cheryl prayed to Joe. He was included in their prayers to God and to their late father. Dennis Burress was a truck driver who had died of an apparent drug overdose ten years earlier, at the age of twenty-eight. The sisters were six and seven at the time. Now their mother had remarried, and they did not get along with their stepfather at all. There were stresses in the home; the family had "problems." This was well known to friends and clergy.

Cheryl had dropped out of high school but was working on her equivalency. For a while she had a job as a hostess over at Callahan's, next to the Amoco station, across from the Foster Village Shopping Center. Her employers described her as cheerful; she did her job well. Cheryl was the outgoing one, lively, friendly, and full of energy. Lisa was quiet. But both sisters had many friends; they were popular girls, responsible babysitters. The neighbors liked them—especially how the sisters spent their free time teaching the younger girls dancing and cheerleader moves.

In the months after Joe's death, the sisters seemed to be doing okay. Like Tommy Olton and Tommy Rizzo, the sisters were "known" to authorities. They had "histories" of substance abuse. But Cheryl also had dates and plans for the future. She told people she was happy about her life. Lisa kept things inside more. She and her sister were very close; they were best friends, almost never apart. Around three weeks before the suicide pact, Lisa had started seeing Tommy Olton and one of her girlfriends started seeing Tommy Rizzo.

Of the four, Lisa was the only one who hadn't quit, but she wasn't really too involved at Bergenfield High. In fact the day of her suicide pact, she was suspended for lateness. She wasn't all that upset about it, according to her friends. That day, she seemed to be in a pretty good mood. Nothing out of the ordinary. She said she was thinking of quitting anyway.

Tommy Rizzo worked on and off as a roofer for his dad's construction company. Periodically he did landscaping too. He had dropped out of high school in 1985 and had been trying to get into the service, but he wasn't really sure it was what he wanted.

After Joe Major's death, Tommy Rizzo started having nightmares; he changed—he just wasn't himself. At one point he was arrested for drunk driving and entered a rehab program. For a while he dried out, and then he tried getting his life in order. Things started to look up for him.

After Joe's death, Rizzo and Olton became best friends. Tommy Olton was also a Bergenfield High School dropout. He worked as a carpenter, sometimes on jobs with Tommy Rizzo and his dad. They were regular Bergenfield guys who liked to have fun, drive around, and look for girls. And they had a lot of friends, good people they knew they could depend on.

Early in the friendship they tried to support each other in their newfound sobriety. They went to A.A. meetings and worked hard at their jobs. But that didn't last. Eventually, they started drinking again, first separately, then together.

If Tommy Rizzo was sweet, Tommy Olton was rowdy. His parents had divorced when he was young, and he had gone to live with his father in Washington. He didn't get along with his stepmother, so eventually he had returned to Bergenfield to live with his mother.

Tommy Olton's father had committed suicide a few years back. Some people said Tommy was in the house and saw his father blow his brains out with a gun. But that was just a bad rumor. Tommy was in a drug rehab program in Pennsylvania when that happened. He was fourteen.

To people who didn't know him, Tommy Olton seemed seriously burnt. They described him as "wild," or "deeply disturbed." But to his friends he was a great guy, the life of the party. He was lots of fun. They understood he had some problems; they loved him.

His mother described him as a "loved child." But he seemed to have carried a heavy emotional burden. Reports of his death fixation go back several years. His biology teacher described him to reporters as an angry young man, often self-mutilating, "gouging his wrists with laboratory scalpels . . . at times, he seemed so depressed, he'd spend the class period with his head down on his desk. If someone touched him, he seemed to growl like an animal."

The teacher said she was alerted by school officials that Olton had tried to slit his wrists. Tommy had called his girlfriend from a phone booth, and she had called the police. That was in the winter of 1984.

Over the six months that followed the death of Joe Major, the four friends seemed to gravitate closer and closer to each other. Bonded together by their common loss, they kept Joe alive, close by. In death, Joe was deified, the way any lost loved one will be. They turned to each other to fill the void. Some of their friends thought this wasn't such a good thing.

People close to the situation said the two boys talked about suicide on and off for a few weeks before they died. But then other people had the opposite impression. They didn't think there was anything unusual, anything to signal a suicide pact. They were convinced that their friends were happy. But the weekend just before the suicide pact, things did begin to turn.

On March 6, a Friday night, a bunch of people were hanging out at the Rizzo home. At one point, Tommy Olton fell down the stairs and cut his head. His friends called for an ambulance, but when it arrived, Olton wouldn't go. According to a friend, Olton started talking about suicide. The friend told him to stop thinking that way.

Later, the group went over to a friend's apartment to watch a fight on television. They had been drinking for a while when Tommy Olton complained of dizziness. They called an ambulance again. When it arrived Tommy Rizzo tried to ride with his friend, but his request was denied. Angry, Rizzo slammed a door of the ambulance, accidentally injuring an attendant. Police arrested him and charged him with disorderly conduct.

Meanwhile, the ambulance attendants noticed three superficial cuts on Olton's right wrist. He admitted to a member of the Bergenfield Ambulance Corps that he had slashed his wrists earlier, that he had been drinking heavily and that he wanted to kill himself. This was reported to an unidentified nurse at Englewood Hospital, where Olton subsequently refused medical treatment. A friend picked him up at the hospital, and then they went to pick up Tommy Rizzo at the police station.

That weekend, friends rallied around Tommy Olton to offer him their support. But by Sunday, Olton had had a fight with his mother and was staying at the Rizzos' home. Mrs. Rizzo had no idea he was suicidal.

The next day, Cheryl Burress called one of her friends, crying because of a bad fight with her mother. She told him that she had hit her mother and that now she really hated her stepfather—things were worse than ever. She asked if she could stay at his place for the night. Fearful of aggravating her friend's girlfriend, Cheryl left the apartment early the next day. Later on that day, Lisa was suspended from school.

By the evening, the sisters were getting ready to go out. Cheryl broke a date she had, telling her friend she was "going to see Joe." He simply assumed she meant visiting his grave in Paramus. A little later on the sisters called the Rizzo house, inviting Rizzo and Olton to hang out.

Much of that night seems to have been spent just riding around Bergenfield. Around 3:00 A.M. Tommy Olton's Camaro pulled into the Amoco station on Washington Avenue and New Bridge Road, right across from Foster Village. They bought three dollars' worth of gas and tried to pull a ten-foot hose from a car vacuum cleaner at the station. The manager, Terry DeRosa, said no, they couldn't take the hose. He said later that he never asked what it was for. Since they were his friends, he wouldn't have questioned their motives. The four kids didn't push it; they appeared to be in good spirits, so he didn't think anything of it.

They left the gas station and then drove across the street to the Foster Village garden apartment complex, at Liberty Road and Howard Drive. Pulling into the complex, they made their way to a vacated garage, recently appropriated for hanging out. Their bodies were discovered by a tenant at around 6:30 A.M. They had died in garage #74 sometime between 4:00 and 5:30 A.M.

When police found their bodies, Tommy Olton was in the driver's seat. Tommy Rizzo was in the back with Lisa and Cheryl. A pack of razor blades was on the right front floor. A single blade was found in the back, next to Tommy Rizzo. But very little blood was found in the car. In the trunk were a purse and knapsacks filled mostly with clothing.

Autopsies of the four kids revealed alcohol and average street doses of cocaine. Authorities speculated that they were on a downside, coming down around the time they died. And they found razor slash wounds on the wrists of both boys. Fresh wounds covered the scar tissue from the old ones.

Nobody close to them understood why they did it. Their parents couldn't understand it. Tommy Rizzo had just signed up with the Marine Reserve; Cheryl had seemed her usual cheery self. No one could imagine her doing it. Mrs. Olton was also sure her son Thomas had been in a positive frame of mind. She was especially proud of him because he had recently volunteered to help kids in a children's rehab program.

Some friends believed it just happened spontaneously. They probably started talking about Joe and their recent misfortunes. They had gotten high and now they were crashing. Maybe they started talking about how life was just a piece of shit. Maybe they agreed it always had been and always would be. So they just decided fuck it, let's just do it. Let's just *go see Joe.*

On a brown paper bag found next to their bodies, the four kids had tried to explain. In a lengthy suicide note signed by each of them, they criticized their families, and indicated that they felt unloved. They asked to be buried together. This request was denied, and their parents' wishes prevailed. There were three wakes, one for the sisters and one for each of the boys.

The crowds in attendance at their wakes proved that indeed they were loved. Tommy Olton was buried in Paramus, in the same cemetery as Joe Major. At his service, they played Whitney Houston's song "The Greatest Love of All."

Before people could even catch their breath, there was a second suicide pact. A copycat. Exactly one week after the first, same place, same way. This time it was a couple—he was seventeen, she was twenty. They were also described as dropouts and friends of the four youths. Boyfriend and girlfriend, both working in restaurants. Two more burnouts huffing octane in garage #74. Also in a Chevy Camaro.

The girl had handcuffed herself to the steering wheel of her 1978 gray Camaro, hoping to make her rescue more difficult. This was her fourth suicide attempt. Apparently, the door of the garage had been locked following the deaths on March 11, but it had been recently broken. According to people close to them, the couple had been extremely upset over the recent loss of their friends—Tommy Rizzo had been buried the day before.

But the suicide pact of March 18 was aborted. The couple were found by police, dazed by the fumes, but alive. According to reports, the couple were taken to police headquarters, where they signed a statement admitting they had attempted suicide. Then they were signed into the psychiatric unit of Bergen County Hospital by court order.

After the first suicide pact, someone had written "Teenage Wasteland" on the garage door. After the second, the door was removed by order of police. Today garage #74 is a storage shed.

In between the first and second pacts, in an isolated incident not far from Bergenfield, John Staudt, twenty, of Clifton, died in his family's garage of carbon monoxide poisoning. North Jersey was now experiencing what suicide experts call a "cluster effect."

Bergenfield police captain Daniel McNulty told reporters, "Every kid who has suicidal tendencies is coming out of the woodwork." Some of the town's "street" officers were badly shaken by the deaths. According to Bergenfield administrator Louis Goetting, a few police were "pretty emotionally involved dealing with [these individuals] over a long period of time and I've got some cops looking themselves in the eye and saying, 'Is there something I didn't do?' "

The deaths of four teenagers who were beloved by friends but alienated from family, school, and community loomed over the town. After the second suicide pact, people in Bergenfield began having the chilling feeling that maybe it didn't all just start the night Joe Major fell from the cliffs.

Within the previous twelve months, in addition to Joe Major, three other local youths had died suddenly and violently. They were all high school dropouts, three were in trouble with the law, alcohol was involved each time, and suicide had not been conclusively ruled out. Following the suicide pact of March 11, and the "copycat" that followed, experts reexamined the previous deaths.

In August 1986, in a death listed as alcohol-related, Paul Brummer, twenty, was found floating in Cooper's Pond. In May, Brummer had been indicted on an armed-robbery charge.

On June 14, Christopher Curley, twenty-one, died in another alcohol-related episode. He was killed after being hit by a Conrail train on the Dumont border (Dumont is the town adjacent to Bergenfield to the north). According to prosecutor Larry McClure, Curley had been charged, with Steven Kesling, in a theft. Curley's older brother Martin told reporters that Christopher felt he had been "set up" by police. He told Martin they had planted stolen items on him.

Then, on September 27, nineteen-year-old Steve Kesling died under a Conrail train not far from where Curley died, on the tracks just north of Dumont. Kesling had been scheduled to appear in court on the theft charge two days before his death. Kesling's brother Jim told reporters that, before he died, Steve had been trying to get away from Bergenfield, that he did not want to go to jail if he was found guilty. According to McClure, Kesling had discussed suicide with friends prior to his death. Steve Kesling and Chris Curley were best friends.

The four individual deaths in the year prior to the suicide pact of March 11 were also among "burnouts." All eight youths were described as friends or acquaintances—ten including the "copycat" couple in the gray Camaro who survived.

After her son's death, Thomas Rizzo's mother told reporters, "They have a pact going here in Bergenfield, and they are dying one after another." Kids in adjacent towns agreed. Long before Bergenfield, there had been a wave of teenage suicides in north Jersey. In less than one year, by January 1980, in isolated incidents, six West Milford youths had taken their own lives. In 1984, in nearby Passaic County, eight persons between the ages of fifteen and twenty-four had killed themselves. Kids from nearby towns laughed nervously, speculating, "By the year 2000 the entire youth population of New Jersey could wipe itself out!" Nobody really knew what to think.

II

In the days and weeks following the suicide pact of March 11, Bergenfield was trying to get back to normal. First there were the jokes: "Did you hear about the car for sale in Bergenfield? A '77 brown Camaro with four on the floor. Garage kept." Then, copies of a rap sheet hit the street. Lyrics to the Beastie Boys' song "You've Got to Fight for Your Right to Party" were retitled, with the last word of each line underlined for the rapper's convenience. This particular bit of folk art made a number of people very angry. It had circulated all over Bergen County. People giggled, admitted it was sick, and thought it was good enough for radio airplay. I had to swear not to say where I got it. Don't even mention the town. Nobody would give out the name of the kid who wrote it. Supposedly, he had already gotten the shit beat out of him.

People elsewhere speculated about the suicides, clucking their tongues. "There's something wrong with New Jersey. All that radon gas. Too much toxic waste, too many malls." In Bergenfield the adults spoke of "something evil in the air," like this was *The Village of the Damned.*

The high visibility of rock & roll kids in Bergenfield gave adults the impression that there were heavy metal–instigated suicide cults in the town. There was talk of Satan and black magic, because some kids listen to Ozzy Osbourne, Iron Maiden, and Motley Crue. And because of some scary song titles on an AC/DC cassette tape cover found on the floor of the garage where the four kids died.

CHORUS "You Got to Fight for Your Right to Park in Foster Village."

BREATHE IN!!

You go late at night and no where to go
Your friend says lets die and you say lets go

You get two girls to go for the ride
They say okay car-bon-monoxide

CHORUS You ask Terry D. If he got a hose
you beg and you plead but he still says no

So you come back later to get some gas
its only 3 bucks but its your last

CHORUS If you live in Bergenfield and your name is Tom
then breathing in fumes is really on

And if you have a sister that looks like you
then killing yourself is just what to do

CHORUS Then you write yourself a note on a paper bag
then you think again life is such a drag

You drive thru Foster Village there is an empty space
your frien Tom says this must be the place

CHORUS   You seal off all the doors just to finish it <u>off</u>
just sit back relax and try not to <u>cough</u>

They find you in the mornin bout 6:<u>45</u>
ain't that a shame your far from <u>alive</u>

CHORUS   They take out your dead carcous and your stiff as a <u>board</u>
First a few pictures then off to the <u>morgue</u>

Now your on the news channels 9 and <u>11</u>
One place you ain't you know is <u>heaven</u>

They're rollin in their grave they say whats that <u>noise</u>
Aw your just jealous it's the B'field <u>boys.</u>

CHORUS   REPEAT

—Anonymous,
Bergen County, 1987

For a week or two, there were tales of rituals—stories of séances, the burning of dead animals, and the lighting of candles—outside the Foster Village garden apartment complex garage #74. Reports of mysterious bowls of water left nearby. Bits and pieces gathered from collected memory. Fictions, images from religion, folklore. Pop-cultural forms cut and pasted into an explanation outside the garage where four close friends had gassed themselves to death. Outside the garage some people cried; others watched or prayed. Some were laughing. People who hadn't known the victims were shocked, annoyed, angry, frustrated. People who had, felt betrayed. Everybody went on about the "senseless waste."

While the four previous deaths had formally been ruled accidental, the suicide pact on March 11 left no doubts. Their deaths meant that the four kids got to call the last shot. They abandoned the people who were close to them without warning. They threw the ball in someone else's court once and for all.

"Why did they do it?" Nobody had a clue. The four kids never said a word. Friends wondered why they didn't see it coming. Across America, parents figured it was the drugs, kids figured it was the parents, but most people admitted they just didn't know. As people in Bergenfield tried to understand how this most recent suicide pact was possible, blame passed from the kids' allegedly "fucked-up families" to their presumably "authoritarian school," to their ominous pleasure in "heavy metal music," to "the wrong friends," and most predictably, to "drugs." Finally, "the media" were held responsible for the "contagion effect" often associated with teenage suicide. In the best of times, parents are confused by teenage activity. Now they were panicked.

By now, enough towns across America had experienced the unthinkable that leading Bergenfield officials rightly understood that the "problem of hopelessness" among youth was national, not local. Still, nobody had been prepared for the suicide pact, and the contagion effect that it triggered in Bergenfield and elsewhere.

The day after the Bergenfield suicide pact, news had come of a copycat suicide seven hundred miles away, in Alsip, Illinois. Nancy Grannan, nineteen, and Karen Logan, seventeen, were best friends, high school dropouts, both waitresses. The two died of asphyxiation in Grannan's car, inside the garage of the Logans' home, an imitation of the Bergenfield suicide pact. Bergenfield officials feared all the media attention might have set them off. This, the aborted copycat in Bergenfield, and the suicide in Clifton, exacerbated the feeling that it would never end.

Then, the four kids' story was buried with them. The police would not release their suicide note, claiming it was too personal. Bergen County prosecutor Larry McClure believed that releasing the note would be destructive. He feared it would "romanticize" the situation —adults agreed.

Like most young people watching events in Bergenfield unfold, my teenage cousins thought this was the worst insult. Even in death, the parents won out. The dicks wouldn't even let them get their last word in. Denied to the bitter end.

Then, friends of the victims asked to have the American flag at Bergenfield High School flown at half-mast. But their request was turned down. After all, they were told, their friends weren't heroes or anything. Some of the neighbors did lower theirs, and then the town held a community prayer service. Not a memorial, but a gathering together, a healing, a statement of community.

The people of Bergenfield turned to the clergy, to the "mental health people," their mayor, the superintendent of schools, the chief of police—the spiritual and political leaders of the community.

Neighbors comforted each other. What did this mean? What did it say about their town? What had they done wrong? "Why us?" Friends of the deceased reached out to the siblings of the suicides. Parents could not fathom that this had actually happened. Friends cried openly in the streets.

Bergenfield was hard-pressed to come up with answers, to curtail the possibility of *more* copycat attempts, to comfort its residents and to pull itself together. The weekend after the suicide pact was ominous: Friday the 13th *and* a full moon. Because Bergenfield claims the largest Irish American population in Bergen County, the annual St. Patrick's Day parade had been scheduled there. Such a celebration could be uplifting, but there was concern about alcohol consumption. Mayor O'Dowd was anxious to restore normalcy and the sense that life goes on. On the advice of mental health professionals, the town went ahead with the parade. Over 12,000 people showed up.

From the beginning, from the day the four bodies were discovered, television cameras were rolling.

"Are you burnouts?"

"Are you gonna commit suicide?"

Kids threw eggs at the reporters, muzzled the cameras with their hands. They yelled and cursed from the smoke line outside their school. That first day, as the news of their friends' deaths broke, the kids just wanted to be left alone. Bergenfield High School officials had to ban reporters from school property. Students were visibly upset by them, crying.

The kids were tight-lipped and wary of reporters. They warned one another, "Don't tell them anything." When they could, the kids tried to convince the world watching them through the lens, "We're not druggies . . . it's not drug-related." Then they'd beg the reporters to leave. "Can't you see you're hurting people?"

The privacy of a town in mourning versus the public's right to know. A town proud of the many resources it has to offer its youth. A community where eight kids had died, and two more had tried. Privacy to heal and to constitute the truth as it must be told to the rest of the world. Privacy and the need to make peace with the unthinkable.

After a few days, the reporters were driving everybody nuts, badgering kids for details, forcing conclusions from people before they had a chance to sort things out, putting everyone involved on the defensive. But people fought back, tried to protect themselves. There was boasting, and tales of local heroism—retaliatory gestures against the media. One rumor had Tommy Rizzo's father waving a baseball bat at reporters. Nobody confirmed that this actually happened, but nobody blamed him either. They figured it was his right to defend his family's honor and the memory of his son against outsiders.

People were also confused. They wanted to mourn but also to avoid giving it too much attention, glorifying suicide. They wanted to talk about it but feared setting off more incidents. They wanted to figure out what had happened but resented how "everything had gotten blown out of proportion" by the news reporters.

But Bergenfield was not the first or last "typical American town" to suffer a media assault in the aftermath of a collective tragedy, to complain that a local event had been "blown out of proportion," that reality had been warped by the leering and gaping of the electronic eye. News reporters, particularly television crews, had surfaced as malevolent intruders in communities across America wherever teenage suicides had occurred.

At first, such towns were on the defensive; after a while they got media wise, learned how to appropriate the technology for their own purposes. The "truth" would be told on their terms or not at all. After a while the school simply refused to talk to anyone. The kids became street-side performance artists; parents and loved ones prepared themselves, becoming practiced at regulating the flow of information.

Then they began laying blame. Under attack, close friends of the victims tried to defend themselves against the more bizarre rumors. They denied repeatedly that they were part of a cult. "We watch each other's backs." "We are like a second family." They described their clique: "We're not a pack like they say. We're just a bunch of guys who love each other."

But parents and officials saw things differently. For them, this bond was disturbing. School superintendent John Habeeb said, "That kind of support system often has a destructive agenda." Tommy Rizzo's mother said she was touched by the loyalty her son's friends showed to her younger son and to the younger brother of Tommy Olton. They offered to spend time with the kids, to play with them, to help them mourn. But Mrs. Rizzo also confided that at one point, she and her husband had considered moving out of Bergenfield to separate Thomas Jr. from his friends.

The school also came under attack. The day after the suicide pact, an estimated four hundred Bergenfield residents packed into the high school auditorium to express their anger at the school for its "lack of compassion in dealing with troubled students." Marian Henderson, a youth counselor from Parsippany, charged that Bergenfield High School's students have a "sense of hopelessness and powerlessness" which she attributed to an "oppressive disciplinary policy that includes no warnings or second chances." Students applauded, and when John Habeeb tried to interrupt her, a man from the audience shouted him down. "Baloney. Let her speak."

Superintendent Habeeb was "visibly shaken by the allegations," and defended the school's suspension policy as "extremely fair." He denied that Bergenfield High School "encourages" students to drop out. "That certainly is not our policy." And he cited the 1.9 percent dropout rate. The school reported an enrollment of 1,150, so that's approximately 22 kids in a town of about 25,000. That's comparable to the dropout ratio in Bergen County. It's not that bad.

But parental anger persisted. One Bergenfield father railed, "I don't see us working to keep them [troubled students] in school . . . I find it reprehensible that this has happened. A look at your suspension policy might be in order." The day after the suicide pact, Bergenfield High School students told reporters that they were still being suspended and "encouraged to drop out."

Yet the school refused to discuss its expulsion policy. Instead, officials stood behind the "terse" six-paragraph statement they had issued essentially defending the school's services, claiming, "The needs of the student body [were] identified and addressed by Bergenfield faculty and staff."

Parents and kids complained that school authorities had been slow to respond to widespread drug use and alcoholism; they had hired the drug counselor only one week before the suicide pact. The school, in turn, charged that parents were dumping their child-rearing responsibilities on educators.

Around the time of the big meeting at the school, a few Bergenfield High School dropouts spoke to reporters. They likened life at Bergenfield High School to prison. There were charges that "the school is all too eager to push out troubled kids for minor infractions." One eighteen-year-old dropout told reporters, "I was a problem so they asked me to leave. I felt worthless."

After the meeting at the school, there was a flurry of activity. To some, the activity seemed exemplary. To others, it was people just trying to cover their asses. Bergenfield officials seemed intent upon normalizing as quickly as possible. All sorts of mental health support services were installed, energized, or trotted out.

There had been a break in the order of things in Bergenfield. And for a day or two competing truths had come to the surface. But the old patterns fell back into place early on. "Mainstream" kids evinced a desire to remain separate from the kids they called "the burnouts." It emerged soon after the suicide pact, and was articulated anytime representative "Bergenfield youth" were given an opportunity to speak publicly.

WOR-TV is a New Jersey television station that features would-be teen messiah David Toma. Toma is the cop on whom the series *Baretta* was based. On his show, Toma sincerely tries to "reach out" to teens. He spends the rest of his time traveling around the country talking to youth in their schools. He combines 1960s rap-group empathy with tough-guy encounter sessions. But more often he talks at kids, rather than to them. And he's at his worst with "burnouts"; he's hysterical about drugs. He's an ex-junkie or something. You know the type—"I've been there, I know!" And he hates heavy metal. He seems to think all metalheads talk to Satan.

On March 22, eleven days after the suicides, WOR-TV aired "Lean on Me," a three-hour special about teenage suicide. Rock stars, parents of victims, failed suicides, and experts were brought in. It was a tremendous effort. Toward the end, though, one teen from Bergenfield was upset because she thought everyone would think all kids from Bergenfield were "burnouts." Toma reassured her. "You happen to be darn fine kids, and I agree with that. But the shame of it is, is that when it's reported they put a couple of kids in the newspaper who are dropouts or something else, and they ask them questions."

The confrontation between angry Bergenfield parents and the school and the news media's subsequent airing of the town's dirty laundry brought about a vigorous backlash. First, against the "burnouts" for putting the town on the map and for giving the school a bad name. Then the community rallied against the "irresponsibility" of the news reporters.

While the "burnouts" soon disappeared from public view, rival factions from Bergenfield High School got the opportunity to air their opinions in the *Record*, a Bergen County newspaper. On March 29, two weeks after the suicide pact, when all the soul-searching had subsided and the kids were buried, a few clean-cut students representing Bergenfield High School came out on behalf of their school.

Steve, it seems, is angry at the media and its responsibility in spreading the suicide epidemic. He is also practical. "Now more than ever, the community must pull together in passing the school budget and getting Bergenfield High on its feet." But Jennifer is livid. How could the press portray her school "as a prison and as a repressive institution"? She continues, "I am outraged that such a fine school is criticized in this way." She goes on to defend the wonderful programs, opportunities, the "excellent guidance offered by the entire faculty and administration . . . the comfortable, congenial environment."

Vincent notes that it is true the town "has not provided for the so-called undesirables and burnouts." But he thinks it's unfair to "go lynching the school board right away." How can the town help people who "have given up on the town"? How can the school help people who "never gave it a chance to do anything for them"? Vincent acknowledges the town has "flagrantly neglected" the "burnouts" but defends his school and town against recent attacks. He concludes, "Now I know that because I'm labeled a 'jock' and a 'brain,' I will be criticized for writing this. But I speak for a great many people—not all of them jocks and brains—who can't possibly lay the blame for this on a town and school that have done so much for us."

Finally, Jeff focuses on the futility of blame and offers these solutions: a twenty-four-hour hotline, communication, and publicizing services. "Before the joint suicides, no one knew there were any social workers at the school." He suggests permanent support groups and calls for better communication.

Parents openly expressed the fear that people would associate all children from Bergenfield—their children—with *those* kids. College-bound students feared their school would get a bad name. School officials worried about budget cuts, liability, and accountability. Everybody was afraid the town would be marked forever. It was obvious nobody wanted to be identified with what the papers described as "the fringe students at Bergenfield High who self-mockingly call themselves burnouts." Yet officials, experts, parents, and Bergenfield High's top students publicly espoused a new ethic of caring about their alienated youth.

Police chief Willard Burkart described the four members of the suicide pact as "pain-in-the-ass kids." Not really bad kids but obviously "going nowhere fast." According to local authorities they were a minority among the town's young people, "members of an insular teenage subculture known as the 'burnouts' . . . many of whom come from troubled or broken homes, drop out of school, and have trouble holding jobs." News reports portrayed them as teens who "hung out with a scruffily disgruntled group put down as the burnouts, sharing a fondness for punk fashion and heavy metal music."

Reporters covering the story after the suicides noted that Bergenfield's "burnouts" wore leather and looked tough standing around together, though alone, engaged in conversation, they found the youths to be polite, even shy. The youths' identification as "burnouts" would be mentioned repeatedly though never explored in any detail. Yes, "the burnouts" were dropouts from the mainstream, but not all of them were high school dropouts.

The burnouts' bond was cultural—not ethnic, racial, or religious —although it seemed almost as strong. As I would later learn, some kids who were labeled as burnouts were actually good students. Yet by virtue of their friends, their clothing, and their interest in a certain type of music, they could be identified and categorized as burnouts. The unabashedness with which the kids in Bergenfield were identified as belonging to an outcast youth subculture was unique to any reported teenage suicide. But nobody noticed.

III

On the first anniversary of the suicide pact, a number of special follow-up news reports aired on local and national television. We saw many of the same faces—officials, loyal students of Bergenfield

High School, mental health administrators. Over the year the town had gained a certain moral authority—it had survived the suicide pact as well as the media invasion. The community had learned something and had grown. By now, Bergenfield's representatives also knew how to work media.

On WABC's *Nightline*, we would learn of Bergenfield's "new awareness," its comprehensive battery of preventive services. We would see signs advertising "help" posted in store windows all over town, wherever kids might hang around. There was a hot line, and Bergenfield police were getting special training for suicide calls. Bergenfield High School would implement a "peer leadership" program. Parents would get involved at the school. There was an aggressive youth outreach program. The town would take pride in itself as a model for other towns to follow. Officials would seek out federal and state funding so that these programs could continue to help Bergenfield's youth. The town had been successful with its rational responses to a serious social problem. This is how Bergenfield would present itself to the television world.

On a local news program, there was a brief clip of a follow-up visit to Bergenfield High, on the anniversary of the suicide pact. Wholesome and alert students selected to represent the school sat around a table with their principal, Lance Rosza, and reiterated what had become *the* story about the Bergenfield suicide pact. The four kids "had nothing to do with the school." They had "chosen" to drop out. They committed suicide because they had "personal problems."

Police lieutenant Donald Stumpf, who had also served as school board president, admitted that Bergenfield was "weak on dropouts." A juvenile officer, Stumpf noted that once the kids drop out, "they go to never-neverland." Maybe that's where they came from, since the school took every opportunity to point out that it had nothing to do with its students' dropping out. Suddenly the "burnouts" appeared in this state of social dislocation, as if by magic. They had no involvement with the school or the town. By choice they turned their backs on all the available support, concern, and care. They were self-made outcasts, disengaged atoms floating in space somewhere over Bergenfield. There was no discussion of the process, only the product.

In the end, Bergenfield High School would be vindicated by its more devoted students, honored for its "involvement" with potential dropouts and their families. Supposedly, the town's "new awareness" and the preventive services had paid off: a few dropouts had been saved, or at least temporarily reprogrammed. In fact, Bergenfield officials had implemented programs so successfully they were now deemed worthy of replication in communities across America. And finally, everybody agreed Lisa, Cheryl, Tommy Rizzo, and Tommy Olton had committed suicide because they had *personal problems*.

Once the event was understood, explained under the banner of *personal problems*, entire sets of questions could be logically excluded. Yes, the four kids did have personal problems. But maybe there was more to it than that.

Some explanations for "why they did it" were formulated with compassion and sincerity, others were handed down contemptuously, callously. There was no organized conspiracy to keep "the burnouts'" own story silent. But it was kept silent—it was now outside the discourse which framed the event. In a sense, the burnouts' story, their view of things, was evacuated from the social text.

Once we all agreed that the four kids had banded together in a suicide pact because they had *personal problems*, we no longer needed to ask what "the burnouts" were alienating themselves from. Or what role their identification as "burnouts" played in the way they felt about themselves, their families, their school, or their town.

With the suicide pact explained away as the result of *personal problems*, it would be reasonable to believe that aided by Satan, drugs, and rock & roll, four "troubled losers" pulled each other down, deeper and deeper, into an abyss of misery until they finally idled themselves out of it.

If we understood the Bergenfield suicide pact as the result of *personal problems*, we would then have to remove the event from its social context. And once we did that, the story according to "the burnouts" would never be known; it would be buried with the four kids.

There were other reasons why "the burnouts" themselves weren't being heard. First, they had little access to the media. They weren't likely to be on hand when Bergenfield High School authorities needed bright, articulate youth to represent the school or the town to reporters. "Alienated youth" don't hang around teachers or shrinks any longer than they have to.

Second, to the chagrin of their caretakers, "burnouts" aren't particularly "verbal." The basic life-world shared by teenage suburban metalheads is action-oriented: best understood in context, through signs and symbols in motion. It would be hard to convey one's thoughts and feelings to reporters in the succinct lines that make up the news.

In the beginning "the burnouts" did talk to reporters, but things got twisted around—"the papers got the story all fucked up"—and besides, they really hated hearing their friends and their town maligned by strangers. So they clammed right up.

The kids everybody called burnouts understood this: Once you open the door, they've got you. You're playing their language game. Whatever you say can be held against you. At the very least, it changes meaning once it's out of the context created by you and your friends. Better to keep it to yourself. So programs existed in Bergenfield but "the burnouts" didn't dare use them. They may have been outcasts, but they weren't stupid. They knew to avoid trouble.

Kids who realize that they are marginal fear reprisals. Over and over again I was asked not to mention names. And no pictures. As a rule, teenagers love performing for the media. It's a game that lets adults think they understand "kids today," and it's fun. But "the burnouts" were now media wise. They knew better. They wanted complete control or they weren't saying shit.

So by design and by default, nobody really got to hear what "the burnouts" had to say. Like any other alienated youth since the conceptualization of "youth" as a social category, they don't like to talk to adults. About anything. After the suicide pact a few "burnouts" told reporters they were reluctant to confide in school guidance counselors because the counselors might tell their parents and "they'd be punished or even sent to a psychiatric hospital."

The idea of troubled youth doing themselves in was especially disturbing to a town that boasted over thirty active programs for its youth prior to the suicide pact of March 11. Yet Lieutenant Stumpf noted that the Bergenfield kids who most needed the services would not make use of them.

Authorities had acknowledged that the more "alienated" or "high-risk" youth of Bergenfield would not voluntarily involve themselves with the town's services. But the kids weren't talking about what it was that held them back, why they weren't looking to confide in the adults.

In the local papers, experts called in to comment on the tragedy referred to this as "the conspiracy of silence"—the bond of secrecy between teenage friends. While there was some acknowledgment that this reflected kids' terror of "getting in trouble," nobody questioned whether or not this fear might be rational.

Yet it was becoming clear that for Bergenfield's marginally involved youth, the idea of going to see a school guidance counselor or really "opening up" to parents, shrinks, and even clergy was inconceivable. It was apparent that even if they had done nothing wrong, they felt guilty.

On those rare occasions when "burnouts" spoke to reporters, it was obvious that any brush with authority carried the promise of trouble, fear of punishment, of getting snagged for *something*. Enemy lines were drawn. "Burnouts" articulated little confidence that they could be understood by their appointed caretakers, and they assumed that fair treatment was unlikely. Even being able to relate on any level of natural comfort was out of the question.

By now it was also apparent that the "burnouts," as a clique, as carriers of a highly visible "peer-regulated" subculture, posed a threat to the hegemony of parents, teachers, and other mandated "agents of socialization" in Bergenfield. The initial blaming of the suicide victims' friends for whatever had gone wrong did take some of the pressure off the parents and the school. This was predictable —after all, "Where'd you learn that from, your friends?" is a well-traveled technique adults use to challenge and suppress a kid's dissenting view.

While some "burnouts" did complain to reporters about feeling neglected by the town, the school, and their parents, some were just as happy to be left alone. This was a loosely connected network of friends and acquaintances who appeared to live in a world of their own, almost discontinuous from the rest of the town.

Readings of youth, from the *Rebel Without a Cause* 1950s to *The River's Edge* 1980s, have explored the young person's long-standing critique of the adult world: Nobody talks about what is really going on. Especially not parents, and never at school. The "burnouts" seemed to understand that very well. Yet the "insularity" of this group of outcasts frustrated adults everywhere. It annoyed them as much as "explosive inside views" might have titillated them.

These kids were actively guarding their psychic space because the adults controlled everything else. Yet, the experts on the scene continued to urge the "burnouts" to purge. Forget about it. It's no secret, you give them an inch and they'll take a self. Bergenfield's alienated youth population already had a different way of seeing things. How *could* they reach out and speak up? When every day up until the suicide pact, and shortly thereafter, they were encouraged to suppress what *they* perceived to be reality? When living means having to deny what you feel, disassociating yourself to survive, you better stay close to your friends or you could start to believe the bullshit. Yes, the "burnouts" carried the news, they knew the truth. They all understood what that "something evil in the air" was. Alone, it made them crazy. Together, it made them *bad*.

Ave of Dreams

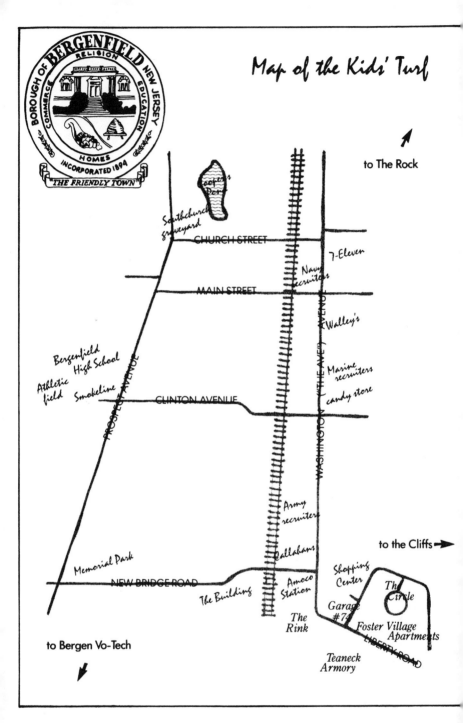

I

The drive from Long Island to Bergenfield moved through the burned-out parts of the Bronx, over the George Washington Bridge, taking me ten miles west into New Jersey. The ride took about an hour, but it went pretty fast with car tapes and fantasies about what might be encountered.

The first time I drove out there, I made a pit stop at a Korean-owned gas station, stepped outside to stretch, and took a whiff that brought me back to reality. Here the smell of nail polish remover from a nearby factory jolts the recent memory of the Palisades, the breathtaking beauty of the cliffs. This is New Jersey, the Garden State of industrial pollution. The reminder of what we've done. But by the time I hit Route 4, I'm in it and this could be anyplace. Redundant gas stations. Gulf, Exxon, Amoco, Exxon again. The Riviera Motel, Shell, a Holiday Inn. I'm two minutes out of Bergenfield.

Bergenfield is an "upper-poor" American town, an anomaly stuck in the midst of scenic, wealthy Bergen county. To get to Bergenfield from Route 4, you turn off into Teaneck. Teaneck is right next to Bergenfield, but with its affluent homes and multicultural face, it's really another America.

Bergenfield and Teaneck. Two different universes, with different social meanings to those who have traveled between them. The contrast between these two towns is most striking at the border. The first thing to hit you as you enter Bergenfield up from Teaneck is the sign announcing the Foster Village Shopping Center. That comes up right after the Teaneck Armory, where John F. Kennedy spoke four days before his election. Now the New Jersey National Guardsmen gather there for monthly meetings. On certain nights these weekend soldiers, reserves in uniform, pour into the shopping center. It gives the place an air of friendly occupation. Soldiers shop in the liquor store, eat at the Chinese restaurant, browse at the card shop.

Outside the pizza place there's a lot of traffic from other neighborhoods. Black families drive up in BMW's, Hondas, and Subarus in fashion sweat suits or business clothes. Asian and Caucasian people shop at the supermarket—Hispanics too, at the deli, and other stores. This is a multiracial enclave that looks a lot like Queens.

According to the 1980 census, Bergenfield is approximately 94 percent white, almost 5 percent Hispanic, and less than 2 percent black. Ask any kid in Bergenfield where the nonwhite people live, they'll tell you, "Foster Village."

The apartments, which go for $300 up to $700 a month, stand at the edge of Teaneck's black middle-class neighborhood on Liberty Road. These sprawling reddish brick two-story garden apartments house a rainbow coalition of families. In the past the 237 units were merely stopovers for transient families—people moving from the Bronx, waiting to buy their house. Maybe they'd stay a year or two.

Now people tend to stay longer. Single parents find that renting an apartment is impossible. Landlords don't like to rent, even if you have a good job. In the last ten years, buying a home in the suburbs —the centerpiece of the American dream—has moved well beyond the reach of many families. So they stay put. Foster Village has lots of young children and teens visibly around.

It is also the only part of Bergenfield that is racially mixed, with whites generally outnumbered. Kids and coloreds. In the newspapers it was described as run-down. It's not.

In the last ten years an Asian community has been growing in Bergenfield, and with it, new Asian-owned small businesses have cropped up—there are two grocery stores that sell Asian, Jamaican, and Indian foods, an Asian-owned gas station, and an Indian-owned card shop. Kerosene is sold all over this town, which resembles rural upstate New York as much as it does other downstate suburbs.

This is truly a family community. In Bergenfield alone there are at least seven churches. St. John the Evangelist Roman Catholic Church and its grade school are up next to the 7-Eleven. The elegant Clinton Avenue Reformed Church is situated in the wealthiest part of town, east on Clinton Avenue, toward Tenafly. From there, the view is splendid. You can see the city lights twinkling through the leaves of tall trees.

Overbuilt commercial horror in some places, lush rural sensuality in others. Bergenfield is architecturally schizophrenic. Alternately homey and harsh, Bergenfield is more homogeneous than adjacent towns: there are very few rich and very few poor in this town.

In some ways, Bergenfield is a 1950s town living in the 1980s. Its stores and homes remain well-kept and ungentrified. No artfully quaint little shops, just the basic stuff, most everything you need with no frills.

Before I started hanging around and talking to people in Bergenfield, I wanted to get a handle on the place. So from a phone booth in Teaneck, I called a friend of mine who once worked as a union organizer all around the state of New Jersey. He knows Jersey. He describes Bergenfield as a "psychotic town." Psychotic, he says, "because its ideology is discontinuous with its social class." Folks in Bergenfield are prole and Republican, he explains, "reactionary . . . too white." Big deal, I am thinking. It sounds like the town I live in. Such contradictions are perfectly normal in the United States.

But my friend says there's something else, a vibe he got when he was there. The spirit of the town. "Dutch Reformed Church all the way . . . fuckin' weird repressed Calvinists . . . tight-assed, really uptight."

It seems my friend once tried to organize a shop in Bergenfield and got run out by the workers. It was the first time he actually feared for his life. "Not the bosses," he explains, "not the management goons, the fucking workers! . . . Ahh, too many churches, too many bars. You know something's gotta be fucked up."

Then he says, "You know, I really wasn't surprised that suicide pact happened in Bergenfield. If kids were gonna commit suicide anywhere in Jersey, it would have been in Bergenfield. That town—they can't deal with those kids at all. C'mon, with the metal and the dope—it's too much. Those kids don't fit in at all . . . if they're arty, or a little bit off, forget it. There's no room for it."

Now I understand what he's saying. Right after the suicide pact I remembered reading about a punky-looking high school student in leathers who told the reporters that in Bergenfield, kids who were different, "just weren't taken very seriously."

Being different was a big problem in the 'burbs to begin with. Besides which, Bergenfield was changing. The population was slowly but definitely becoming more integrated. There would be harmonies, hostilities, antagonisms, adjustments to be made.

In the newspapers Bergenfield had been described as a town "past its prime." Local libraries provided official histories of what the town might have been like in that prime.

Bergenfield was the kind of place people moved to from cramped apartments in the Bronx, away from the relatives. In this town, you got to know your neighbors. Each policeman was appointed by the mayor and the town council after he was recommended by a police committee and passed a civil service exam. They were neighborhood cops. In fact, many were your neighbors, had graduated from your high school. Everything was for the kids. In 1949 the Bergenfield Police Association began sponsoring the Police Athletic League. And by 1957 you'd have a Juvenile Conference Committee to "screen minor juvenile infractions without publicity."

There were seventeen parks, including a duck pond, playgrounds, baseball fields, basketball courts, and a raw spot on Halberg and Spring for Girl and Boy Scout camping. The new high school was built on S. Prospect, off W. Clinton. The first class enrolled in 1959. Wide-open spaces, and room to move, sometimes two to three graduations up the class ladder. Young, white, mobile, and free in postwar America, Bergenfield was full of promise.

Moms could stay home with their kids, take them to Brownie meetings, get active with their school, join the PTA. Dads coached the Little league. All the serene and pleasant activities oriented toward building a future.

Families cultivated their homes and gardens and hoped to become rich enough to join the country club, maybe even rich enough to move to a really big house in Alpine or Ridgewood. That was Bergenfield in its prime.

But the Newark race riots of 1967, and even closer to home, the anarchy on the streets of Englewood, pushed people against the wall. Suddenly the tranquil gardens of their suburbia had been trampled. "They" wanted in. If property values went down, people worried about losing everything. This was America during the 1960s. (This history was not on file for me at the libraries in Teaneck, Bergenfield, and Dumont. These were oral histories, revealed through people I would later encounter.)

By the 1960s there was electricity in the air and Bergenfield's rebel kids got inspired. Tear down the walls, kick out the jams. Remove the shackles of adult authority. Do what you want; whatever happens is right. Bergenfield's rebels were romantic then.

If you grew up in Bergenfield as a third-generation-nation baby boomer, with grandparents from the old country and a mom and dad who moved out of the urban enclaves after the Big One, you had dreams of your own. End of the 1960s and on into the 1970s, if your parents gave you shit and you hated your fucking town, you could just leave and look for America. Head out on the highway, split for the West Coast, find an alternative. You could hop a train or hitch a ride. Townie or college-bound, you still felt born to hit the open road. You were born to be free and wild like Kerouac or Kesey or anybody else. That was your American dream.

To this day, Bergenfield calls itself "The Friendly Town—Religion, Education, Homes, Commerce." Words that fill the circle around a picture of the Municipal Building—the Bergenfield seal. The town's colors are a composite of the best designs submitted in a competition among Bergenfield High School seniors. It was adopted by ordinance in 1957. You see it on the police cars.

There are still many civic-minded neighborhood people who are involved in family-oriented activities—they participate in Little League, parents' associations, read the local paper, *Bear Facts*, support the Arts Council, and boast about the new, modern public library near the high school.

The state Municipal Building is north on Washington Avenue, just up from 7-Eleven. It houses the police department, court, and a workout bench where the cops and the town's younger athletes press iron. There are memorial stones and tributes to local veterans, including those who fell in the Korean War.

For a stranger like me, Bergenfield was in fact a friendly town. People made eye contact, they smiled, they were patient about giving directions. In my town, if strangers smiled we would just look, we would wonder what they were up to. But in Bergenfield it was different.

From north to south, Washington Avenue gets pretty packed with cars, but people still yield right-of-way. It's a good old town, with people whizzing through, tending their property, bent over working on cars. Down-home country moms with neat hair sets and glitzy glamour moms do their shopping, pick up the kids, greet their neighbors, go to work.

The police keep their shotguns nose up to the dash at all times. At first I thought this was fascist, but it is a rural tradition. It's no big deal. Bergenfield police look more like New York State Troopers than the New York City cops or Nassau County police I was accustomed to.

The town is visually intriguing. In the center of the shopping district, Woolworth's has an extraordinary art deco façade. It sells the usual stuff, and also miniature rebel flags and Confederacy bandannas. That's because the manager comes from Alabama and he's a little homesick. But walk out of Woolworth's and turn the corner and there's a wide-open sky and it feels like a sleepy upstate town. Back the other way, this could be Levittown.

A variety of beauty shops cater to the old world and the new. Clothing chain stores like Dress Barn sit next to mom-and-pop specialty shops. The Silver Spoon is a fifties-style coffee shop that would come off trendy if it were situated in SoHo.

On the avenue there are beauty supply stores, auto supply stores, and your pick of car dealerships. A modern video store, and plenty of places to eat: Magic Wok for Chinese takeout, the Tavern Inn, Carvel, the Wagon Wheel. Bergenfield has lots of bars. Singles spots for the newly over-21 set, divy sports-oriented gin joints, workingmen's bars with good hot lunches, and the more sedate cocktail lounges. There are many secular and religious service organizations, and plenty of thrift shops if you happen to be on assignment and think you need a quick costume change.

Like many American towns in recent years, Bergenfield has experienced its share of economic pressure. In one of the wealthiest counties in the nation, the average income in 1984 was $37,236, placing Bergenfield forty-ninth from the top among seventy Bergen County towns. When interviewed by reporters, Bergenfield residents had described their town as "upper-poor" or working-class, even blue-collar. But Bergenfield was not industrial. In the Reagan years, as the rich got richer, home-improvement-sector and related service trades flourished: tree surgeons, electricians, contractors, plumbers, and landscapers found work with wealthy customers in surrounding communities. Many people here did well in those years.

But most adults in Bergenfield are not employed in skilled trades, or as manual laborers. More typically they work in nonprofessional or semiprofessional jobs in offices like the ones that have recently sprung up around Secaucus. Bergenfield is not a bedroom community. While some people do still commute to New York City, more and more, people are able to work in or near the towns they live in. Landscaping and carpentry trades are passed from father to son, brother to brother. Automotive and grooming trades remain very popular among young people. Many people found work at the new malls. Some of the shipping plants closed down, but the fast-food, supermarket, and home-improvement-center employment opportunities replaced them, and people moved on.

From an adult's point of view, Bergenfield appears as a warm, modest, close-knit community of well-kept, compact single-family homes.

Like all towns, Bergenfield has no "real" history. There are several histories running concurrently, overlapping as each generation imposes itself upon the terrain. There are familial ties that have crossed generations, intermediary generations that have wedged their way into this history. There are the histories of the wealthy and the poor, of the leading and marginal families. There is the history of the town according to the adults—the statistical, official history according to the state. Oral traditions—when people came here, where they were from, and pride in where they have ended up. Reasons, excuses, silences cover disappointments. Human dreams. What people hoped to accomplish, their desires.

Then there are secret histories known only to kids who grew up in a town—the young people who have been born here, who have no memory other than through the experiences they have gathered here. Histories gathered in stories handed down through siblings and cousins and young aunts and uncles. Lived histories shared in places coded with secret meanings, on grounds that have been held for so long they are sacred. Legends, tales of famous teenagers, preserved linguistic and spatial and sartorial practices, traditions carried over the decades, impenetrable to the outsider.

Now, from a teenager's point of view, Bergenfield looks especially cool: six pizza places, four record stores, two car washes, two billiard halls, a dozen hair and beauty places; the walls of dark, narrow alleys testifying to immortal true loves and to the greatness of bands, remnants of prior generations that have ruled these streets. There are grand parking lots; most famous is the one in front of Foster Village Shopping Center and then the one behind the 7-Eleven.

Most important, Bergenfield has a 7-Eleven right in town. The convenience stores of America are a focal point of suburban teenage street culture. Among them, 7-Eleven reigns supreme. It's full of rites-of-passage stuff, though one's relationship with 7-Eleven may continue on into early adulthood, where, after a long night of drinking, pleasure is found in a freshly microwaved atomic burger. And don't forget your last beer of the night, or that cool cherry Slurpee on a hot day. 7-Eleven goes one step beyond the normal panorama of teen junk food—beyond White Castle, Micky D's (McDonald's), or Taco Bell, 7-Elevens are so essential to the life that several hardcore and thrash metal bands have honored the chain store in songs.

At five bucks a shot there's always the Rink. For local kids this roller-skating arena provides what bowling alleys once offered adolescents in the early sixties. The Rink is right across from Foster Village Shopping Center.

With approximately 25,700 residents in Bergenfield, there are always plenty of kids hanging around. Washington Avenue, the main commercial street, has two lanes and clocks about two miles if you're driving north from Teaneck to Dumont. The kids call this strip of turf "the Ave" because of its notoriety and centrality among the towns of North Bergen.

Everything ultimately connects to Washington Avenue: Foster Village, the Rink, Memorial Park and the armory to the south, the schools and the stores in the center, 7-Eleven, Cooper's Pond, and the Municipal Building to the north.

Explore the Ave from the Campus Candy Store to 7-Eleven, and you'll find a store to buy leathers, skateboards, makeup, T-shirts, jewelry, posters, patches, magazines: total rock and roll.

Several sporting-goods stores supply everything necessary for jock life—equipment for football, baseball, soccer, bowling, basketball, running, and swimming. Sports are a big squeeze in Bergenfield. On the Ave, in the center of town, a roster of Bergenfield youth who've won presidential fitness awards is on display.

On any day by mid-afternoon, carloads of young people from towns across Bergen County—Demarest, Hackensack, Oradell, Maywood—cruise through and stop to hang. Kids from Bergenfield don't have to leave the Ave to meet new people!

After I had done foot patrol on this strip for two days, I already recognized the cars, the faces, and the police. I'd seen the teal-blue 1967 "mint" Mustang, and the red Mazda pickup truck with the Harley Davidson stickers. And the guy who looked like ZZ Top who worked at the gas station near the 7-Eleven. I found out later that he could do nice customized lettering for a good price.

That particular year the IROC-Z was premier on the Ave. Car regalia in Bergenfield was hip. Most guys had a biker bandanna hanging from the rearview mirror, and maybe an air freshener— Rolling Stones Lips ruled. Also hanging were roach holders with tails or feathers. Ladies had feathers too, along with little stuffed animals, festive bracelets or beads.

Then there were the recruiters who just happened to be stationed strategically around the most obvious "burnout" strongholds. Marines right next to Campus Candy Store—that's across the street from the Roy Brown Middle School, just down the road from the high school. Then, the Navy recruiting station, directly across from the 7-Eleven on S. Washington. But the Army had the best catchment spot on the Ave: right across from the Foster Village Shopping Center.

Towns rise and fall, but Bergenfield was established way back as "kids central." In the secret history of Bergen County's youth populations, affluent Teaneck was arty and intellectual, but lame, too safe. Dumont was nice, respectable, and boring. But Bergenfield was different. It was an exotic town where anything could happen. Bergenfield has long held its prestige among the towns of north Jersey. Half the people I met hanging around Bergenfield didn't even live there. They came to see their friends or were going out with people from Bergenfield. So it was their town too. When you hang around somewhere, you own it. Each corner, every store, all the faces you see are cathected with memories, details only you and your friends share.

Bergenfield High School is at the bottom of Clinton, about a mile down from the Ave. If you walk west on Clinton from the Ave, past the Roy Brown Middle School, you'll cross the railroad tracks, pass the new, modern library, the Sears outlet, a car wash, and find the two-story brick building. The high school is set in a relaxed residential area. On the side of the building, classrooms face a green courtyard. The athletic field, behind the school, is on a dead end, which minimizes traffic noise. There are ample areas for students to congregate.

On a typical school day, parents come to meet with teachers, or to pick up their kid for some special appointment. Younger students wait for the bus. In the front of the school, on S. Prospect, a few Hispanic and Asian kids wait for their friends. Lovers argue, kiss, and stroll arm in arm.

I walk inside the building. It's after school and "the jocks" are gathered around the commons—a group of couches in the center of the building. Two guys carrying gear talk to a guy who must be the coach. This is jock turf—here, and behind the school on the athletic field. The road adjacent to the athletic field is used for drag racing. The races start farther back, usually from the smoke line, a space allocated by the school where students are permitted to smoke. No jocks at the smoke line, though. That's "burnout" turf. Jocks don't smoke.

In 1986, the school's football team was New Jersey's state champion. The athletic prowess of its youth is the pride of Bergenfield. According to Bergenfield police chief Burkart, half the police department is involved with sports. Two officers are football coaches at the high school. The rest are involved in junior football and Little League.

"Burnouts" don't play sports and jocks never hang out. Not on the Ave, at least. It's the "burnouts" who own the streets of Bergenfield. For those inclined toward hanging around, the best thing about living in Bergenfield is that within minutes, you can find your friends. On foot! It is a terrific advantage, offering an urban sense of independence often missing in sprawling suburbs. With typically inadequate public transportation systems, local mobility in the 'burbs is always difficult. But everything is central in Bergenfield. That means you never have to hit your parents up for rides if you want to see your friends. You just *go out*.

But there is a downside. The particular geography of Bergenfield is such that by car or on foot, you always feel highly visible. In fact, you *are* highly visible. And if you've got a mark of any sort, if you're known, you cannot hide from it. Ever. This is a small town. People know who you are. Unless you have a car, plans, and money for gas, you're shipwrecked here, you're under suspicion, under surveillance.

I felt this cloying sensation immediately. At first I dismissed it as my own paranoia—I was an intruder, a spy on assignment. Bergenfield felt weird because of the suicide pact, because I knew *it had happened here.* It was impossible not to think about all the kids who had died in this little town. But it wasn't "the haunts" or even "the vibes."

Bergenfield simply has this horribly oppressive geography that makes it different. Different from my town, different from Levittown, and from the town I grew up in. It is just too fucking close. There is no reprieve, no refrain from the burden of this relentless landscape. With only two lanes for cars, Bergenfield's corridor of teens can get narrow pretty quickly. The town just moves in on you. After a while, it is suffocating you.

II

"Where They Partied They Mourn." After the suicides, the headlines described the turf the kids held in Foster Village, told how they partied in the empty garages. They often gathered around a big bush in the center of the complex. The neighbors complained, but there wasn't much anyone could do. The Circle at the end of Georgian Court is a round mound of grass on a cul-de-sac. Safe for young children to play on. Today, empty beer cans and mangled cigarette packs decorate the grass, but no teenagers. It's the middle of the day in a pleasant American family town.

A few mothers are sitting on their stoops. One of them, with rolls of fat, tits swaddled in a stretch light-blue tank top, blond stringy hair tied back in a ponytail, drinks from a tall plastic orange cup. Sitting there with her neighbors, she keeps her eyes on a four-year-old boy riding a plastic motorbike near the curb. "Billy, get back up here!!!"

I walk back around Howard Drive. A couple in their thirties argue in Spanish outside garage #74. The door to the laundry room is open. Two aging hippies park their truck and head into the back building. Standing back there, behind the building, facing the garage, I wondered what it felt like to be tired and cold, a suburban street kid with no place to go to be left alone in peace, walking into the Foster Village complex hoping maybe something was going on and you could find a place where you felt accepted, where people didn't stare at you and watch your every move, convinced they had your number.

In early March the nights are wet and chilly. I tried to imagine what it felt like, pushed out of the house with no place to go to just sit and be yourself except here. Your haven—an empty garage in a low-budget garden apartment complex behind a fading shopping center.

It occurred to me that Tommy Rizzo, Tommy Olton, and the Burress sisters weren't the only kids who had died on "burnout" turf. So had the other four. Cooper's Pond, the railroad tracks, Foster Village. Eight youths had died on holy terrain, in party places well traveled by prior generations of uncooperative kids. Places they knew as sure bets to find friends, to get away, to have a good time, to be left alone, to think.

Soon, this relationship between free space and the recent teen deaths in Bergenfield became overwhelmingly apparent. Every place people partied, they mourned.

A century ago much of the territory I now explored was called Schraalenburgh. That was before the railroad built a station on the southern half and people had to give their settlement a name. When the railroad came in 1873 there was still no official name, so a railroad official stamped a ticket "Bergen Fields." Over time, the name was changed to Bergenfield.

Before the Civil War, before this railroad brought in the English, Scottish, and Irish, the Dutch immigrants and French Huguenots got their land from the Hackinshacky and Tappen Indians. The Indians traded for guns, blankets, hatchets, barrels of lead, knives. By the time of the Civil War, Bergenfield's industry included a tannery, a sawmill, and a chair factory.

Now preserved as a historical landmark, the red building at Cooper's Pond serves another purpose for the descendants of Dutch farmers, pious Huguenots, and latter-day immigrants. Today an American flag waves prominently in the wind over Cooper's Pond. This is hallowed ground, long appropriated as a burnout sanctuary. By day you can feed the ducks amidst voluptuous trees and relaxing greenery. Night falls and it's a place to sleep for someone with no place else to go. People like to spook around here, playing in the graveyard of the church next door. If you've run away from home, the historic landmark offers shelter from the storm. A kid can stay here for a while and feel safe.

Its legacy as a youth safety zone dates back to the turn of the 1970s when Cooper's Pond was famous as dealer's cove—acid, pot, mescaline. While the jocks were busy listening to southern rock bands and drinking Buds over on the south side of town, at Memorial Park, freaks and greasers could score drugs over at Cooper's Pond. Just outside of New Milford, it was a pretty place, the perfect setting for coming on to your trip.

It was here, in this free space, that almost twenty years later, on August 14, Paul Brummer walked into the pond and drowned. Like so many kids before him, Paul had been partying at Cooper's Pond with his friends.

Then there were the freight trains. Around the time when freaks and greasers rivaled rah-rahs for turf, before the burnouts and the jocks, when the ruling bands were Cream, Blind Faith, the James Gang, and Steppenwolf, Bergenfield youth legends tell of the Railroad Kids. In their Army jackets, engineer caps, and painter's pants they walked on the tracks, hopping the freight trains out of Bergenfield. Before the Conrail trains, the Reading Railroad came through here. The tracks run north to south through Bergenfield. Same side as the high school, same side as the Municipal Building. On the west side of town if you're facing Dumont.

The Railroad Kids were high-spirited rebels. Anarchistic, politically minded, mechanically gifted greaser kids, the Railroad Kids were the next permutation out from Bergenfield's strong postwar car mechanics culture. Prole kids. Their girlfriends didn't hop trains, they spent time speeding around in cars up along Clinton—racing on the drag strip. Antiwar, the girls wore Army jackets also.

The guys were freedom riders who could book school to make more money buying, fixing, and reselling cars. Longhairs. At the school you could spot some of them dealing from "freak hall," where people hung out, sold drugs to Teaneck kids. "Freak hall" is the courtyard right behind the smoke line; in the eighties it was undisputed burnout turf.

The Railroad Kids had a band—the Ballzwick Band, which had a strong cult following. Though they seem to be remembered more for the time they spent hopping trains than for playing music. A white blues band, the Ballzwick Band's insignia was painted all over town, especially around the train tracks. The Railroad Kids would pick up and move out at any time. Ride as far as they could—into Pennsylvania, or maybe they'd go all the way to California. That was years ago.

More recently, the railroad had figured in the lives of Steve Kesling and Chris Curley, the two best friends who died on the Conrail tracks. Hit by trains, Kesling and Curley died just a few months apart, almost to the day, the same way. People said each one just lay down on the tracks and waited for the train to run him over. Some think the guys were just drunk with bad judgment, they died on dares. But others say they were drunk and trying to leave town—suburban outlaws, with dreams of another time and place, hopping freight trains like the Railroad Kids.

For a kid growing up now, in a town like Bergenfield, or a town like mine, the dreams of prior generations are lost. The suburban frontier no longer exists, there is no sure place to move to find a better life. Land is increasingly unavailable, unaffordable, or unusable. Home ownership is becoming unimaginable. The trend of remaining at home into adulthood drags on, making the dream of independent living seem impossible. You feel stuck in your hometown forever, like it or not.

In the 1980s, the great promise of suburbia or the wild urban adventure moved well beyond the grasp of most people. The world out there seems less welcoming than it once was. It has less to offer, and the road is harder. There are fewer free spaces, no buffer zone of affluence, no surplus cushions to fall back upon.

And your family can't help you out; they're just hanging on themselves. Twenty years ago you know that any rebel kid in Bergenfield would have just split, walked, and not looked back. But the harsh street life of today's American teenage runaway is not the glamorous life promised to you in dreams.

But maybe you hate it here so much you will try anything to escape—to an abandoned garage, to the railroad tracks, to Cooper's Pond. Desire now leads you straight to nowhere. You're high but the streets are ugly and cold. The world "out there" is shrinking. The possibilities of suburbia are exhausted, and your capacity to dream has reached a dead end. But nobody cares, nobody gives a shit.

Children of ZOSO

From now on let no one trouble me,
for I bear in my body the marks of the Lord Jesus.

—Galatians 6:17

t's Thursday afternoon. After-school activities are in progress.
A group of about seven teenagers are sitting around a truck in front of the 7-Eleven. Burnouts. I know from the pose, the clothes, the turf. Yep, in another age they'd be hitters or greasers or hippies or heads or freaks. On another coast—they'd be stoners. Archenemies of jocks, dexters, rah-rahs, or socs for all eternity.

Guys with earrings, crucifixes, long hair hanging over a concert shirt or a hooded sweatshirt. Walking in threes with boom boxes blasting AC/DC, Bon Jovi, or Zep. Suburban rocker kids are patriotic—everyone wears denim jackets (a prized commodity among international rocker youth, proof of America's pop-cultural world supremacy). Back panel is painted, a shrine to one's most beloved band: Iron Maiden, Metallica, the Grateful Dead.

Ladies have bi-level haircuts. Long shags blown, sprayed, clipped to one side, teased, sometimes bleached. Grease & glamour. Where Farrah and Madonna meet Twisted Sister. Bergen Mall trendy, but informed by the careful reading of albums and metal magazines. Earrings, junk jewels, eye makeup, leggings or spandex pants. Oversized cotton shirts hang down past a more stylized, unpainted denim jacket. Heavy cotton athletic socks slouch over white or black leather ankle boots or white sneakers.

Street-corner society in suburbia. Hanging around minding your business until you get banished by the cops. Archaeological leavings include empty cans of Bud, bottles of St. Pauli Girl. Slurpee containers, and the remains of other 7-Eleven delicacies: buttered rolls, beef burritos, beef jerky wrappers.

Cave renderings appear on walls, or else they're carved into wood: THE DEAD LIVE, a peace sign, KISS, and lovers' initials united 4-ever. Recently the 7-Eleven contracted for graffiti-proof paint jobs, so stuff on the side wall is now transitory. A guard patrols the parking lot next door, behind the bank, until it closes. This sign is posted in the window of the 7-Eleven.

Troubled?
Need a Direction—Advice or Just Someone to Listen?
call Bergenfield
HELP-LINE 387-4043
Talk To Someone Who Cares
24 Hours A Day

Right now it's a warm spring afternoon. A good day to cop some rays, get an early start on your tan. The guys are in casual repose—the world-historic teen lean on one's own vehicle. Three guys sit up in the crib, another in the cab. Two more at a forty-five-degree angle on another car. A couple is clinging, shadowboxing and making out. At the center of all this is this deep blue Bronco with its big fucking wheels. Huge. The cab is high up from the ground. Tons of shit hanging from the rearview mirror. Stickers on windows and bumper. Music playing very loud. They're talking. All guys except for the couple making out. The girls are huddled closely together a few feet away. I walk up to the guys.

"Excuse me, I'm writing a story about your town." They look at me cold. One guy reminds me of Mr. T, but he's white—turns out his name's Bobby. He's sullen in his gray hooded sweatshirt, jeans, and white high-top sneakers. Earring. Hands deep in pockets of jeans, shoulders up, head down, Bobby pulls out cigarette, sucks it lit, sneers. "Look, they were our friends—we don't want to talk about it, okay?" I start rambling on about having friends who died too young and growing up in a town . . . and halt. Bobby's friend spots my "Ace of Spades" lapel button. "You like Motorhead?"

"Ah, yeah . . . I mean . . . like . . . Lemmy's god . . ." Off guard and completely disoriented, I answer a guy with clumpy layered hair and a Grateful Dead T-shirt. He spots my mini–tape recorder piled with my junk on another car, grabs it, turns it to record. He introduces himself to the condenser mike. "Nicky Trotta from Dumont." His friend, a bigger guy with longer hair and a faded Ozzy T-shirt, snaps, "Don't tell her your name!" But it's too late, Nicky's on with the show.

"Okay, so what's the meaning of Bergenfield?" Three guys sing, "five letters—*p-a-r-t-y* . . . party!" Nicky gives my ring a side glance. A big silver skull. Pulls my hand toward him. Subtle tone, doesn't look up, swallows the first word: "That's cool." Soon after, Joe, the Ozzy fan, introduces himself, we shake hands.

Nicky slaps his girlfriend Doreen on the ass. A few feet away, out by the main road, another girl walks by. She hurries past the store. She is spotted by Doreen. Her friends, Susie and Joan, rush over to her. "You gonna fight her?" Doreen knows that Nicky went with her the other night. She'd like to kill her. Bitch. Nothing happens. This is my first introduction to the girls.

We settle in. I say that I'm not really interested in interrogating them about the suicide pact. I understand they are sick of the reporters. I explain that I wanted to check out the town, to know what it's like to be a "burnout." Nicky understands my purpose at once. Pointing to his friends, he says, "Yeah, well, you got the right ones." No doubt about it; they are "burnouts."

Now, as it turns out, some of Nicky's companions knew Tommy Olton, Tommy Rizzo, and the Burress sisters merely as acquaintances—from school, from having seen them around. Others knew them well, as close friends. One guy had dated Lisa Burress. But everybody had strong opinions about the way the "burnouts" were treated.

At this point Joe takes over as informant, tells me the cops are on everybody's ass. They know his car. He grabs my tape recorder and makes a dedication to the Bergenfield police officers. "Go screw yourselves because you're not getting me again." The cops are all crooks. Totally corrupt. Bust your ass, flirt with the girls. (But then a day or two later, he tells me the cops are really okay as long as you don't fuck with them. Be polite. Don't bust their balls.) Cop watching, skateboards, and car races are the burnouts' idea of sports.

Nicky and Doreen are making out. The Bon Jovi tape plays "Runaway" on the truck's stereo. I check out the system. Impressive! More talk about music. We compare favorite bands. I ask if they like Metallica. Heads bang back and forth and we play air guitar "Batterrreee!" Nicky figures yeah, if I like Motorhead, I'd probably like Metallica. We are now at a regional hardcore–heavy metal–thrasher convention. What goes on next is a rock and roll version of "Paisan . . . landsman . . . you like Anthrax?" You sniff out cultural heritage. Then you talk. This is the centerpiece of suburban street culture. I could be doing this in my own neighborhood. But music subcults are esoteric. You either know or you don't; you can't fake it.

Someone asks, "What about Suicidal Tendencies?" I had just seen them at City Gardens, a club in Trenton. "Unbelievable," I say, then ask if anyone is going to see the Butthole Surfers. They were playing the Ritz in New York City pretty soon. No, but Nicky says he's heard of them.

"Yeah, they're from Texas," I say. "Psychedelic noise band, completely mentally ill . . . Fire marshal always comes down to close their shows . . . happened in Jersey, San Francisco . . ." Bobby is watching, Joe is listening, but the quiet guy, Randy, could care less about this entire rap. And the girls have now gone inside 7-Eleven. Lots of motion. They're after cigarettes and gum.

By now we have established lineage, and favorite bands in common. Okay, I don't care for Bon Jovi and they aren't too motivated by my noise bands. They've never even heard of Test Dept.—that's another world. But we agree about Motorhead and Suicidal Tendencies and that is enough to establish an understanding.

Right at this moment Nicky has something important to ask me. Opening his flannel shirt to expose the T-shirt, he wants to know, what about the Dead? Did I see them? They had played recently. My ring, the skull, is a Grateful Dead icon. But it's an accident. I'm not a Deadhead. I could never lie about something like this. I explain, some guy in a bar gave me the ring.

I ask Nicky about the famous north Jersey Deadhead town I had heard about. Is that the town he comes from. Nicky and all the kids you see at Madison Square Garden who travel in for the shows. You see them hanging around the Path trains around Penn Station dressed in tribal regalia. They're looking for tickets, waiting for friends. New Jersey kids, Long Island kids traveling to Mecca. Yes, Nicky does come from that famous town.

The next thing I know, three kids are showing me razor blade scars on their wrists.

Immediate memory recall is the police report about the razor-slash wounds on the wrists of the two guys who died in the suicide pact. Nicky says, "Every one of us has either tried it or contemplated it." Nicky's scars look old, healed. So do Joe's. But one of the girls has her wrists freshly bandaged. She's much younger than they are. She's just starting out.

Suddenly Joe grabs my arm, there is great excitement. A scar and some red ink on my right wrist. They look at me and smile, making a deeper connection. "No," I explain emphatically, "it's from a jar of mayo I rammed too hard into the trash."

Nicky starts talking about a recent family altercation. "Look, I blame myself. I fucked up, I blew my curfew and my father beat the shit out of me, it was my fault," Nicky understands these things. He knows his father loves him. We all agree, everyone understands about that.

But the other day he beat the shit out of his little sister for smoking. He made her nose bleed. It was a really dumb thing to do, he admits. And he feels bad about it. Last year he was thrown out of school for fighting. He almost killed a kid for bothering his sister. "Attempted manslaughter," he says, looking somber and grim. Now he's in another school.

Joe talks about family life. "My dad pulled me out of bed by my hair this morning, at 5 A.M., and called me a scumbag." Joe's had run-ins with the law. No details, thank you. Won't talk about it. Hates everyone, wants to say fuck it. Everything sucks. "What's the answer?" he asks. Joe takes center stage.

"It's the system," he answers himself. Randy flicks a butt, slouches into the car, smirks, and pumps up the volume.

"I don't know." I hesitate, trying to give Joe some kind of answer. "But if you kill yourself all it proves is that you buy their bullshit . . . I mean the system—it's just other people, most of them are assholes, why give them the edge?"

"I know, but what can you *do* about it?" Joe asks. Doreen and Nicky come up for air, he taps me. "Hey, don't you like us?" He's insulted, I'm ignoring them! "I'm being respectful, you're on a date." He laughs. "A date!" And offers me gum.

I get serious. "You have to fight back." Joe asks me how. I have no answer but I have to answer Joe. "I don't know, but you can. You have to, or they win. *They* get to write history."

This was my moment to explain everything to them, but I couldn't. I couldn't say anything. This is stuff you can never put into words. It's a lack, something you dream of reclaiming when you grow up. You're looking for something, but you don't know what. It is an emptiness, an ache, and it is unspoken. These are the hidden injuries of youth, the scars that don't show. The creepy feelings that will follow you through life. Set up from the start to carry the burdens of your fucked-up family and your stained class, you play a loser's game and then you blame yourself, you're worthless. I wanted to stop them from feeling this way by saying something very real and strong to make them proud of being themselves, rather than ashamed.

I had spent years trying to figure out how to put this into the words that might have made some sense to me when I was a teenager and I felt like this—like Joe and Nicky did now. But I couldn't say anything.

I thought about my friends who didn't make it out alive. Some died: heroin overdoses, car crashes, suicide, Vietnam, murder. Some got locked up, still breathing with the life beaten out of them. Out of the Army and into a psychiatric prison. Out of dope and onto Methadone. Back from the psychic wars by the grace of perpetual Haldol. Bad feelings, bad choices, bad luck, and bad lives. These people were once my friends. Over time, they become my vendettas.

Little Bull, we called him. His brother sang in a rock and roll band that used to play the circuit at South Shore Queens high school dances. Their mother got remarried and there was a stepfather. He used to beat the boys. He was a gorilla. The older brother was athletic; he got along better with the stepfather. But Little Bull just hung out. To outsiders he wasn't anyone special, but he was a central figure on the street. At one point he got busted. They sent him up somewhere for a while. When he came back he was really paranoid, and he was still dealing.

After he got arrested, his girlfriend wasn't allowed to see him. We all hung around the Wavecrest Apartments, doing routines to "The Letter," a song by the Box Tops. "Gimme a ticket for an air-o-plane . . . ," dancing in the parking lot off Beach 20th Street in Far Rockaway. We'd walk around with tissue boxes and small bottles of Carbona cleaning fluid, sticking wet tissues under everybody's nose until the whole parking lot saw the holy buzzwheel.

The last time I saw Little Bull he came to my house. He was sure he was being followed. My mother gave him some coffee. She noticed that he seemed skittish; his eyes darted from side to side. A few days later I heard they found him in an incinerator closet in one of the apartment buildings. The needle was still in his arm. That was over twenty years ago.

So now try to explain it? All the schooling, the theories and facts just make it sound more idiotic, academic, abstract, and patronizing. Yes, I could give them practical advice. A positive attitude is important. Keep a clear mind. Have faith. Get a job. Say no to drugs. Get away from your family and their stupid shit. Leave Bergenfield. Don't take things for granted. Trust your own feelings. Have faith in yourself. Don't judge yourself by rules you didn't make.

But the cops come. We'd better move on. Twenty minutes have passed. We drive a quarter mile north on the Ave to Roy Rogers parking lot. Fine unless the neighbors call the cops. But that only happens at night. Also a great place to take a piss if you're street-bound. The four ladies come into my car. They introduce themselves formally.

Nicole wins out, takes top position. Gets the front seat. That means control of the radio. She's more outgoing than the others. But everyone is nice. Joan and Susie say nothing, Doreen is good-natured and laughs a lot. It's fun having them in my car.

Rule is, the street belongs to the boys. They are more public in orientation—they'll talk to anybody about anything. That's the art of the street hang. Telling stories, throwing the bull, smackin' your gums, blessed with the gift of the gab.

But the girls are a little different. They're insular; they mostly hang out in pairs, rarely more than trios. They won't let you penetrate unless they see you every day, and then it's just friendly and polite. You have to be a best friend to get really close. Their conversations tend to be more local, personal, private. The girls are a subculture within a subculture.

At first the girls seemed impossible to approach, so I didn't. Knowing my way around these matters, I waited for the guys to "approve me" and then the girls became more friendly. They weren't at all hard or cold or posturing like the guys. Even from the first, they were sweet, shy, and lively.

Nicole wants to know what I am writing about. She had a cousin who spoke to the reporters. "He told them not to call us burnouts." But they did anyway. I said, "I thought that was really fucked up." Nicole looks out the window. "Yeah, that really hurt."

Nicole explains that Cheryl and Lisa Burress were her friends, that they were very good people. It really bothered her to hear them talked about by people who didn't even know them. It was disgusting. The things people said—the way everyone just called them burnouts and druggies. Nicole looks out the window and says, "If you knew them, what they were, inside, they were so good—they were the best. How could people say those things?"

Nicole Shea is a petite and pretty sixteen-year-old. She smokes cigarettes. In her school, that's enough to qualify her as a burnout. But she doesn't care, she hates school. All the teachers do is yell. What she loves is clothes. Her mother is divorced; she has seen her father twice in the last year, but she's hoping he'll spring for her first car. Her mom is her size and borrows her clothes. But Nicole hates the way her mother washes them, so she does them herself, just so. She irons her jeans and her shirts are starched, immaculate white. Hairstyle: full bangs, sides brushed forward on her face. Her secret? A curling iron and lots of hairspray. Her makeup is soft except for the eyes, which she loads with electric blue mascara. She's adorable. She looks like Tiffany. She wants to be a nurse.

The ladies switch my radio from K-Rock to Z-100. Doreen likes music for dancing. Joan likes the gorgeous guy bands like Motley Crue and Bon Jovi. Jon Bon Jovi is from Jersey and he's *hot!* What about Bruce? "Ugh!"

Usually, the girls go for the grooming; the guys go for the riffs. Joan cuts hair; her other brother Bobby plays in a band. They save up from part-time jobs to buy guitars, cars, and clothes.

The kids rave on and on about school, the police, the town. Joe is holding court over ten square feet of concrete behind Roy Rogers. We keep watching the road. A blue car drives past with a rebel flag draped across the back window. A red light on the dash. Volunteer firemen.

Back here there's lots of room to simulate karate chops. Joe keeps moving, talking. A pipe stands in for a bayonet. Bomb this fucking town. Playing soldier while Hendrix wanks a chord on a tape I have playing in my car. Someone knows a guy who fought in Grenada. "No dude, not Cubans, fucking Russians, man!"

Twenty minutes into this hang, the police cruise by. "You better move on." Bobby's mother is at work so we can go there.

The apartment is one of several in an old house with popped dormers. We have to be very cool; the neighbors are home. The apartment is cluttered with the many artifacts of lively teenagers living with a single parent who works. Kids have chores. Socks everywhere. The rooms are normal teen messy—piles of unfolded clothes, grooming artifacts, stuffed animals, and a collection of assorted beer cans.

Many religious icons. Pridefully, these things are displayed: school photos, diplomas, and sports trophies. A family lives here—Mom, Bobby, Joan, Doreen, and Timmy. Wall-to-wall pasteups from magazines of cute metal-hair bands and I'm in Joan's room. Revlon skin-care lotion, Jean Naté powder and bath splash, a decorative bottle of Le Jardin by Max Factor, economy-sized cans of extra-hold Final Net hairspray, zillions of combs and hair clips, three sizes of styling brushes, jewelry, shoes, and makeup. There's a boom box and blow dryer in every room.

Back in the living room, where we are sitting, the color TV is on with cartoons. Timmy watches with no sound. This is really burnt, somebody tells him, it's such a gorgeous day outside. He's about twelve or thirteen and this is his bedroom but he's having a good time. The guys are crawling out a window onto the roof. Joan and Susie discuss the mechanics of layered haircuts. Joan decides maybe she really needs a root perm. Doreen is collecting empty cigarette boxes. Has at least fifty on her windowsill. She tries to explain to me why. Her friend is sick. Something complicated having to do with building up credits for the kidney dialysis.

The girls seemed to have several of these community-oriented things going on that periodically command their attention. As I got to know them, I saw that they were often engaged in sororal, social things like distributing invitations for a confirmation party, or sewing a new dress for a close girlfriend, neighborly arts-and-crafts stuff. They were civic-minded, like women in small towns have always been.

Meanwhile, nearby, Nicky is teasing Doreen. "Here, Rover." She walks out in a huff but returns giggling and sits on his lap. I ask to use the bathroom.

When I come out, I sit down, and my host, Bobby, decides it's time to cut the deal. "Look, I let you into my home. If you want, you can hang out with us. We'll show you the town, where we hang out. But no names and don't ask us about the suicides." Some of this secrecy was just drama on Bobby's part, but the kids were obviously uneasy, trying to lie low—stay cool with parents, the school, or court. Their voices were silenced in the discipline of youth. I understood that I was welcome but that I shouldn't push it.

I wanted them to feel comfortable with me, so I never asked them for their last names, or where they lived. It was fine if I just met them around. They had my phone number if they needed me for anything. And when it came time to tell their story, I made up their names from their guitar heroes, or from people in my own life.

We sit there in the living room, eight or nine crowded around, smoking Marlboros. It is a beautiful day outside. We keep the noise down; Bobby supervises the action and watches the clock. He doesn't want any hassle. A girl comes over who has a crush on him. She's goofy-looking. "My sister's friend Toni," he mimics. Then he cuts a full-blown Celtic brood and remains aloof till she leaves. He doesn't have a girlfriend. He's "free." He's had girlfriends, even gone out with older women. But he's avoiding it now. They take advantage.

In a cultural exchange with the youth of Bergenfield I play my noise tape for them. It has Butthole Surfers, Sonic Youth, and a band called Big Black from the Midwest. I advance to my favorite song of the week, "Bad Houses." They hate it—"It's droney." College-radio dirge from the indie labels of America. Nicky tries to be nice, says he likes the drums. Politely the tape is removed and replaced with Hendrix. Then Bon Jovi. Pensive, Bobby taps my arm. He says, "Look, if you just hang out, you'll see everything, you'll understand what's going on."

Randy puts on Joe's black leather jacket. Here among friends jewelry, food, clothes, and cigarettes are shared. A treasured item shows up on someone else a day or two later. For a few days my skull ring, a black leather wristband, and a silver sword earring circulate into this pool. I am offered cigarettes, a glass of instant iced tea, more gum. The two couples start making out on the couch with the faded floral pattern. Bobby and Joe motion to me to "go into the kitchen."

Sitting around the red linoleum dinette table, Joe and Bobby talk about the time they ran away from home. Bobby says, "You know you can live in the woods." Stuff they learned in the Boy Scouts kept them alive for two weeks. They ate plants, killed wild rabbits and birds. Jersey is the Garden State, and parts of Bergenfield are very rustic. You can disappear here if you have to.

Joe grabs my arm and draws a tattoo: an iron cross with a snake in the center in purple felt pen; "F.T.W." on the top, "M.O.D." on the bottom. He explains as he retraces his artwork on my arm: "Fuck the World" and "Method of Destruction." Then he draws the bleeding heart. He's got the blood dripping, an iron cross inside. He says I should call him "Warlock."

But I end up calling him "Joe" after "Bazooka Joe," another song on the Big Black album ruling my turntable that week. It reminded me of him in the refrain: "Hang with me, Joe, hang with me, Joe . . ." Sometimes it's hard to explain how these connections are made. From the start, Joe and I had emotional rapport. He was street wise. I trusted him.

Joe and I are sitting around talking about tattoos. I want to get a lizard on my forearm. I flex my favorite muscle. Everyone says girls should get them in private places. Shoulders, backs, behinds, hips. I'll probably never do it, though, I confide. "Me neither," says Joe. "Too permanent."

Bobby leaves the room and Joe starts talking about suicide. He thinks about it every day. This morning he wanted to. Why? "I feel like shit." Once you do something, you can't live it down. In this town people don't forget. What? Anything. Joe feels that the kids in the suicide pact did it because they "got pushed down as far as they could go. They were exhausted, tired of fighting, man. They just gave up." Joe can identify, he says. "I mean, how much can you take of hearing people call you a waste case, a burnout, a dirt merchant? After a while, you start to believe it."

I understand, I think. "But Joe, you call yourselves burnouts." He laughs. "That's different. In this town, you're either a jock or a burnout."

We are sitting there in the late afternoon, serene, looking out the window at the emerging foliage on the trees. Joe asks me what I think about God. Do I believe? I tell him yes, I do, sort of. Not in religion exactly, but I know the spirit is there, and that faith is a powerful force. We talk. About how God helps us to have faith, and about the power of love. Then about drinking and not feeling well.

He's been thinking a lot about God lately. He's just not sure. Me neither, I say. I've never been too sure if we invented God, or God invented us. But who cares, I say, either way, we *need* God. A little faith can make a big difference. Joe says he needs something to hold on to. Maybe God can help.

I agree. I start talking about A.A., how it's a very spiritual community. It not at all like regular religion—no crap about sin and evil. No one punishes you or anything. It's very cool. Gives you strength, helps you to feel forgiveness, to let go of pain. You find the joy of sobriety, good people who are on your side. Maybe he could go to a meeting. He had been thinking about going. His father had been going to meetings for years.

I have to be really careful not to come off like I'm twelve-stepping Joe or anything; it would be disrespectful. I go on about how alcohol confuses your thinking, how it can put you into a bad mood. There are ways to avoid that, though. First rule, don't try to do any deep thinking when you've had a long night. Bad news. Better to give it up for the meantime, and just keep things light. Think of it in terms of chemicals. When you're feeling too raw, just go home, eat something, take a hot shower, and get some sleep, like you have the flu. But he can't go home; he's supposed to be out looking for work.

Joe's been up for more than a day already. He's fried, his clothes are getting crusty, and he points to his armpits and says he smells (he doesn't). He's broke, he misses his girlfriend. He says he can't make it without someone. His girlfriend dumped him last year. He's gone out with other girls, but it's not the same. And he knows he can't win in this town. He's got a bad name. What's the use. He's tried it at least six times. Once he gashed at his vein with an Army knife he picked up in Times Square. He strokes the scars.

Tonight, he says, he's going to a Bible study class. Some girl he met invited him. Shows me a God pamphlet, inspirational literature. He doesn't want anyone to know about this, though. He thought the Jesus girl was nice. He's meeting her at seven. Bobby comes back in the room with Nicky, looking for cigarettes.

Later in the living room Joe teases Doreen. Poking at her, he gets rough. Bobby monitors him. "Calm down, Joe." We are just sitting around playing music, smoking cigarettes. Fooling around. "Did you see those Jesus freaks down at Cooper's Pond the other day?" Randy laughs. Nicky tells Joe to forget it. Jesus chicks won't just go with you; you have to date them for a long time, pretend you're serious about them. They don't fuck you right away. "It's not worth the bother."

Suicide comes up again. Joan and Susie have razor scars. The guys make Susie show me her freshly bandaged wrists. I look at her. She's such a beautiful girl. She's sitting there with her boyfriend, Randy, just fooling around. I ask her quietly, "Why are you doing this?" She smiles at me seductively. She doesn't say anything. What the fuck is this, erotic? Kicks? Romantic? I feel cold panic.

Nicky slashed his wrists when his old girlfriend moved out of state. His scars are much older. I motion to him about Susie. Discreetly he says, "It's best just to ignore it, don't pay too much attention." Throughout the afternoon I try every trick I know to get Susie to talk to me. She won't. She's shy, quiet; she's all inside herself.

And I really don't want to push too hard. The kids say they're already going nuts from all the suicide-prevention stuff. You can't panic. But I have to figure out if this is a cult, a fad, a hobby, or something I'm supposed to report to the police. I'm afraid to leave.

I wonder, do they know the difference between vertical and horizontal cuts? Don't their parents, their teachers, the cops, and neighbors see this shit going on? Maybe they feel as confused as I do. Maybe this is why they didn't see it coming here, and in the other towns. You can't exactly go around strip-searching teenagers to see if they have slash wounds.

Bobby brings me back into focus with The Plan. The kids have decided that they'll take me out on the town. Joe says we can stay out all night! Watch the sunrise from the cliffs. But there are instructions. First get a blue denim jacket. They say I look much too straight to blend in. I am horrified. I've taken abuse all my life from people for the way I dress. I flip the bird, throw the evil eye, curse them in a snotty tone: "You know, someday I hope someone says that to you!"

It's too bad. They mean business. Off with the red oversized nylon shirt, the unstructured gray jacket, my black cotton leggings and boots. Forget the long scarf I put on to make it look "professional." I was ac/dc fashion-wise, that day, not sure what I was going to do, planning to drop in on a priest in New Milford until I saw the kids standing around. Bobby laughs. He says I look "too adult" in these clothes. Joe is afraid the other kids will think I'm a narc. They don't want too many people to know I'm writing about them. Don't want to make their friends nervous. If it comes up I should just say I'm Joe's cousin from the Bronx.

We go over the costuming. I must wear sneakers. But all I have are some old navy blue basketball sneakers. Fine. Do I have a denim jacket? "I can borrow one." I ask Susie if I should cruise Mandee's, the main fashion source on the Ave, for ideas. Maybe a Motley Crue hot pink sweatshirt? Turq and pink are good, right? "Just any old shirt," she says. Susie has that classic "dirty sweet" pretty girl look. Neighborhood beauty. Like the English girls Marc Bolan sang about in T-Rex's "Bang a Gong." She assures me no big fashion situation is needed.

Bobby says, "Look, don't groom too much, we just put on what we have around that's clean." A lie. The guys are definitely *dressed*. Classic dirtbag—ripped jeans, long hair, flannel shirts, concert jerseys, denim jackets, sneakers. They look like hippies, like Neil Young. It's strategic, an ethical conviction, a radical statement of refusal articulated in the decade of greed. The anti-look. But of course, there are rules.

Just the right T-shirt, the thick socks, very specific rock regalia, hair perfectly unstyled. Male and female, everybody carries a big hairbrush. Certain brands only of high-top sneakers, details to precise fit of the jeans, cuffed at just the right angle to the foot, but okay I get the point.

I tell them I don't want to lie to other kids about who I am, so if the conversation gets heavier than hair or music I'll have to explain my purposes. They ask if I have a press card. I don't. Get one. Why? "Because if the cops nail us they'll think you're buying us alcohol." The kids figure they have nothing to lose and it will be fun. They advise me to stay underground. They are wise to "contamination effects." Don't want the dicks on their best behavior, Bobby says. Then I wouldn't get to see what it's really like. But Joe is more practical. He reasons that my presence "might get the cops off our backs for a while."

Everybody has to clear out by 5:00 P.M., when Bobby's mother gets home. His sister, Joan, is allowed to have her friends up, but no guys can stay, so we have to leave. Bobby has something to take care of, but I should meet him in a half hour. He wants to show me something. Joe considers blowing off his meeting to come with us. "Fuck it, I'll go tomorrow." We could pick up some beers and hang out. But he'll feel much better if he goes tonight, I tell him. He likes the girl, they sound like good people, and this won't be anything really, an early night. I say, "Bobby's just showing me some building." Apparently, this is not cool. "No way," Joe insists. "You can't take her there in the daytime, what if the cops see her car?" But then Joe backs off, and decides to drive Randy home and head over to his meeting. I take a drive toward Teaneck.

I am freaked out about the scars. I don't know how to read them. What are these collective razor scars, the martyr's ecstasy? Wrist cuts. The suicide pact signifier? Mutilation and negation as community? The poetics of suicide? Literary and religious themes go through my mind. To live and die in Bergenfield. Burnouts. Nailed. The stigmata.

It was getting heavy. But how real was this? Joe was very intense, a real drama queen, I could tell. But he was also pretty strung out. His life wasn't working. Susie was accessible only indirectly, through her friends. For Nicky, this "suicide stuff" was behind him, he had plans. And it just didn't seem like Randy's style. Bobby also appeared more explosive than self-destructive. That was comforting. Joan had the wrist bandages too. I had looked at her flesh carvings—superficial, but what was she saying? Doreen seemed fine, but that's what people thought about Cheryl Burress. I didn't know what to think.

I had ended up at a grocery store in the Foster Village Shopping Center. I was here just killing time, waiting to meet Bobby, aimlessly shopping. Interesting, I thought. Fresh soy milk, fruit salads, tofu by the pound, and a wide variety of fresh produce. Some Jamaican spices, canned fish products from Thailand, seaweed from Japan. Almost looks like a Teaneck gourmet shop or health food store, but actually, it caters to the needs of the local Asian community. I pay for the malted milk balls, some curry powder and chili oil. I put the stuff into my trunk; I'm going to pick up Bobby at Dunkin' Donuts.

But something gives me the creeps. I am standing there in the parking lot, facing the Amoco station. Behind me are the garden apartments and, farther in, that garage. I had been on foot patrol in Bergenfield for a while, but it now occurs to me that I live in a two-story garden apartment complex on a famous turnpike of suburbia, across from a faded shopping center, and an Amoco gas station. Up the road a piece is the all-night convenience store, the one the local kids call Metal 24.

Gimme Shelter

For thy waste and thy desolate places
And thy land that hath been destroyed
Surely now shalt thou be too strait for the inhabitants,
And they that swallowed thee up shall be far away.

The Children of thy bereavement
Shall yet say in thine ears:
'The place is too strait for me;
Give place to me that I may dwell.'

—Isaiah 49:19, 20

From the first time I went with Bobby to check out the Building, I thought it was a pretty cool place. But I really didn't understand how crucial it was in the scheme of things until I had gotten a chance to scope out all the wonderful activities the adults kept boasting about. All the resources they felt they had made available to their town's younger citizens. A few weeks after my initial visit to the Building I had the opportunity to do that.

Some missions were better carried out alone, and this was one of them. By now I had been spending most nights on the streets, so I wanted to see the alternatives for myself. Most kids dismissed these "resources" as hopelessly lame, but maybe they weren't so bad. I wanted to be fair, so I planned out my itinerary based on the places the adults sanctioned and tips from some of the kids.

So on this particularly nasty, rainy night I pull into the 7-Eleven parking lot and wait in my car for a while. Friday night after supper, around 7:30, and 7-Eleven is hopping. Six or seven cars are parked, filled with kids out to party tonight. Drivers sit with their engines idling. The police are there. These are the rules: You can stay as long as you leave the motor running and make a token trip or two into the store. Beer runs, cigarette runs, whatever, but remember to keep the open beer cans out of view. Everybody knows that as long as you keep up the appearance of having a purpose, a business transaction at the store, you are cool. You aren't "loitering," you are shopping. Who in these United States could hassle you on that account? When you are not in the store you have to stay in your car, rain or shine, else there could be trouble.

Two police cars are stationed at critical points in the parking lot, one car in the front and one on the side. They wave at kids they know, make small talk with them. They tell others to move, all the while alert for the sight of a six-pack hidden beneath underage arms. The engines keep idling. I wait there for about a half hour. The rain keeps up. Nobody I know shows, so I decide to cruise.

I drive up the street to Walley's. Something different happens here every night. Sunday night is comedy night. Monday and Tues-

day the DJ spins. Wednesday Yasgur's Farm, then Bystander, ladies' night. Tonight Flashback is playing. It's early yet. The band
won't go on until 10:30, if only I can survive the DJ. Long-haired, I
hope they're loud but uh-oh, the drummer's wearing white Capezios.
That's a bad sign.

At the bar, mall babes drink festive cocktails. Spiked heels,
thickly belted jumpsuits, hair like Heather Locklear, fierce, nails to
death. There's a framed poster of a Nagel print on the wall. A pair
of new-wavesters across the bar in skinny ties and MTV hair. Most
of the guys look too clean. These places always have dress codes—
collars on the shirt, no jeans, stuff like that. Too regimented for the
burnouts.

Restless, I leave after a half hour and head south on S. Washington, one mile to the Rink.

Moms across America would love the heavily supervised Rink.
It's the pride of Bergenfield. After the suicide pact the Rink was
often cited by town officials as proof that the town does provide for
its youth. There was a letter posted from Ronald Reagan, commend-
ing the Rink for providing good, wholesome, modestly priced "family entertainment."

The Rink isn't just for kids from that town. Like Long Island,
towns are small, and very close. So at any given time people from
other towns will be there. It is an ideal spot for preteen socializing.

Friday night at the Rink kids from nine to about sixteen roller-
skate to a great sound system. Loud, thumping. Much better than
Walley's. Rap, pop, and disco music. The design of this place recalls
the great rock palaces of the past. It is fantastic. There's a graffiti-
style sign in the center, "The Rink." The DJ prods the preteens
into a "ladies only" roll around the rink. Hardcore 1950s retro-
heterosexuality. The guys are told to make their move. "Ask for her
number . . . Ladies! They want you! They're dying for you!"

I am horrified, my more puritanical sensibilities now under siege.
They're too young for *that* kind of stuff! Besides, it's bad training
for future feminists of America. But I catch myself and loosen up
when I see a shy twelve-year-old girl with a mouth full of braces
cover her giggling. The Rink could be renamed "Iron Maiden Rink,"
since every other fourteen-year-old boy wears Maiden colors proudly
on his back.

In the ladies' room a most serious encounter is under way. Two girls named Jennifer and Melissa run into each other and chat. "I just came in to fix my eye makeup," says Melissa. They primp at the mirror and talk about some cute boys who are outside. One's really gorgeous, says Jennifer. Melissa points out to a disinterested Jennifer that her eyeliner has smudged onto her light blue shadow. Melissa manages again to reiterate that she's wearing makeup.

This is because tonight is a very special night. Probably Melissa's first night out with a painted face. She hasn't hit puberty yet, not a day over ten, but she is a lady.

There are millions of things to see and do at the Rink. With a disco ball and a neon sculpture hung against a flat black backdrop, it is truly grand. The pro shop sells, among other things, skateboards, funky laces, and T-shirts. There's another shop where you can buy the great neon junk jewelry of the teen ornament industry.

Moms can watch the action on the rink and sip Perrier in a snack bar under hanging plants. On the extreme opposite side, far away from the moms and the Perrier, there's a video arcade with hot & heavy make-out action. Visible only if you're bold enough to look underneath the machines.

Meanwhile, the "Troubled?" sign is posted everywhere you look. But I can't really imagine a troubled teen on a night out at the lively Rink with pen and sheet of paper, inconspicuously jotting down this telephone number. A whole table of pamphlets suggests various priced parties one might organize using the Rink facility. An especially festive brochure seduces, "Your Sweet Sixteen?" But not one small pamphlet an upset kid could just slip in her back pocket.

The kids skate around. Carpooling moms sit up in the back. They're well dressed, my age, in all colors, shapes, and sizes, just like the kids. The Rink is the only turf that is jointly ruled by athletes and rockers. This is mainly because people here aren't usually older than sixteen. They don't *really* hate each other yet. It costs five bucks to get in. There's some hardcore/punky-looking kids loitering in an alcove in the rain. They look older, less spunky than the kids inside.

Everyone I knew from hanging around 7-Eleven says the Rink "is for little kids." For young people in Bergenfield, the years from seventeen to twenty-one, especially without a car, are the hardest.

(This is true across suburbia.) At the edge of seventeen, the action at the Rink starts to get stale.

II

After seventeen in this town and in all the places like it, this is your scene: You're too young to drink in the bars, and you don't have enough money to afford your own place. Most likely, you aren't going to college. Male or female, you're not too sure about the military. You live at home like you did when you were in high school, but it's different. You're supposed to be on your own now. But you aren't, really. Maybe you have a job, and if you're lucky, someone has an apartment you can party in once in a while. When it's warm out, if you have a car and a few bucks for gas, you can drive out to the cliffs, scope out the view.

By nineteen you've hit the brick wall and you really need something. Because there is *nothing* to do here, and there is *nowhere* to go. If you're from Cleveland's West Side suburbs you might be spending your wasted years down at the Lake. If you're in Washington County or rural northwest Florida, police will chase you out to Riverside Park, outside city limits and their jurisdiction.

It's like that in my neighborhood too. Kids aren't allowed to hang out by Metal 24. For a while they did. Some in their teens, others their early twenties, with their bikes and skateboards, doing flips and turns, playing music. But that's all over. The new manager put an end to it. They can play the video games inside if they behave. But "no cursing, ladies come in here to shop." Then the neighbors complained about the noise. The kids made a mess in the parking lot. It was bad for business.

Young people "just hanging out" seems to annoy, even frighten adults everywhere. Sea Cliff, for example, is a fairly affluent town on the North Shore of Long Island. Many of the homes are Victorian restorations, and the community is known for its crafts fairs, local artists, and antiques stores.

From the road Harry Tappen Beach just looks like a waterfront parking lot. People don't swim there, though; they say the water in Hempstead Harbor is too polluted. But for kids from Sea Cliff and surrounding communities, Harry Tappen Beach is still Turf.

In the late 1970s they had a street-work program up at Tappen.

The town voted to put social workers on duty as babysitters, keep the kids under control. Most of the kids had the same problems then as kids do now. Bored kids with nowhere to go and nothing to do, substance abuse and aimless loitering. I had friends who were street workers there, elders who had put in their wasted years at Tappen. Hoping to alleviate the pressures of dealing with their disaffected youth, the town would periodically spring for entertainment. Sometimes local bands played on the beach. One summer the Grinders played for the kids.

Regardless of the season, over ten years later the kids still come to Tappen looking for something. It's a tradition: they come in double shifts, on foot, by car, after school and again after supper. Buzz around the parking lot during prime time, around 7:00 P.M., and you'll hear Led Zep, Slayer, the Dead, or Lynyrd Skynyrd blasting off the car stereos. Some nights skateboard ramps are up, but usually the kids sit on their cars, play hacky-sack, talk, flirt, or show off new body art: custom automotive paint jobs, fresh tattoos.

But by 9:00 P.M. every night someone calls a "5-0!" That means the police have arrived and Tappen Beach is now closed. According to police, they have no real problems with the kids at Tappen except for the beer and complaints about the noise.

Today, as ever, the kids at Tappen range from fourteen to their middle twenties. They understand that by paying beer fines, they are supporting their town's local economy, but still, fifty bucks is a hefty price even for a patriot. Then, New York raised the drinking age from eighteen to twenty-one, turning more kids into beer outlaws. But even the people who are over twenty-one, as well as ones with fake proof of age, prefer the parking lot to the local bars.

There's no littering, because Mean Jean the Bottle Queen—the little old lady who collects empty beer bottles—keeps the parking lot immaculately clean. The kids at Tappen admit she really helps them out. She loves them too, calls them her grandchildren.

Tappen is far away from any residential area. It's impossible to hear noise, even from the road. For a while, Tappen Beach was kept open until 11:00 P.M. But there were complaints. So it's the same story every night: Evicted by 9:00 P.M. from Tappen, the kids drive down to Sea Cliff Beach. By 9:20, "Hawaii 5-0" will arrive, and with them the threat of parking tickets, beer tickets, and formal charges of disorderly conduct. So, risking technical DWIs, they migrate over to Garvie's Point, where police have set up roadblocks, demanding proof of residence in their town. Once expelled from Garvie's by the Glen Cove police, the caravan of cars finally travels south to Roslyn, parking under the viaduct. That's it. The next day, the kids are back at Tappen. Just like they always have been and always will be.

Actually, I don't think this wandering of American youth across the deserts of suburbia has changed much in twenty years. Where I grew up, we'd meet up in "town." That's what we called Central Avenue in Far Rockaway. After a while we'd have to move. You'd have to walk all the way up to Mott Avenue to cross or Benny the cop would snag you, and issue you a ticket for jaywalking. From Gino's Pizza we'd go to the State Diner parking lot, then back to the one behind the bowling alley.

If it was cold out, we could go upstairs to the Chinese restaurant that overlooked Gino's. All you had to do was order wonton soup and you could sit up there all day, smoking cigarettes and surveying the land. At night, you'd hike south on Central Avenue to the Wavecrest parking lot. From there you took the bus home.

In the summer there was the beach. Guzzling Colt-45 Malt liquor and dancing to the Four Tops. At night on the boardwalk at Beach 35th Street you could roll rubber balls for money at Lenny's Fascination, or just sit up on the benches and talk. On a cool night you could build a fire and hold all-night acid vigils. You could always relax under the boardwalk. In the winter it was good too. Late at night you broke into one of the empty bungalows down around Beach 35th Street. You'd get the oven going, light a candle. Three or four friends sitting smoking reefer and harmonizing to Mamas & Papas songs.

There was perpetually *no place to go and nothing to do*, but it wasn't so bad. You could work around the lack of autonomous space because there was city transportation. For a quarter you could take a bus over the Marine Park Bridge west to Brooklyn or six miles east into Far Rockaway and be left alone. Nobody knew who you were. You were free. You didn't need a car. You didn't have to hitch a ride or hop a train. The Green Bus Line and the New York City subway system were cheap. They ran all night, so you could make the scene and get home if you had to make curfew. Having this option, you could always escape.

If you didn't like the way you were being treated at home or on the streets, you could leave at a minute's notice. Here, in Bergenfield, without a car, it's not that simple.

Before the suicides, New Milford, just west of Bergenfield, was the reputed "burnout" capital of Bergen County. New Milford youth are notorious around north Jersey as "headbanging psychotic warriors." Like the kids in Bergenfield, New Milford kids were shifted around from spot to spot. Finally, the cops there came up with one brilliant solution to the youth problem: the kids were allowed to hang in the parking lot behind the police station.

Now, with Bergenfield hosting as unofficial street teen haven of Bergen County, Bergenfield police not only have to babysit the teenagers from their own town, they mind the ones from other towns too. And because the town is so small the policing of nomadic teens roving up and down the densely concentrated commercial streets must be more frequent and more excessive. It's like a bad movie loop—over and over and over again with the police.

Over the years, the migration pattern of Bergenfield's street youth has involved being shuffled by police from Washington Avenue to Memorial Park, then Cooper's Pond, the National Guard Armory, and finally the free spaces in Foster Village. After the suicide pact, that particular population resettlement plan also came to an end.

But in their diaspora some of Bergenfield's wandering teens managed to carve out autonomous space. Some terrain where adults did not make the rules, could not shuffle them around at whim, disrupt their cultural activities, persecute them in the name of law and order. They had the Building.

The Building stood off Newbridge Road, behind the Rink, on the west side of S. Washington, just past the railroad tracks. By day the site looks like any other abandoned factory on the commercially zoned outskirts of a modest suburban residential area. Afternoons you can see Asian families in a nearby field foraging for good soil, filling endless plastic bags and buckets.

I remember how awesome it seemed the first time I went there. It took me several return visits to comprehend the space—this flat, vast, concrete oasis, where the children of ZOSO had created a collective "room of one's own." In fact, they had a sprawling hotel to play around in.

That first day we were very careful, slowly traveling south on the

Ave, clandestinely making a right turn just before the Rink and then a quick left, through the gates. I found myself parked between two industrial structures. Even when we were safely inside, Bobby still worried that the cops might have seen us drive in. Every three minutes we thought we heard them.

I have always liked the police. Even when I was arrested they were nice to me. Many of my father's friends were on the force, and they were like uncles. In the town I now live in, there are many city cops, sometimes two generations. They are my neighbors, my friends. But the Bergenfield police started to get on my nerves early on. This constant threat of the police always intruding upon anything that was going on was a source of chronic anxiety. What if they see the car, what if they followed us in, and on and on.

Like most of the kids, Bobby was used to it. Besides, he had special protection—a relative on the force. Bobby enjoyed some immunity vis à vis the other kids; nobody would dare to fuck with him in this town. He often boasted. But a relative on the force is a mixed blessing; Bobby had to watch it, he had to behave. Because if he fucked up in any serious way, he would get it twice as bad.

Once inside the Building, if the cops didn't intrude, everything was cool. I spent my first visit inside what looked like a military aircraft hangar—a one-story shed, huge, empty and aluminum. Bobby was giving me the grand tour, pointing into the distance and telling me what it's like at night—"Back there is where you go with someone." In alcoves, behind partitions, and up against the corrugated metal you nail the one you're with. Teen sex. A little alcohol, whatever. You switch around fast, hot, and fleeting. It's not exactly an erotic environment but it serves its purpose.

The floors are a dull black, gunked up by footprints, cigarette butts, and random drippings from now-empty beer cans. There are still cartons and bundles of trash, but nothing that really interests anyone. I pick up a souvenir: a dirty, tattered white envelope addressed to *Parents Magazine*—a subscription form filled out by a Mrs. James Goad in Indiana. The address is crossed out in ink. Oh, so that's what this is. *Parents Magazine* used to be here. Bobby says the place has been closed for a year or two.

Up around Newbridge and Woodbine there used to be swamps and woods, wild places for the kids to play. But by the middle sixties there were the warehouses—*Parents Magazine,* New American Library, General Sportcraft Company, and Color Plus. Structures clumped together near another little shopping center, one with a family billiards hall.

There had been plenty of jobs at *Parents Magazine*—filling orders, loading trucks, shipping out packages. Maybe you'd work there after school. If you had no shop skills or leads into a small home-improvement business, and if the Army and college weren't in the cards, you'd take a summer job in shipping, and come fall, you'd stay on.

But now, Bobby and his friends had appropriated the *Parents Magazine* building for their own purposes. "They'll tear it down soon," he informed me. General speculation among friends: "Probably another mall." But Bobby had a vision. Wouldn't it make a good youth center? The town could contain its nomadic youth population here, install some street workers, trusted elders of prior generations of hanging out to keep things cool. Back at the house, that first day, Bobby had decided that it was very important to take me here. He had a plan: I was to publicize the deplorable truth of what "youth are reduced to" here in Bergenfield.

Actually, I thought they had it pretty good. Many towns just have the usual nooks and crannies, a couple of parking lots and street corners for a scene. It was generally impossible to acquire this much space so close to town. People could always find someplace, illegally, to hole up. But the Building? It was grand.

For as long as it lasts, an abandoned anything is a real break. The loss of industry in your town might fuck up your future but it might make your here and now a whole lot better. So the kids in Bergenfield had lucked out. The Building was used by young people from nearby towns as well. So it was, in effect, a teen center. Except the kids felt that they, and not the adults, made the rules.

To the kids, the Building never represented lost opportunities for work. Bobby told me there were always jobs in and around Bergenfield. Not great jobs, or interesting jobs or high-paying jobs, but there *were* jobs—Bobby was pumping gas.

Bobby and company were completely unconcerned with the lost possibilities for brilliant careers in shipping that might have attracted their elders. And for the moment, they could care less about whatever it was that would replace *Parents Magazine*.

Yes, life was a little simpler thanks to this change in the local economy. The time in between the closing of *Parents Magazine* and the opening of whatever would replace it meant that for a while the kids had a free zone. A hideaway to bring girls, to blow off steam, to party undisturbed. The police knew about it, Bobby explained, but most of them just looked the other way. As long as you didn't throw it in their faces.

According to Bobby, the police figured that at least here the kids couldn't bother anybody. But still, he felt, you had to be cool. They could get you for criminal trespass, vandalism if they wanted to. And there were some cops who didn't want you here at all.

"They'll probably get a lot of money for this place," Bobby figured. He wasn't very specific about who "they" were, but the daily removal of trash and dismembering of structures on this property was a reminder: their ballroom days at the Building would soon be over. Their sanctuary was to be dismantled. It was coming down, and so again they would be cast out in the wilderness.

Bobby clearly understood this situation and he was planning ahead, negotiating on behalf of future generations. This was why I had to politicize their plight, he said. Plead their case to the adults. They just wanted autonomous space somewhere in their town, nothing too fancy, just a place where they could be left alone, out from under the gaze of adult authority.

We spent a while hashing this out. What he had in mind for himself and his friends was fairly radical—something between a squat and a youth center. A squat is an abandoned building taken over by runaway and throwaway youth, a pioneer settlement for homeless people. During the 1980s many punks appropriated such dwellings, created centers for cultural and political activities. It was bold of Bobby to dream of a place allocated by the town to the nomadic youth population, where the kids themselves would make the rules. Up to then, the Building had been used mainly for partying, but the guys did hide out here periodically, when things got rough at home.

I recall Joe saying to his friends, "You know the story is basically going to be about us." They were willing to let me into their lives, but they wanted my efforts to serve some higher purpose. Bobby and Joe had discussed using my story to persuade adults to take their demands for a space of their own seriously. Bobby said he was willing to compromise, to let them open up an adult-authorized teen center here. "You know . . . nothing faggy like the one up around Dumont, it would have to be cool." I agreed; otherwise nobody would go and then they'd be back where they started, sneaking around like they were on the lam or something.

Bobby envisioned something like a clubhouse, where older youths would be on hand to supervise the action, offer guidance to younger kids. "How else will they learn how to take care of themselves once they get out into the world?" he asked rhetorically.

At sixteen, Bobby didn't want "another stupid teen program." People should have the "right to party," he felt. With or without permission, they would anyway. They could handle it. Sure, sometimes things might get hairy, but a peer-regulated situation was the only acceptable form of discipline. Otherwise you might as well be sitting around in the parking lots waiting to get chased by the police.

A youth center, in Bobby's opinion, had to be on kids' terms. We didn't come out and say it but we both knew the adults would never buy it. A legitimate place for "burnouts" to commune and groove by their own rules? Forget about it, I thought, adults are never going to trust these rocker kids to do their own thing. We understood that regardless of what was actually going on, there would always be adult hysteria about the possibility of drugs, sex, fights, and loud music.

Clearly, the kids' experiments in chemical intoxication and sexual arousal at the Building were already peer-regulated. To impose some outside Adult Law on kids who were used to setting their own limits and looking out for each other would be regressive, it would never work. But "technical support" in the form of peer counselors as providers of practical information, positive vision, and mediation might.

Bobby and his friends liked to hang out and party but they weren't just wasting their unstructured hours. They often spent their free time teaching themselves to play guitar, skate, draw, and write poetry. One of Bobby's crowd had turned a woodworking hobby into a lucrative part-time carpentry job. Because the "burnouts" had no legitimate space in Bergenfield, the bulk of this creative activity went unrecognized by adults.

The idea of a center for Bergenfield's alienated youth wasn't new.

After the suicide pact, parents complained that the kids really did need somewhere to go when school let out. The after-school activities were limited to academics, sports, or organized school clubs. Even with part-time after-school jobs, a number of the town's young people did not find the conventional activities offered by the town particularly intriguing.

But according to established adult reasoning, if you didn't get absorbed into the legitimate, established routine of social activity, you'd be left to burn out on street corners, killing time, getting wasted. It was impossible for anyone to imagine any autonomous activity that nonconforming youth en masse might enjoy that would not be self-destructive, potentially criminal, or meaningless.

Parents understood that the lack of "anything to do" often led to drug and alcohol abuse. Such concerns were aired at the volatile meeting in the auditorium of Bergenfield High School. It was agreed that the kids' complaint of "no place to go" had to be taken seriously. Ten years ago, in any suburban town, teenagers' complaints of "nothing to do" would have been met with adult annoyance. But not anymore.

In Bergenfield, teenage boredom could no longer be dismissed as the whining of spoiled suburban kids. Experts now claimed that national rates of teenage suicide were higher in suburbs and rural areas because of teen isolation and boredom. In Bergenfield adults articulated the fact that many local kids did hang out on street corners and in parks looking for drugs because things at home weren't too good.

Youngsters have always been cautioned by adults that the devil would make good use of their idle hands. But now they understood something else: boredom led to drugs, and boredom could kill. Yet it was taken for granted that if you refused to be colonized, if you ventured beyond the boundaries circumscribed by adults, you were "looking for trouble." But in reality, it was adult organization of young people's social reality over the last few hundred years that had *created* this miserable situation: one's youth as wasted years. Being wasted and getting wasted. Adults often wasted kids' time with meaningless activities, warehousing them in school; kids in turn wasted their own time on drugs. Just to have something to do.

So by now whenever kids hang out, congregating in some unstructured setting, adults read *dangerousness*. Even if young people are talking about serious things, working out plans for the future, discussing life, jobs, adults just assume they are getting wasted. They are.

Us and Them

Us and them is a game, there is you FIRST and then
I am what you let me be.
—Charles Manson

I

In the social order of the American high school, the athletes are always at the top of the heap and they are probably the most persistent of the cliques we have known. Over time, preps become yups but they've always been clean-cut. Greasers became hitters, then dirtbags, but they were typically working-class kids. Lames were replaced by nerds and dweebs, but they were always socially inept. Brains, or dexters, they were the smart ones. Browns, then goody-two-shoes were busy sucking up to teachers. Sexually adventurous females used to be whores, now they're sluts. Preppies, J.A.P.'s, buppies, and guidos are stereotypes based on combinations of ethnicity and class culture. But through it all, with or without steroids, jocks have remained jocks.

The social order of Bergenfield High School was pretty normal except for one thing: the place was unusually polarized between the jocks and the burnouts. There was not one conversation among the outcast that did not include de rigueur dissin' the jocks.

Because Bergenfield's teams have made their mark at the state level, giving the town extraordinary prestige, the jocks here stand high-and-mighty. For putting their town on the map, jocks are the elite, the golden boys, the cream of the crop in a high school not known for producing many great scholars.

So the vendetta between the jocks and the burnouts was very serious in Bergenfield. Rockers in general are not famous for liking organized athletic activities, but I had never observed this degree of hostility. For example, in my neighborhood members of the burnt population sometimes play baseball; it's no big deal. Some even support our local Police Athletic League.

Sports are usually the average American mom and dad's best connection to their kid's world. They may not be too big on the books; science and technology may also be over their heads. But competitive sports are something most any parent can relate to. The whole family can be involved. It may be the only time they are.

On the other hand, suburban rocker kids or arty types engage in cultural activities that are usually generationally bounded, alien to the parent culture. Nicky and his father, for example, both like Pink Floyd, but they don't party together, and Dad definitely is not into Motley Crue. Mostly, Nick's interaction with Dad is focused around how his car is running. The parent whose kid is deeply into music or some other esoteric scene may have no common ground with that child beyond automotive small talk, or asking what the kid did to stay out of trouble on that particular day. But organized sports can keep families together across generations.

Spend a few minutes outside of any American public school, and you can figure out who makes up the enemy camps. It's visually apparent: different races, ethnic groups, classes. And subcultural affiliations are expressed through clothing and music, coded in signs. So at the high school in Glen Clove, Long Island, white Italian-American and black African-American teenagers play out their adjacent communities' racial and territorial rivalries. Like any place, Bergenfield had its social schisms.

Of course there were many smaller rifts, and many "unaffiliated" kids around. But the principal rivalry among the youth of Bergenfield was played out along lines of participation and refusal in adult-orchestrated athletic activity.

In most high schools the politics of conformity and defiance are not this clearly articulated. At Bergenfield, in political terms, the jocks were "hegemonic," and their arch rivals, the burnouts, were "transgressive." So the closer Bergenfield's burnouts were to the adult-prescribed action, the worse they felt about themselves. The further away from the mainstream they could get, the greater their self-respect. Whether that meant nonparticipation, obliteration through drugs, or contemplating suicide, it was a matter of psychic survival.

The burnouts' point of reference was their "scene"—whatever subcultural activity they had going after hours, outside of Bergenfield, apart from the status hierarchy expressed at school. So something like a night at an Iron Maiden show was not only weekend fun, or a thrilling pop-cultural experience combining Kabuki-style theatrics, horror-movie effects, and video-game adventure. It could also help get you through the next six months by restoring your dignity. When Maiden's lead singer, Bruce Dickinson, bleats out, "Run to the hills, run for your lives," in a huge arena to thousands of suburban refugee kids, he's singing about the American Indian under siege—Cree, a proud people facing imminent decimation by "the white man." But the kids identify. Who cares if arena shows are corporate, commercial, or mass, Dickinson's singing their anthem too.

For the duration of my stay, in almost every encounter, the outcast members of Bergenfield's youth population would tell me these things: the cops are dicks, the school blows, the jocks suck, Billy Milano (lead singer of now defunct S.O.D.—Stormtroopers of Death) was from a nearby town, and Iron Maiden had dedicated "Wasted Years" to the Burress sisters the last time the band played Jersey. These were their cultural badges of honor, unknown to the adults.

Like many suburban towns, Bergenfield is occupationally mixed. Blue-collar aristocrats may make more money than college professors, and so one's local class identity is unclear. Schools claim to track kids in terms of "ability," and cliques are determined by subculture, style, participation, and refusal.

Because the myth of a democratized mass makes class lines in the suburbs of the United States so ambiguous to begin with, differences in status become the critical lines of demarcation. And in the mostly white, mainly Christian town of Bergenfield, where there are neither very rich nor very poor people, this sports thing became an important criterion for determining "who's who" among the young people.

The girls played this out too, as they always have, deriving their status by involvement in school (as cheerleaders, in clubs, in the classroom). And just as important, by the boys they hung around with. They were defined by who they were, by what they wore, by where they were seen, and with whom.

Like any other "Other," the kids at the bottom, who everybody here simply called burnouts, were actually a conglomerate of several cliques—serious druggies, Deadheads, dirtbags, skinheads, metalheads, thrashers, and punks. Some were good students, from "good" families with money and prestige. In any other setting all of these people might have been bitter rivals, or at least very separate cliques. But here, thanks to the adults and the primacy of sports, they were all lumped together—united by virtue of a common enemy, the jocks.

There are other towns where it is understood that high school athletes will be granted immunity for their "youthful" transgressions. Only in the face of some public scandal will adults fess up to this preferential treatment and the damage that often results from it. An example of this occurred in spring of 1989 in another New Jersey town.

In jock-ruled Glen Ridge, a quiet, affluent suburban enclave southwest of Bergenfield in Essex County, a group of boys—"Ridgers," as the town's jock elite were known—were implicated in the sexual assault of a seventeen-year-old girl, using a broomstick and a miniature souvenir bat. Thirteen boys were reportedly present at the event. Five were subsequently indicted as adults—four were charged with conspiracy, aggravated assault, and aggravated criminal sexual conduct; one with conspiracy. All five pleaded not guilty. Three other boys were charged as juveniles.

Apparently, the boys had known their victim since childhood. She was generally (though inaccurately) described by her peers as "retarded." Long before the story broke, people gossiped about what had allegedly happened that afternoon in the basement of the home of the captain of the baseball team, who, with his twin brother, was also co-captain of the high school football team.

After the story broke, in May, some people in Glen Ridge admitted to reporters that the case would have been buried but for an anonymous tip that brought a television news reporter to town. This gash in the order of things gave some residents the opportunity to express their moral outrage over the community's unspoken conspiracy in denying and suppressing the episode.

Because the town seemed so much more concerned with protecting the "futures" of their stellar athletes than with the rights of the alleged victim, Glen Ridge became known in the newspapers as the "Town of Shame." Around that time, other long-festering hostilities were articulated: local graffiti read "Thrashers Against Jocks."

In addition to cliques, which have traditionally served to obscure as well as to emphasize social inequalities based on sex, class, race, and ethnicity, 1980s American high school kids also carried banners of "subcult" affiliation. Subcults are far more specified and differentiated than subcultures. They are essentially cliques *within* subcultures—subcategories within the "outcast" population.

Subcults are tied to highly exclusive scenes, organized into shared systems of music, language, style, and ideology. Each sub-cult carries a different status in the high school. Often, membership in one's high school clique is modified to a great degree by one's "after-hours" subcult affiliation. Most high school students can decipher these sign systems; they can read peer subcult affiliation on the spot. Most adults can't.

And this can be a problem for adults, since the institutional prerequisites of the high school demand that adults know "who" they are dealing with so they can get on with the business of sorting and labeling kids into categories. Some categories will be more worthy of adult attention than others.

Aversion to some social types, bias, and hierarchy are built into the system; they are functional imperatives. Schools could not operate without these codes since their main purpose, along with "surplus absorption" (keeping kids out of the labor pool for as long as possible) is to prepare young Americans to fill positions in the work force. Ultimately, schools help to plug you in where they think you belong in our class structure.

And since the ideology and institutional culture of most high schools is still fixated at its zenith—in the 1950s—many educators tend to fall back on values of an idealized past. So even though it struck me as rather amazing, in the 1980s, as the resources for education dwindled, a key code adults used to figure out how much effort they should devote to a particular kid was whether or not that kid *smoked cigarettes.*

Always suggestive of some type of stigma, smoking cigarettes became a venial sin in suburban high schools during the 1980s. In the 1950s, it was a mark of juvenile delinquency for boys, trampiness for girls. In the early 1960s we did it to be cool. In those days, smoking *reefer* upstaged cigarettes as the mark of the in-crowd. In the 1970s, the status of smoking began to change. And by 1980, as we became obsessed with physical fitness and the rest of yuppie culture, cigarettes once again had symbolic power. Initially it had to do with the Surgeon General's findings about smoking and cancer. But in the high school, cigarettes could again mark a kid instantly as bad news.

Throughout the decade smoking cigarettes became a sign, a pivotal category in the status hierarchy of the high school. Yes, it was bad for your health. But adults always said that about everything—premarital sex, masturbation, fried foods, dial-a-porn, nail-biting, and drinking.

By the early 1980s adult antismoking campaigns had renewed 1950s-style schisms among students. Now smoking politicized the 1980s high school student body, sharply drawing the line between good and bad kids. In some schools, this line was more absolute. The painted white smoke line outside Bergenfield High School was one reason the area had become known as burnout turf. Another was that the spot had a long tradition of hosting teenagers famous for refusal and defiance. The smoking area is where the action can be found in any high school. Ask any kid where you can have a smoke and you'll find some kind of a little scene going. Taking your smoke break is a big deal, the highlight of the day, it's *the thing*.

Even though experts say that more girls smoke than boys, and that fewer college-bound youth smoke than those with no such plans, smoking was taboo for anybody hoping to move up in the world. Often cheerleaders would be thrown off the squad for smoking. In some schools, they weren't allowed to smoke or even stand near the smoking section. It was the forbidden zone for school elites.

Like every other social transgression, unless you were very wealthy, or looked like it, your cigarette could cost you your reputation. Preps and brains who smoked were not that easily labeled, but unspectacular kids who could have gone either way were quickly stigmatized. "Oh, she's smoking, well we've got her number."

So smoking cigarettes became a label, a mark of the uncooperative teen, the rebel, the troublemaker. A signal of dissent in the 1980s, smoking in Bergenfield came off like an act of civil disobedience—an intentional statement of alienation and the possibility of dangerousness.

Sometimes it was hard to believe this kind of stuff was going on, that the kids in Bergenfield were dealing with crap like this at this late date. Now, in my high school there wasn't much social distance between the drug-taking and the sports-participating population. I got out of high school in 1968, one year before girls were allowed to wear pants to school. It was a transitional year, and the "freak" population was just beginning to flourish. For a while, the traditional status hierarchies of high school were preempted by the larger youth culture "out there."

Under normal circumstances the status hierarchy of the American high school has reflected white, middle-class adult values—the kids most talented at being cooperative, who excel in the activities dictated by the school, will be the most rewarded. Kids will compete for their teachers' attention, the respect of peers, popularity, and social approval. Set up to perform prescribed rituals, they will be attractive, from "good families," and well-behaved.

But in 1968 there were other choices. If you weren't very spectacular in the eyes of the authorities, it meant nothing and you could care less. Because you knew you were part of something much more grand, you could care less about the bullshitty cliques in your dumb old high school.

The idea of a huge, media-celebrated hippie counterculture made deviance, alienation, and local anarchy fashionable. Intellectuals and activists at the universities stood behind you. They encouraged you to believe that you had a handle on the truth. That you knew better than your parents and your high school teachers. Always question authority.

Education liberated us, emancipated us from adult domination because it validated our intuitive perceptions of the world. There was no pressure to deny what you saw, so you felt sure of yourself, directed. You had an inner power, and a larger power than yourself to rely upon. You had Marx and Marcuse and Fanon and de Beauvoir behind you. And you didn't even have to read them or understand them to have them on your side.

The high-tone social location of this subculture was intimidating to our parents; many were suspicious and resentful of "book smarts." Nobody in my home "read"; we watched television. But the power of formal knowledge was understood and was often embraced across class lines—by the disenchanted angry children of corporate elites as well as the sons and daughters of European and third-world labor pools.

Even though polarities on the basis of race, class, sex, and sexual preference did persist, to the adult world, the youth of America appeared organized, integrated, and unified under a higher, more eloquent authority. So even marginal affiliation with the youth subculture gave you permission to feel that your instincts were correct. And because of the ties to the universities, you were intellectually, culturally, politically, and morally very cool.

Even in high school you had power, the charisma of a national affiliation that scared the shit out of adults at the local level where your battles for dignity were being waged. If your teachers didn't fess up to the hypocrisy and join in the critique of the dominant order—"the system"—you had reason to suspect that they were scared or even stupid. At a certain point, you simply did not trust a teacher if he wore a tie or she wore makeup. They were plastic people, straights, to be easily dismissed, their authority undercut.

As in any scene, people were there for many reasons. Some people just got into it for the sex and the drugs, or to have something to do. Other people were busy reading Mao, fashioning themselves as politicos. And even though the universities supported you in your rebellion against your overly regulated teenage life, you didn't have to read that much to get a handle on things.

To participate in this social movement all you needed to do was to get dressed, remember your hash pipe, and take change for the bus.

Twenty years ago, alienation from adult rules was so accepted in my high school that the night of the senior prom there was an anti-party, with everybody getting high on the beach. The prom is the premier middle-class "coming-out party," a rite of passage into the American working week. Kids get to dress up like adults, take limos, dress formal, and stay out real late. It costs lots of money, offers a glimpse of what is to come if you continue to play the game. We rejected it and everything it implied about "growing up," which we essentially saw as "bourgeoisification." The prom was shunned as politically incorrect and totally lame.

But that had changed. By the 1980s—after the Reagans and *Dynasty*—every kid dreamed of going to the prom in high-glam style. The limos would pull up to Metal 24 and people would get ready to party down, rent hotel rooms, play rock star or millionaire, get fancy. Everyone was dressed for glory. Fast money and good times. Some even skipped the prom and just did the drugs, the limo, and clubland. The prom now was strictly party time!

By now adults had stopped viewing kids as part of a social movement. The importance of "youth culture" had diminished. Subculture was just something recreational that kids did, and overdid when they failed at what adults figured they were supposed to be doing. In the adult imagination, young people were returned to their status as an overly regulated, dependent population. Adults went back to viewing high school students as either good or bad kids, winners or losers. Conforming or troublemaking, fine students or juvenile delinquents.

Some youth advocates lamented what they called the return of the 1950s. As the country seemed to split into rich and poor, privileged and disenfranchised, the kids themselves were also polarized, dichotomized as winners or losers. With everybody telling them how little there was to go around, kids in the 1980s had two choices: be very good and win, be bad and lose.

But American youth culture evolved over the postwar boom years so that by the eighties "bad" kids could draw from quite a lot to buffer themselves from the adult world. Kids are now empowered by a strong collective memory. They can easily live in their own world, sleepwalking through stale family life, boring school, and bad jobs. The dullest, most apathetic students will come alive when left to their own devices.

The "burnouts" and "dirtbags" occupied a specific place in the status hierarchy of the 1980s high school. Where some of their equally alienated but more politically motivated peers—rads, skins, and punk/hardcore kids—shunned drugs, and practiced nihilism with purpose, the "burnouts" and "dirts" didn't ascribe their actions to some higher principle.

As stereotyped by their peers, "burnouts" are in the zombie zone of existence. Their main activity is getting high, being oblivious. It is this, not their clothing or music, that sets them apart as a clique.

For adults, "burnout" is synonymous with "dirtbag," but in local teenage linguistics, the two labels are analytically distinct. You can be burnt and dirt, dirt but not burnt, or burnt but not dirt.

While dirts (dirtbags, dirtballs, dirtmerchants, dirtbombs) dress like they just walked out of 1968—"freaks"—they are wholly "today's kids" and full of contradictions. In my neighborhood, for example, dirts may shun designer jeans *and* pay up the wazoo for sneakers and concert T-shirts. They get high and harbor an innate, populist mistrust for people in power and big corporations. But they hang out at malls and support major arena shows. They think Ronald Reagan was the best thing that ever happened to America. They say they hate what happened to American soldiers in Vietnam, how the government "wimped out" and left them hanging. They refused to register for selective service but were ready to fight in Grenada.

Typically, dirtbags and burnouts are near the bottom of their school's status hierarchy. Teachers have given up on them; so have many of their peers. It's not just the jocks and preps who dismiss them for how they look; even severely alienated rockers from other subcults find them contemptible. Disaffected dirts and burnouts have problems with authority. They may look like rebels and be viewed as outcasts by adults. But as a rule, they don't have a program, they won't organize or even *try* to "fight the power." Theirs is an individualistic, atomized form of "resistance."

Dirts defy the mainstream game through rituals of style and attitude. Anger is expressed in random episodes of violence—vandalism, fighting. Burnouts, on the other hand, are more passive, inert. They withdraw, they just wanna get wasted.

During the 1970s the notion of a *person* experiencing "burnout" emerged as a clinical diagnosis of human exhaustion, the human soul temporarily on the blink. This condition would involve a feeling of fatigue, helplessness, hopelessness, and lack of enthusiasm about work, people, and life in general. It was described as an insidious, gradual erosion of the spirit. It occurred among the most enthusiastic and idealistic.

What had once described the drug casualties of the late 1960s' counterculture was now applied to the overzealous human services practitioner. Many such practitioners came out of the 1960s still hoping to do good work, to change the system from within. Researchers emphasized that burnout was situational, not personal, although some personality types were more susceptible to burnout than others. Certain institutional settings were likely to destroy human emotions. The more you could feel, the more you cared, the higher your risk of burning out.

By the mid-1970s the verb "to burn out" had entered our dictionaries. Certain occupational groups (nurses, police, airline hostesses, social workers) were at high risk for burning out. Human services, especially the "emotion work" involved in traditionally female occupations, were notorious. Some people burned out in bureaucratic settings, from frustration with rules and regulations that worked against their professional ideals. Others were overwhelmed but kept trying to meet relentless demands without adequate resources or appropriate expectations. Many books were written about burnout; special seminars were offered. Staff meetings usually included some mention of "burnout syndrome," as it was sometimes called.

Burning out means you are getting frayed around the edges. Stress continues to build as you feel yourself less and less capable of controlling your environment. It is an individual response to a collective problem. Atomized, each person suffers in isolation, and in isolation the problem gets worse. At some point you are lost—to those around you, to your loved ones, even to yourself.

Somewhat like a nervous breakdown, burnout involves a change in your ability to function, to "perform." You numb out, hoping to lower anxiety by shutting down, denying access to your feelings. The body, the organism, is overwhelmed. Burnout is a way of slipping out the back door with your body still present. You can still go through the motions of living, but you feel dead.

The burned-out individual protects the self for the moment, but in the long run the self is estranged. The ability to relate in any way at all is compromised. You are living at half speed in a world you cannot handle—shut down, tuned out; you're gone.

This estrangement from feeling, this disowning and disengaging from feeling, is a form of *alienation*. According to Marx, in the process of laboring, human beings enjoy the creative activity of transforming the world. If the product of this pleasure is taken from you, alienated (as in the process of capitalist production), you experience deep loss. You become detached from your world because your connection to that world, your power to create and transform in that world *through your own efforts*, has been taken from you. So you are living in the world in a state of detachedness; you no longer feel viable.

Powerless, useless, ineffectual, you are only remotely connected to life around you. The most you can hope for is to get through the day—at home, at work, in school. Drugs and alcohol will help to kill the pain, protect you from things that would, if fully perceived, drive you crazy. But then you have to deal with the secondary effects of your anodyne solution. Either way, you know you're not well.

It is not surprising that the Alcoholics Anonymous doctrine

advises never to let yourself get too hungry, too tired, or too lonely. Being emotionally strung out often leads to desperate self-medicating. The active alcoholic, overworked professional, and emotionally overwhelmed kid all appear to be wasted. Often, they are. Whether stressful life experiences or excessive drug taking has wasted you is unimportant—a burned-out soul feels empty, the spirit seems depleted.

For a bored, ignored, lonely kid, drug oblivion may offer immediate comfort; purpose and adventure in the place of everyday ennui. But soon it has a life of its own—at a psychic and a social level, the focus of your life becomes *getting high* (or *well* as some people describe it). Ironically, the whole miserable process often begins as a positive act of self-preservation.

Both the dirts and the burnt may understand how they are being fucked over and by whom. And while partying rituals may actually celebrate the refusal to play the game, neither group has a clue where to take it beyond the parking lot of 7-Eleven.

So they end up stranded in teenage wasteland. They devote their lives to their bands, to their friends, to partying; they live in the moment. They're going down in flames, taking literally the notion that "rust never sleeps," that it is "better to burn out than fade away." While left-leaning adults have valorized the politically minded punks and right-wing groups have engaged some fascistic skins, nobody really thinks too much about organizing dirts or burnouts. Law enforcement officials, special education teachers, and drug treatment facilities are the adults who are concerned with these kids.

Such wasted suburban kids are typically not politically "correct," nor do they constitute an identifiable segment of the industrial working class. They are not members of a specific racial or ethnic minority, and they have few political advocates. Only on the political issues of abortion and the death penalty for minors will wasted teenage girls and boys be likely to find adults in their corner.

Small in numbers, isolated in decaying suburbs, they aren't visible on any national scale until they are involved in something that really horrifies us, like a suicide pact, or parricide, or incest, or "satanic" sacrifice. For the most part, burnouts and dirtbags are anomic small-town white boys and girls, just trying to get through the day. Their way of fighting back is to have enough fun to kill themselves before everything else does.

II

In post-Vietnam America, on the streets, the original burnouts were the junkies, the townies, the unemployed Vietnam vets shot through the heart. This is the social origin of the 1980s burnout. In pure form, the dirtbag can be considered a cultural descendant of the late 1960s' freak, with residual elements carried over from the 1950s, the Age of Grease.

Burnouts and dirtbags have distinctive social histories and strong cultural legacies to fall back on. These are American kids, armed for everyday life with the lipstick traces of all prior generations of rebellious teens. Life is harder for kids nowadays, so a robust attitude is needed. Attitude in a moment of severe humiliation might make the difference between keeping on and giving up. It is crucial.

Attitude is also a very personal matter, customized through a series of historical details—whatever you have at your fingertips. Here's an example of how attitude, style, and borrowed traditions make one kid's life a little better.

Randy Masterson has relatives living a few towns east of where I grew up. They told him all about surfing in Long Beach. He used to watch them when he was little.

The traces of surfer in Randy's worldview are obvious, yet Randy doesn't identify himself consciously as such. In Bergenfield Randy is identified as a burnout. Yet in his sartorial opposition to the jocks, and since he had recently curtailed his drug use, Randy could also be identified as a dirtbag. Either way, he's proud to be guilty.

Yet beyond this particular north Jersey situation, Randy has something else going for him. Beyond his devotion to Ozzy and Metallica, Randy has something that makes him special. So does everybody. That's what style is all about.

And so even though Randy was born and raised inland, mostly in New Jersey, his clothing carries traces of a surfer style. He is a free spirit, with the mythos of the beach bum in his back pocket. Based on the bands he listens to, Randy is a thrasher, not a surf punk. There is no skateboard, no baseball cap over long hair—images borrowed from a scene, inspired by a record or a specific surf punk band. No, Randy's beach sensibility comes down from his rebel father and his uncles; they were surfers from the western end of Long Beach, New York. He carries this with him like a family recipe or the tradition of drinking dark ale. It sets him apart.

Randy as a thrasher of Bergenfield looks very different from thrashers in, say, my neighborhood. He is even different from thrashers in his own neighborhood. He is unique by virtue of his interpretation of these styles. He is one in a million. Mass production just lays the groundwork. Homogeneity in the 'burbs is an urban myth. The kids just look alike if you don't know what you're looking at. Within Randy's community of friends, no two people dress the same. Each is as customized and individualized as the once-identical houses in Levittown are today.

Some people have said that 1980s youth cultures are warmed-over 1960s leftovers. That's not true. Burnouts and dirts live and breathe in a world that is very much rooted in their everyday lives. But they have taken something from everywhere, and redefined it for their own purposes. They simply borrow what is needed and synthesize it with the present.

Kids have always done that. That's what culture is—a living re-definition of the past in the present. As "freaks," we loved the Beach Boys and we wore safari jackets. Woke up in the middle of the night to prowl around our peninsula, hunting for cigarette machines. We got drunk, listened to Donovan, and smoked baked banana peels. Our local culture was a collage of endless rituals borrowed from everywhere—other eras, social classes, and our parents. So we put spells on people, went "copping" (shoplifting), learned how to drive, and prayed to God to get our periods on time.

Because we lived near the ocean, we streaked our hair like the surfers on the West Coast. We wore bells and flowers, and danced to the music of the Spencer Davis Group. After a while we got "political." And soon we laughed at our predecessors, the older "hitter chicks" we used to idolize. They now looked bland, like Barbie dolls; their toughness seemed like ignorance.

The main thing for us was getting high and feeling very alienated. That was the only way to get a handle on what was really going on. Most of the people in my graduating class had gone off to college but I was still hanging around the neighborhood in 1969, the year Far

Rockaway High School supposedly came in second in heroin addiction rates in the city public schools. I remember we were very proud of this. Rumor was that only Harlem High School beat us out for title. Whether this was ever true was irrelevant; we thought it was very cool.

But actually, it wasn't cool. By 1969, it had become dangerous to hitchhike; drugs were cut with bad medicine, getting people sick. It wasn't really fun anymore. Most people who were stranded in the neighborhood had serious drug problems.

Helter Skelter was upon us; drugs replaced possibility. Once a vehicle for transcendence, getting high became an end in itself. Things got ugly out on the street. People lingered on long after there was anything happening; they got desperate. Guys would beg quarters, the white crust forming in the corners of their mouths, skinny, dirty. Girls I grew up with became junk whores, turning tricks down by the wino hotels near the train station. Their faces aged, they got pregnant, their kids disappeared. People were willing to do anything to get high. They shot dope, lighter fluid, or wine, or various combinations of crushed-up pills, especially downs. People overdosed, looked dead alive, and died young. It seemed to be happening all over America.

The great decline was beginning. The bad acid and beat pot of Woodstock were upstaged by the alcohol and barbiturate overdoses of Watkins Glen, another upstate New York Festival that occurred just a few years later. The veterans were coming home more and more shattered each year. Some went into drug rehab. Some of the guys who had been drafted were back in my town. They looked old, wasted, and tired. They hung around the boardwalk and the train station panhandling, drinking beer, their teeth rotting out from methadone. The girls were gone. Half the people I grew up with ended up dead, in detox, or on a sad, endless vacation.

They were hollow, empty, finished. Burned-out. This appeared as a generational condition. A loss of faith, nothing to believe in anymore. We already knew about adult mendacity. We accepted that. But then the list of our political heroes who got shot down became a familiar litany: King, the Kennedys, Malcolm X, the crucifixion of Lenny Bruce. Anyone who dared to speak out or tell the truth would be killed.

Our most beloved rock heroes also died one after the other—Moon, Joplin, Morrison, Hendrix. Songs were written about rock and roll heaven. "Live fast, die young" was the cornerstone of teenage wasteland. Early death allowed us to make legends and martyrs out of drug casualties. Going down in flames had more honor than getting beaten down by the assholes.

There were marginal cases we now call survivors—David Crosby, John Phillips, Grace Slick. Then there were sellouts, the makers of Michelob commercials and Pepsi tours. The baby boom selling itself to itself.

My lasting impression of burned-out 1960s idealism was the sound of Jimi Hendrix cranking the national anthem as the sun rose over Woodstock. The sight of a few weather-beaten strays picking through miles and miles of garbage, debris left behind from our "three days of peace, love, and music." The culture of consumption had peaked. On a noise guitar note you understood the American Century was fading; the dream was over. In that moment Hendrix sounded the death knell for an economy predicated on consumption and waste. All our commodities, our knowledge, our beliefs, our civilization itself—everything was disposable.

And so a new concept had emerged from the graveyard of the Woodstock generation, this idea of being *burned out*. This was a metaphor borrowed from machines, aerospace jargon for the termination of the powered portion of a rocket's flight upon exhaustion by the propellant. Personified, the burnout lives in our collective memory in the image of the Vietnam veteran as a dislocated psycho, the 1960s' drug casualty, the overworked "dedicated" professional. True believers engaged, exploited, and then discarded. This is the nuclear core of teenage wasteland America. This is the cultural heritage of the 1980s burnout. Post-Vietnam, twenty years after Woodstock. Wired in the free world, wasted, rusting, going nowhere in overdrive.

III

In teenage wasteland America, new kids have always replaced old ones. Scenes have graduated some people and wasted others. The sign over the train underpass in Seaford, Long Island, has read "Teenage Wasteland" for the past twenty years.

So right now, in Bergenfield, Randy and I are sitting around the 7-Eleven waiting for something to happen. He sees a guy named Percy standing there with big a silver ankh pendant around his neck and a white shark's tooth earring. His long, stringy, reddish-brown hair covers crossed knife wounds, warrior scars from suburban scuffles and street feuds. Randy goes over to talk to him.

Meanwhile someone taps me on the shoulder and asks if my companion is the notorious Randy Masterson who twisted some girl's arm until it broke because she wouldn't go out with him. Before I can confirm, the guy tells me he is that girl's cousin. In fact, he jumped Randy, beat the shit out of him. But he tells me Randy was cool, he didn't press charges. Now sure that this is indeed *the* Randy Masterson, the guy goes over to him, shakes his hand, and they reminisce about their legendary fight.

I join the group, start talking to Percy. He's wearing these faded sweatpants, inside out; they were once a bright red, but now they're worn to shreds. He's taken the Sign of Jock and thrown it in their faces, fighting back with fashion and flair. Traditional rocker sartorial aggression. I tease him. "Percy, aren't you afraid somebody will think you're a jock?" He laughs, "Hell no, they know I'm burnt." Bad little rock and roll nigger of Bergenfield knows he's cool.

Percy wants to know if I am a narc. Everybody wanted to know that at one point. Some guy once flaunted a packet of herb in my face. But Percy pushes it. Half playing with me, half creepy, he examines my car. I never saw any serious drugs out in the open in Bergenfield. And I never asked about it. Periodically I would be hanging around and people would just leave and then come back. But nobody was ever sloppy. Drunk maybe.

Sometimes Joe would introduce me as a "street psychiatrist." But if I wasn't formally introduced, or if they saw the state trooper's sticker on my window and nobody told them who I was, they would whisper around. Finally someone would approach me and ask if I was a narc.

At first this was very entertaining—I couldn't believe American high school kids were still suspecting every stranger of being an undercover narcotics agent. This was a tradition. Accusing someone of being a narc was like saying your mother wore combat boots. Anyone who looked a little culturally off was suspect. Once people trusted me, even I would be warned to "watch that kid, I think he's a narc, into that Crime Watch." It was also a way of saying, "Who are you and what are you doing hanging around here?" Sometimes it created drama. Just a harmless game. Calling someone a narc was more of a put-down than an accusation.

The kids understood that I didn't get high. I was inclined toward sobriety. But I didn't push it. One time I did ask Joe why he never accused me of being a narc. "The vibes," he said. Randy also noted, "Think about it, we've never gotten high around you, have we?"

Still, I didn't take this narc business lightly. By the fall of 1987, it wasn't just a joke. In Midlothian, Texas, police officer George Raffield was allegedly executed by a group of high school students who figured out that he was an undercover cop sent to "do something" about the drug problem in their high school. Nothing much was happening in this small blue-collar American town. Everyone agreed Midlothian was boring. According to the kids all you could do for fun was look for sex, cruise, blast music from your car, and get high.

The kids in Midlothian used drugs like crank, coke, pot, hash, angel dust, and LSD. Small, regular quantities. A steady flow, the same as in any other suburban town. The boys now under indictment on the charge of capital murder were metalheads: Slayer, Metallica, Anthrax, and Iron Maiden were favorites. One of the boys wore a pentagram necklace and used a Ouija called "Terry's Heart." He told people he worshiped the devil.

Over time, some of the details attached to the new student who called himself George Moore just didn't jibe—his car was way too expensive for a high school kid, he never seemed to play his classy car stereo, and no matter what happened, he never got busted. On a tip from Terry's Heart, and out of fear of going to jail for drugs, one of the boys blew George's brains out in the middle of a pasture seven miles from town. At the time the narc was murdered, the three boys were between fifteen and seventeen years old.

Sometimes people in Bergenfield were stoned. Their eyes were glassy, bloodshot, they were slow, and you could smell the reefer. Nobody ever tried to hide the fact of marijuana consumption. Periodically people would be tripping. They would be laughing a certain way. They would be feeling especially tickled. Compared to standards set forth by the United States Army or the acid dons of the 1960s, the effect of the acid now available is fairly mild, more physical sensation than psychedelic. No hallucinating colors or lights—people just giggle and feel good. I was surprised to learn nobody was into sniffing glue—"too degenerate."

"Partying" here usually meant joints, beers, liquor, and if it's a good night maybe something a little stronger—coke, dust, crack. From what I could determine, the kids on the streets in Bergenfield weren't that bad. Ironically, they never seemed "burnt" by the standards of other kids I knew, say, from the beach on Long Island. People down there were dusted night after night.

On Long Island, mushrooms were the big thing for metalheads and Deadheads alike. People wore trip bracelets: three trips for each woven multicolored bracelet. You slept in them, showered and partied with them on. They didn't come off once you tied them. They were tokens of friendship. Some people made them to sell at shows. After a while you could buy them anywhere. I noticed people wearing them in Bergenfield too.

Percy had some. But he was now busy waiting to turn eighteen so he could get a tattoo. Percy is only fourteen but he's wanted a tattoo for years. Especially likes the one on the arm of one of the big guys he's been hanging with lately. I'm introduced to one guy who's freshly inked. Percy has me examine the grim reaper holding a crystal ball on a muscular arm. He's knocked out. "Yeah, whoa . . . show them suckers off down the shore, dude." He shows me the spot under the cut-off rim of his flannel shirt, it's just waiting for his design. "Snoopy smoking a doobie!" Yep, the little kid in Percy's heart was gonna be with him forever.

The situation outside of 7-Eleven has now been altered by the influx of many friends. School's out and it's a whole new scene. There are several little cliques within the untouchable sector of Bergenfield's high school population. A cranky, dumpy, mean-looking woman in her fifties is annoyed by our presence, scowls at the police —"Can't you do something about this?" Cops move out the herds. Gently, almost sympathetically, the officer tells them, "Come on, kids, you know you can't stay here."

Instinctively, we migrate to the next safe spot, across the street to the stone wall that wraps around St. John's R.C. Church. I've lost Randy somewhere in the relocation. Now I'm sitting with Doreen and Nicole.

It is usually impossible to get a quality hang going with the girls if the boys are around, because they always dominate the conversation and distract our attention. Unless they are with their girlfriend, in which case they will just be distracting her. If they cut into the train of thought it is usually to mimic or tease. It was fun, but it was also nice to be left alone with the girls sometimes.

Doreen warns me, "You shouldn't hang out with Joe and them. Real bunch of thieves." Nicky and Doreen aren't speaking now at all, and so the stories are starting to fly. It seems the week before, she heard they were all over at Susie's house, and her mother called the cops on Randy. He hadn't mentioned any of this, but that means nothing. She figures I should just know what I'm dealing with. I ask about Susie. "Same shit." By now her friends seemed more annoyed than worried about her razor-blade fixation.

There's more important gossip. Bobby, Doreen's brother, got dropped right after Nicky and Doreen broke up. Bobby had instigated another big fight down at the Rink that left a bad taste in everybody's mouth. He hadn't been around in a while. Bobby was now staying with a relative in another town. He even had a new girlfriend. After a while it got hard to follow their stories; they were always moving around and then politics could get tricky. If someone was excommunicated you had to be very careful not even to mention that you spoke to or saw that person.

Eventually, Nicole and Doreen became enemies. Doreen said something nasty about Nicole's feet being pigeon-toed. But tonight Doreen and Nicole were still the best of friends and Nicole was talking about her mother's new boyfriend. He was now in A.A. and Mom was helping him to get sober. Nicole was happy for her mother. They were more like sisters. Nicole was tight with her mom but pissed off. She had borrowed a blouse Nicole really wanted to wear tonight.

We are feasting on greasy potato chips. Nicole introduces me to Jeanne, who asks if I'm a Jesus freak since I'm obviously not a local and also not a teenager. "Oh, are you wearing that Led Zeppelin T-shirt as part of your cover?" We laugh. Jeanne is wearing a commercially tie-dyed T-shirt, lots of Indian beads, and some silver necklaces. She has a huge cluster of wool and leather friendship bracelets, and an old but clean and pressed Army jacket. It has her last name on it. Turns out it was her dad's, "from Vietnam!" He's still in the reserves, mostly for the extra cash, but he's into it, she says. "He likes going out on his little military maneuvers."

Sensing I'm a relic from the age of the hippie, Jeanne asks if I went on peace marches. "Did you ever get arrested for protesting the war?" Not for protesting the war, and yes, I explain, I went, but mainly to hang out.

Jeanne looks like she just walked out of 1969, except she's got a real clear head, is politically minded, organically so, in the true spirit of the Railroad Kids. But she's got some other ideas too. She wants to open up a youth center, dedicate it to the four kids who died in the suicide pact. She gets angry.

"Look, suicide is a disease, and those kids had serious problems, they came from messed-up families. But someone could have helped."

It's been a while since officials started hyping the suicide-prevention stuff but I wondered if anyone was actually seeing shrinks, using all the services that were advertised after the suicide pact. Jeanne laughs and mimics in shrink doublespeak: "Oh, you're feeling depressed?" Feigning seriousness, "And how does that make you feel? That makes you feel depressed . . . ?"

Jeanne's mind surfs across several subjects in the course of this brief street-side episode. She would like to become a vegetarian but her mother says she can't do that until she has her own apartment. Meanwhile she sneaks the meat under the table, feeds it to the dog.

Jeanne says she identifies with the 1960s. And she's also interested in magic. She saw someone levitate once. We get into a whole long conversation about tarot cards. "Forget black magic," she says, "it always comes back to you."

Religion, God, and spirituality are always big topics on the street. Everyone says the Bible says the world is going to end. But Jeanne is a Lennonist, after John. Pantheistic, she takes the best of all the formal religions and rock and roll and lumps it all together into a positive scheme that offers her some hope for the world's getting its act together in her lifetime.

Kids on the streets here as elsewhere are skeptical about organized religion, about the established definition of "god." They think it's phony, corrupt. Some just say it's stupid, just another scam. But they are secretly also afraid of going to hell, of maybe being innately evil, of getting punished for their sins.

And they try to be good in funny ways—to their friends; to be fair and speak truthfully. They are, for the most part, very moral, decent people. Sometimes, when things get hairy, they grasp at particular elements of their religions of origin. But always, they supplement what they were formally taught with their own ideas. Just to help get a handle on things.

Even though it's always the guys in suburbia who get the press for being "Satanteens," it is usually the girls who really are talking about the occult. Hourlong discussions about Wicca and Stevie Nicks, whether fire is stronger than water, if there is life after death. What the nature of God is. Jeanne is very mystical, spiritual. She has a world faith—nothing too organized but it's there, and it's strong. She thought she "saw" her friend Lisa Burress last week.

Now she starts to get angry. Like her friends, Jeanne hates her school. "They judge you by the way you look. Forget it. If you smoke a cigarette then you're considered a burnout. And then the teachers treat you like you're stupid." But she knows she's not. Because she dresses unconventionally, she understands that it means she will systematically get less. She is clear about it.

I ask about the jocks. "I know they rule the school because of the teams, but are they smart?"

Jeanne shows visible contempt. "No! they just sit there with a glazed look in their eyes. Neat little jockish collars all spiffed up. They just do whatever the teacher tells them. They never disagree." That was the way to win at her school and she just didn't buy it.

So Jeanne gets disposed of in a snap decision that says, Well, you're smoking, you must be stupid after all, look how you dress. And your friends, well, they're losers, truants, druggies, dropouts. It was all too easy to be dismissed around here. But Jeanne will fight for her ground.

A triad of boys nearby breaks into our conversation, joining in a rant fest about the jocks and the way teachers treat you if you don't impress them the right way. I am introduced to Roy.

I had seen him around, although we hadn't met. Jeanne knew Roy from Bergenfield High School, but she hadn't seen him there in a while. That was because Roy was now studying auto mechanics at

Bergen Vo-Tech. He says he actually *likes* school now. "I wanted to do something with my life besides sit there and have my teachers yelling at me." He's just stopped by on the way to the store, to pick up some motor oil. Roy has no time to waste on the corner today. He's got stuff to do. Has to get some things for school. On his way to get the motor oil, walking fast and tall, Roy is straight ahead on the Ave.

The Rock

Problem Child

That nice vice principal said,
My dear, look here, I don't want to sound too dramatic
But we gotta get rid of your bothersome kid
He's too problematic
He won't answer questions, he's never prepared
He's got all the little classmates scared
He won't answer questions he won't change for gym
We just don't know what to do with him
He's smokin' in the bathroom and screamin' through the halls
He's drivin' all the teachers right up the wall.

Don't blame us if he's out of control
It didn't happen suddenly when he was enrolled
We should have seen it coming, now it's out of our hands
The other mothers all demand that we take a stand
We never could have reached him, he's too far gone
Every time I see him, he's out of uniform
We try to discipline him and he just throws a fit
And we ain't paid to babysit.

We've tried detention
We've tried suspension
He needs attention
He's a problem child

Don't blame yourself it's beyond your control
It's got something to do with drugs and rock & roll
Just remember any time the kid could crack
He's a dangerous, raving little maniac
We know more about your son than you think
I've seen him after homeroom with an eight o'clock drink
Are we supposed to interest him in science and math
When he's coming on like a psychopath?

He's a lyin', cheatin', hopeless cretin problem child
And we can't have him runnin' wild.

—Raymond Jalbert

I

ne Saturday afternoon I pull into town to find Nicky, Randy, and Joe parked behind 7-Eleven in what is now referred to as "the office." It is out of view of the police, offers easy access from side roads, a quick, convenient checkpoint in either direction. I park my car there when I'm in town. When we are supposed to meet, that's where we hook up. Messages are left on windshields.

My car is especially useful for our espionage since it is a Honda. Like most kids in turnpike suburbia, these guys have American cars. Mine is Japanese, it's new, it looks "adult." I have a New York State Trooper's sticker on the back window. The fact of a foreign car, the New York plates, and that sticker are a real asset, very good cover. We can travel around freely and keep our low profile. That is good, because both Joe and Nicky have cars of notoriety.

Because it's the weekend, the guard from the bank isn't around to chase us, so we stand around for a while sipping Slurpees—the first of the season. My informants scrutinize my outfit. "That's cool, black is always cool," adjudicates Nicky. "Oh! But what have we here?" He is poking fun at my leggings because the seams are on the outside. "It's the style," I reply, attempting to be smug. By now they made fun of me the same way they made fun of all the girls.

And by now it was usually the guys that I hung around with. It was easier to hook up with them. If I saw them anywhere, any time, with rare exception, I could be included. Mostly we did nothing. The girls, though, always had a mission pending: some shopping, an errand, a planned chance meeting with "him" which meant they had to travel light. If they saw me, they would be polite, friendly, talk for a few minutes. But they were reluctant to actually include me in any of their activities.

I never took this personally; there were reasons for it. Street-corner society in suburbia is often made up of younger girls and older guys. Gender cliques are ever-present; although girls and guys can also be best friends, on the street people do tend to gravitate to their own sex. Unless they are involved in some heavy drug scene, girls will normally be gone from the street by the time they reach legal age. By twenty-one, if they're still free, they're hanging out at the bars.

But at twenty-one, the guys may still prefer the street. So a typical curbside soiree would include a few fifteen-year-old girls, one or two of the younger guys, like Bobby and Randy, and then the older ones like Joe and Nicky. Then there were friends from neighboring towns. Sometimes people in their mid-twenties hung out.

Because I was much older, and very tall, I looked really out of place hanging out with the girls. But with the older guys, I fell into an appropriate, existing street role: older, possibly divorced female burnout from another town, maybe involved with one of the guys, but mainly here for "business" (drugs). This was much better for my cover.

On the streets, there are some girls who are "macho." In addition to having severe crushes and boyfriends they also hang out in the boys' "sphere" of music, bands, and action. But when the guys go to see Slayer, for the most part, the girls will stay home. This is boys' night out. Some of the guys would rather the girls kept out altogether—one street soldier confided to me that the girls were "stupid about music . . . they'll say they like some band, they get all excited—'Oh yeah, yeah, I love Anthrax'—but then they don't know any of the songs." Others worry protectively about the girl-friend's safety, in case things at the show "get out of hand."

As rock widows, on the night of a big show, girlfriends may decide to get together at someone's house to engage in traditional American girlcult activities: shopping, pigging out, talking, playing Stevie Nicks albums, watching videos, getting high, drinking beers, cruis-ing. A few, though, will join the boys at the show for serious busi-ness. Such girls dream of *being* their rock heroes, not marrying them. They identify with the bands, and are encouraged by no-nonsense guitarists like Joan Jett, Lita Ford, and Chrissie Hynde. In Bergenfield I did meet one or two females who were involved with music on such terms, but for whatever reasons, they didn't hang out.

Because of these "methodological constraints" and because I was sort of "macho" myself about bands, the boys moved to the center of my daily narrative early on. Ironically, all my previous street work in Levittown had been with teenage girls. And in my own life, with my friends, I was deeply into "girlcult" with the other wives and girlfriends of the guys in the Grinders. We happily maintained our separate spheres: the guys went off to play music, and we sat together discussing grooming, family, jobs, cats, movies, books, and our homes.

Right now Joe and Nicky are busy carrying on about the other night. "You should have been there. We spent the whole weekend at the Building." Nicky continues, "Buds for breakfast, Buds for lunch, and Buds for dinner. Buds and Doritos. Smoked about fifty packs of cigarettes. Yeah, met some girls and just partied!" This was a major pastime. Unless you had seen a beloved band, an arena show, you'd elaborate about how fucked up you had gotten the night before, who you fucked, and all the damage you caused.

It's quiet today in Bergenfield but the spring weather makes us restless. "Feel like taking a drive?" Joe smiles and whispers something to the guys. He wants to take me to visit his alma mater. Nicky is still a student there, but Joe waxes nostalgic: "I haven't been back to that shithole in years!" We take my car and head north to the Rock.

It's only about a twenty-minute drive, and you go through some lovely towns. The Rock is rural, situated up on the New York State border, right off the Palisades Interstate in Rockleigh, New Jersey.

There are no grade levels at the Rock; you graduate when they say you're ready. Nicky explains, "They can keep you there until you're twenty-one." Of course you can always drop out, he says, but then you'll never get a decent job. Nicky's had it, though. He told them he'd quit if they didn't graduate him this June. That straightened them out. They don't like it when kids quit; it looks bad. And so his threat worked. He's definitely graduating in June, assuming he doesn't mess up in any major way. "Fuck them." Nicky is nineteen. He gets worked up just thinking about the possibility of getting stuck there for another year.

Meanwhile, I'm trying to figure out about the Rock. Why do they have to go to a school all the way up in Rockleigh? What kind of school is it? Randy and Joe explain, singing along in unison, "Well, from the Rock you go to Conklin. From Conklin you go to Jamesburg. From Jamesburg, you go to Rahway State Prison." The guys are laughing, proud to share in the power and prestige of real hard convicts. They flaunt this with style and purpose.

They presented themselves as bad boys, juvenile delinquents who riled adults and sometimes broke the rules. Usually they just did what they wanted to do. To be young and doing what they wanted to do was taboo, even after the hippies had reframed "youth defiance" as "intergenerational politics." But that was a long time ago. Once again, to mess with the social order of the high school, the community, or the family was forbidden. Adult authority was absolute. Sometimes adults viewed troublesome young people as outlaws, resenting them. Other times they viewed them sympathetically as "troubled teens," figuring that if kids broke adult rules, they must be fucked up, since the laws were for their own good. The kid must be self-destructive. Maybe even emotionally disturbed! Such kids, of course, needed help.

Once upon a time, kids like these got sent away to the warehouses upstate that were known as reform schools. In 1965 we called it "getting sent up." I remember guys I knew from the towns near where I grew up in the Rockaways. These were boys who got in trouble, usually for fighting or stealing cars. Guys with bad attitudes and long records were shipped off to places like Hawthorne Cedar-Knolls, or worse, to Elmira and South Courtwright. Reform schools, "600 schools." Grim, total institutions that isolated unruly young people far away, out of sight of their more cooperative peers. Harsh discipline, rigid work routines, and low-level vocational education were offered in the name of rehabilitation.

At the turn of the century, juvenile delinquency was almost exclusively male. Boys outnumbered girls fifty to one. But by mid-century there were bad girls too. Rude, truant, and "trampy," with hard-looking makeup and tight clothes. The bad girls in my town usually didn't get sent up, they got sent away. They'd disappear, to live with relatives in another town, to another school, sometimes to have a baby. Bad girls usually dropped out of school, went to work, and devoted themselves totally to the boyfriend—ankle bracelet, I.D. bracelet, fighting off other girls.

This was right before the Beatles, just before drugs, when the Ronnettes and the Shangri-Las instructed you on what it meant to be a woman, and the car-crash teen-death anthems ruled the AM radio airwaves.

It was very high status to have a boyfriend in serious trouble with the law. Like everybody who hung around, the guys who got sent up were tough kids, often identified as the black sheep of their families. But we looked up to the hoody older guys singing their late-night storefront harmonies in the alcoves. Especially the guys that got sent away.

State reform schools were not viewed as prisons, and the guys were not being punished, they were being "trained" in industry, reformed by ethical activity—work, school, beatings, and detention. Fucked-up families had been preempted by the court. *Parens patriae*—the court as guide and protector, benevolent, stepping in after the family, the school, and the community had failed. The new guardians would be harsh, harsher than families had been. This plan was supposedly in everyone's best interest. *Parens patriae* and the idea of adolescence worked well together to keep wild boys and angry boys behind bars.

If we periodize the history of youth by when they were most troublesome to adults, the 1950s are the decade most people associate with the idea of juvenile deliquency. The "600 schools" that housed my neighborhood cronies were formed in 1949, with the stated purpose of rehabilitating "disturbed, disruptive and delinquent children."

Adults know wild boys are a little crazy and that's why they are always fighting, partying, looking for trouble. But their caretakers have always been confused about what makes kids act bad. By the 1980s any of these things could explain teenage badness: antisocial tendencies, moral indifference, psychotic rage, anomie, parental neglect and abuse, malnutrition, borderline personality, emotional deprivation, lack of self-esteem, divorce, substance abuse, poverty, dysfunctional or disorganized family life, failure at school, labeling, racism, class bias in the institutions. In short, whatever tag was media-trendy, funder friendly, or hot in the professional journals.

By the time I met up with Nicky and his friends there were many new and creative ways for adults to warehouse troublesome kids. They could throw them in jail, remand them for drug treatment, lock 'em up in a mental institution, or dump 'em in places like the Rock. Sometimes the civil rights of young people were protected under the law, sometimes they were violated under the law. Mostly, the law was there to get them out of the way.

The famous *Gault* decision, which came down from the Supreme

Court in 1967, challenged the notion of *parens patriae* and the idea of a benevolent, paternalistic court. While *In re Gault* asserted young people's basic civil rights—to be informed of charges against them, to counsel, to confront and cross-examine witnesses, to the protections of the Fifth Amendment, to obtain a transcript of court proceedings, and to appellate review—it only protected juvenile delinquents, kids who did something bad. Under the best of conditions, there was still very little "help" available for them. And subsequent *Gault*-inspired reforms improved nothing for the dependent, hapless throwaway kid. They made no provisions for the status offender, whose crime is only a crime because of his or her status as a minor. So the truant, runaway, or "incorrigible" teen often found him- or herself warehoused in adult jails or, for lack of any alternative, in juvenile detention centers. And while the *Gault* decision looked great on the books, the courts did not readily part with the notion of *parens patriae*.

By the 1970s, the juvenile justice system would be viewed as a punitive, patriarchal, authoritarian mess. There were media exposés, and the public was outraged by reports of teen-on-teen brutalities *inside* correctional facilities—some had ended in death. A number of critical books were written. Films and television dramatizations followed. In the early 1970s the teenage suicide rate in the jails was more than three times higher than the rate of the general youth population.

Humanistic approaches to young people's "problems" were geared toward deterrence. Kids were "at risk" of going bad and programs were set up to prevent that. Reformers understood that the juvenile justice system was arbitrary, discriminatory, and biased on economic, social, and racial grounds. The idea of "kids in jail" was a national disgrace. So the Juvenile Justice and Delinquency Prevention Act of 1974 was designed to deter juvenile crime and delinquency, to set up services for runaways, and to remove juveniles from adult jails and nonoffenders and status offenders from detention facilities.

But "prevention and deterrence" could mean anything. Educators believed in teaching kids to read because illiteracy led to failure and failure led to crime. Social workers did street work with potential dropouts because dropping out would lead to idleness and idleness led to drug addiction which led to crime. Or they did "counseling" to raise "self-esteem" because low self-image led to "acting out," which might mean fighting or drug taking or cursing or anarchy, or even violence! Prevention and deterrence were not supposed to be punishment, but when such services were "mandated" by the court, they were commonly perceived as such. In turn, members of the "helping professions" often regarded such clients as "resistant."

By the 1980s, kids in jail were mostly poor, male, minority youth. Dealing drugs, assault, burglary, rape, and gang activity now came to the attention of the court as "juvenile crime." There was now a category for "urban" youth crime—a euphemism for Asian, black, and Latino kids breaking adult laws. Girls, now too, were getting into more violent crime.

Most suburban outlaws aren't in jail. At twenty-one it's not unusual to have been in and out of substance-abuse-treatment programs three or four times. The effectiveness of such programs depends on many things. My teenage neighbor Scott has strong opinions about these programs. "They try to discipline your whole life, to embarrass you out of being yourself, they put you to a routine, to make you get normal." He feels this structured approach can be helpful to some extent. More often, he feels it gets abused. "Every petty thing gets blown out of proportion."

Scott says, "Parents don't give a shit, they don't want to face problems until things blow up. Then, when shit happens, they panic, they think you're nuts. But they still won't help you out." He feels that parents may overreact to situations where drugs are involved, because of all the hype and hysteria—the media, the shrinks, the school—parents become "overeducated." But instead of becoming sensitive or acting rationally, they get hyperalert to "signs" of a "drug problem." They start reading pathology into every little thing their kid does.

Many people Scott's age are skeptical about drug programs. One alum said, "Either you get clean and then walk around feeling superior to everybody else, or you just sit around and talk about drugs all day until you want to go and get them, or you get high with the people there." Many people do it to avoid jail. Most kids know the score. "If you're rich and you get in the way, they send you to a mental hospital. If you're poor, your parents throw you out and forget about you. If you're in the middle, they send you to these stupid rehab programs."

Kids agree that rehab programs help for a while, but that they are in the long run pretty ineffectual. For the most part, drug programs operate on a "born-again" model: admit it was drugs that fucked up your life and your sins will be forgiven. Drug treatment is also a good scam for avoiding jail, for getting over on DWI charges, and for patching things up at home and in school.

Randy had a better feeling about this particular form of "help." His program was out-of-state, residential. "You have rap groups and shit, a lot of rules." He had made friends from there but eventually lost contact. These programs do have a really high recidivist rate, and this wasn't Randy's first. But he felt he'd been doing "pretty good" since he came home. He was still getting high, of course, but not like before. The program had been a nice break for Randy, had made life easier at home and chilled him out considerably. "It was pretty decent," he said.

At the very least, going into a drug program doesn't carry such a heavy stigma. Of all the places they could send you, drug programs also seem the least terrifying. First of all, they are usually short-term, and ultimately focused toward some identifiable goal—"sobriety," "recovery." And one thing is certain: a few weeks in a drug program that you don't really need is a whole lot better for your mental health than jail or a psychiatric hospital.

Poor and minority kids who act up are more likely to end up warehoused in jails, but kids from "good homes" who are out of control, mischievous, defiant, and willful may be banished from sight just as arbitrarily as their less affluent peers. While still very protected and private, by the end of the 1980s experts agreed that mental hospitals were becoming the teen jails of middle-class kids.

Considered the "biggest child welfare scandal of the last fifty years," according to a 1989 exposé by *Newsweek* magazine, the private mental hospital is viewed by middle-class parents as a desirable alternative to jail. Feeding into parental hysteria over drugs, suicide, and "alienation," the mental hospital seems a better place to send a seemingly "troubled" kid.

In the 1980s mental hospitals began to take over some of the caretaker responsibilities shared by parents, the schools, and the courts. This most recent entry in the services on behalf of "difficult" children was most frightening. See, if you're bad, at least you're hip. But if you're mentally ill, you're really a loser. You're on your own. You're disturbed, but it's not romantic. You're isolated, removed from the context where your actions have meaning. It's not social, it's *your* problem.

Until you got into the hospital where, if you lucked out, you could meet lots of other cool people to get high with, possibly to hang out with after you're released. One girl in my neighborhood said the mental hospital she went to wasn't really so bad because there were a lot of other metalheads there—"cool people, into Metallica." Sometimes you can even fall in love!

But even under the best of conditions, parents and caretakers seemed dedicated to conspiring against you, to saying all this was going to help you. So if you let on that something was bothering you, that was it. You'd be sent away.

Once upon a time, when juvenile delinquency alarmed the adults of the 1950s and 1960s, if you fucked up at school, they threw you out. If you were unspectacular they just ignored you. Maybe they tried to pick your brain with some of their psychology, but if they picked on you too much, you just quit and got a job.

On the streets if you gave the cops a hard time, they took you in and you were punished. The judge was pissed off at you. They would "rehabilitate" you. It was just a game. Everybody knew you'd get locked up and maybe you'd get a beating. But there would be no question in your mind about what was going on. You were bad and they were the law and you were taken down. Over the last twenty years, it's gotten weird.

Today, unless they're involved in hard-core juvenile crime, most kids would rather talk to a cop than a shrink any day. Consensus holds that shrinks are slippery, they dupe you into going along with them, then they fuck you up. "Nosy sons-of-bitches." The very idea of psychotherapy makes kids nuts. Besides, most shrinks are perceived as real dweebs—"We know they weren't hanging out when they were our age." Kids sense the cultural distance between themselves and their newest cast of self-anointed saviors.

But the kids have gotten their revenge. While inner-city rappers sang about gangster life, police brutality, guns, fatal beatings, and jails, the suburban-based white punk and hardcore bands crafted hilarious critiques of life in shrink-o-rama.

New York's punky Ramones spent a good part of the 1970s singing about being "teenage lobotomies," "going mental," needing "psychotherapy" and "shock treatment." They exposed the whole scam as the ridiculous cartoon that it is. By the early 1980s hardcore bands had become even more radical, making fun of adult hysteria over adolescent psycho-trauma. Among the most brilliant was L.A.'s Suicidal Tendencies' 1983 classic, "Institutionalized." In a rambling shamble of chords and narrative, a seemingly good-natured, average American kid is incarcerated after a series of parental misreadings stemming from his pensiveness about life and his request for a Pepsi. The parents tell him, "We're afraid you're gonna hurt yourself, so we decided that it would be in your best interests if we could put you some place where you could get the help that you need."

The kid, now actually ready to snap from parental psychosis over possible drug use, replies, "Wait, what are you talking about? *We* decided? *My* best interest? How do *you* know what *my* best interest is? . . . What are you trying to say? *I'm* crazy??? When I went to *your* schools, I went to *your* churches, I went to *your* institutional learning facilities? So how can you sit there and say . . ." And whenever this song played at shows throughout the 1980s, kids would regularly bleat the lyrics out, line by line.

In 1985, Metallica sang "Welcome Home (Sanitarium)," a moving tale of individual suffering in an institution. "They think our heads are in their hands but violent use brings violent plans, keep him tied it makes him well, he's getting better can't you tell . . . no more can they keep us in, listen damn it, we will win. They see it right they see it well, but they think this saves us from our hell . . . Sanitarium . . . leave me be . . ."

All over the country, youth-generated fanzines and street sheets were full of letters to peers asking for and offering support, public messages with advocacy tips, reprints of state laws. Kids had to do their best to help each other from psychiatric persecution.

Finally, by the end of the eighties, some adults began to listen to the kids. Youth advocates, now being heard, warned parents of what was going on. There were media exposés, and more people were made aware of mental hospital dump scams through television shows and movies.

Newsweek reported that in-patient hospitalization for children under eighteen had increased from 82,000 in 1980 to more than 112,000 in 1986. This was mostly in admissions to private hospitals. Roughly 43,000 kids were admitted to freestanding private psychiatric hospitals in 1986 compared to 17,000 in 1980 and 6,452 in 1970. Four out of five kids were white, and they were mostly middle- to upper-middle-class, diagnosed with minor but scientific-sounding personality disorders such as the infamous "adolescent adjustment reaction."

This was the new teen gulag. Reform schools used to represent coercion to obedience through beatings and authoritarian discipline. Now we had psychotropic drugs and therapeutic mind control. Advocates have called these practices the worst violation of young people's civil rights to come along in years.

This is nothing new; it has been creeping into teenagers' lives little by little. Jail if you're poor, mental hospital if you're rich. This puts guys like Nicky between a rock and a hard place. If his crime of brutally beating up a neighborhood boy is juvenile delinquency, is he bad or is he sick? Should he be in teen jail or a mental hospital?

From a sociological point of view, Nicky's sort of in a contradictory class location—he is white and suburban. His family owns their own home, a few cars, a small cabin upstate. He sees himself as middle-class; most suburban Americans do. But by his habits and attitudes and interests, and the fact of his father's blue-collar occupation, Nicky is working-class. He is Republican, and very patriotic. So where does a bad boy like Nicky fit in?

Between the black male juvenile prison inmate underclass and the privileged white suburban psychiatric hospital there is a place for Nicky: the Rock.

My immediate reaction hearing about the Rock was that it was a reform school, except more fancy because Bergen County was rich. On a good day, Nicky and his friends did still see themselves as juvenile delinquents. It was nothing to be ashamed of, to have had a brush with the law.

Nicky and his friends were kids with records, known to the authorities. They were troublemakers; they had been thrown out of their local high schools, mainly for fighting. They were academic failures, identified losers in the community game.

Yet most of the jargon Nicky and his friends mimicked when describing their situation did not come from reform school. I had been out of "youth services" for years, but I knew mental health lingo. The whole country is saturated in it—psychotherapy is now firmly established as *the* panacea. Our visit to the Rock was a real joy ride as long as the idea of delinquency operated. But once that wore thin, and the truth of their situation emerged, things got uncomfortable. The joke was turning on them.

As we approach the campus, Nicky recites "Child Study Team" from a sign that leads to the area where their classrooms are situated. I ask him about the child study team. Nicky isn't too clear about what it is. He just says impatiently, "It's a team. You know. A Child Study Team." I had never heard of it. But it sounded like mental health. As it turned out, "the Rock" was special education in New Jersey.

In the adult mind, describing a kid as "special ed" is a cue that something's just a little bit wrong with the kid. Maybe not quite retarded, but not normal either. It implies the kid's missing something, or that something's just not working right. It does have a stigma, although most parents are still relieved by the possibility that the damage is organic. If it's psychological, they are to blame. If it's a hardcore birth defect, they may never forgive themselves. But if it's slightly chemical, curable by Ritalin or something, they're off the hook and there's hope! It's the least of all stigmas to bear.

Everyone would agree that what is now the special-education empire began with the best of intentions. Before its creation, many American children were being denied education. Children who did not fit the middle-class norm were invisible. Kids with handicapping conditions were generally denied access to public education. Often, schools simply did not have the resources or facilities to accommodate their special needs.

Various special-interest groups—parents of handicapped children, adults with disabilities—had fought for equal treatment and the right to access for over a hundred years. But the Kennedy family's commitment to the retarded stirred public awareness of the invisible minority. Parents pressured legislators, organizations and advocates lobbied, and the federal government responded. In 1975

Congress passed the Education for All Handicapped Children Act and Gerald Ford signed it into law. This was hailed as a "bill of rights" for handicapped students. Federal funds became available for each state by 1978. Any school that did not provide equal educational opportunities to disabled kids was now in violation of the law.

States were mandated to establish procedures for the identification and evaluation of all kids with disabilities in school settings—public, private, residential, or correctional facilities. The school district's level of federal funding would depend upon the number of its special-education students. The evaluation was to be a fair assessment of the student's abilities. The law was intent on protecting the rights of handicapped students, and was based on an ideal of "cooperation" between parents and educators.

The school was to provide free and appropriate education for all students aged three to eighteen who were identified as handicapped. The related services—psychotherapy, physical therapy, speech correction—that were required to meet the individual educational needs of each child would also be provided. Each state was required to design and implement an educational plan for handicapped children.

On paper, special education was great. Each kid identified as having a handicapping condition would get the personal attention of professionals, generally a social worker, a school psychologist, and a learning disabilities teacher-consultant. Parents, and where possible the child, were to play a big role in this ongoing process.

Along with the mentally retarded, the hearing-impaired, the visually impaired, the physically disabled, and the multiply handicapped, children with behavioral and emotional problems, learning disabilities such as the inability to express ideas, and communication disorders like stuttering or high-pitched voices came under this law. Once classified, the child's right to special education was set in motion.

The federal government was willing to put a lot of money behind education for the handicapped. It was one of the four largest long-term federal programs for kids. Even under Reagan, this federal program fared well. Funding continued for special education as other programs and opportunities diminished in the 1980s.

Teachers were happy too. As the baby boom moved into adulthood, and the population of school-age children declined, school buildings were empty. The overpopulated teaching profession flooded a diminishing market—there were fewer kids in school. By 1978, as special education went into operation, it was seen as a real boost to a dying industry.

Special education would require the creation of a bureaucratic state apparatus for the purposes of interpreting and implementing the law, program development, research, and evaluation. There would be "direct service providers," including special "resource room" teachers, supplemental teachers, home instructors, school psychologists, social workers, nurses, psychologists, neurologists, ophthalmologists, optometrists, audiologists, recreation therapists . . . and on and on and on.

Then, an ancillary market was generated in degrees in special education. Like any organizing profession, special education had developed a distinctive body of knowledge, and claims of scientific-ity and professional ethics; it had its own jargon, and a unique shop culture.

As the special-education empire flourished, careers were built; people would go to conferences, publish in the journals, join new professional associations, and participate in "networking" to perpetuate and advance their positions and the prestige of their own territories within the empire. Stars would publish books, innovate new conceptual models, share new findings, strategize for collective aggrandizement, publish books, speak to the public, even appear on television and radio talk shows.

As one of our more recently established semi-professions, special education is actually a patchwork of white-collar workers, experts, specialists, and altruists grouped together, mutually dependent. They cooperate to keep the empire going, for the personal rewards of good work, professional prestige, local power, and job security. In the fifteen years since it was created, special education has become big business under a banner of high purpose.

Early on, special education showed a destructive side, particularly for kids identified with behavioral, emotional, and learning disabilities. First of all the law formalized the socially constructed "learning disability" as a matter of fact. It could now be taken for granted as a natural condition, albeit so minimal that often it could only be measured by the kids' weird behavior, as per the teacher's observations. Established as medical phenomena, nobody would question that these handicapping conditions were organically based, that they *existed*.

Second, there was growing evidence that categories such as "learning disabilities" were ideological, not biological. Critics of special education have pointed out that the discovery of "LD," as it was nicknamed, dovetailed with America's recognition that its children were not keeping up with their European and Japanese counterparts. The learning deficit created during the 1980s was now to be blamed on the kids and their parents—not on the failure of the American public school system, or this country's lack of economic commitment to its children. America's stupid children couldn't learn because many of them were actually brain-damaged! They needed special attention. At the very least they had to be removed so educators could do their best with the little they had to work with in the way of raw materials.

Parents were reassured that the brain was a very intricate entity, so their child's "brain damage" wasn't always measurable—but it was there. Because the kid was having all these problems in school. Experts had it all figured out. And weren't parents so lucky they had? Relieved parents now understood why their kids were losers in the classrooms. They had "learning disabilities." They weren't bad, they weren't even dumb. They were simply working against the odds, burdened by a hidden handicap.

And because of the alleged disabling condition, parents were advised, such children often "acted out" their frustrations of not being able to be like the other kids (read obedient, normal, cooperative) because their brains were slightly imperfect. Like needing glasses, or braces for your teeth, it could be corrected.

From the beginning, the gaps between the ideals and the reality of special education for kids identified as learning-disabled, hyperactive, and emotionally disturbed bothered people. Even within the professional community of special education, practitioners were aware that the classification systems used to identify such special kids were not precise, that they were grossly unscientific and unstandardized.

Arrogant and defensive about their new, untested expertise, special-education administrators and practitioners devised their own impenetrable and arbitrary classification system through which such American children could be evaluated, tested, tracked, monitored, and coerced. Obtaining funds for special-education services depended on it. The child who would not be classified, or labeled, identified as having a handicapping condition could not be serviced. Well-intentioned service providers knew that the law provided for handicapped kids and that if the power of the label were to diminish, the leverage of lobbying groups would be weakened. Advocacy on behalf of kids with special needs would be hampered. By the 1980s everybody also agreed that labeling children was damaging, that it led to self-fulfilling prophecies of failure and hopelessness. But they also understood that the funding game depended upon it.

So administrators would train their direct-service providers (teachers, guidance counselors) to be alert to "identifying" the more socially constructed "symptoms" of the behaviorally and emotionally impaired child. Programs were mandated and waiting for kids "at risk." Research directors developed "instruments" to substantiate the observed "conditions." Kids could be set up to fall right into these categories. And in spite of the safeguards provided for parents' rights under the law, there were seductive methods of bullying parents into going along with "expert" assessments of their child. Special education today is helping many kids who really do have special needs. It also is damaging many kids—intransigent kids, kids who simply don't and won't fit in.

So along with the "learning-disabled" and "hyperactive" child, the child like Nicky Trotta, who is diagnosed as "emotionally disturbed" ("ED"), becomes a subject of bureaucratic domination at its most sophisticated. And despite the legislation stating that the child's evaluation shall not be tainted by cultural or racial biases, special education is often about the containment of minority and working-class male children. Everybody knows "who" is in special-education classes.

Under the Public Education Law, this is essentially what Randy, Nicky, and Joe have done to earn their tag. To be certified "ED" kids, you must be "exhibiting seriously disordered behavior over an extended period of time which adversely affects educational performance and may be characterized by the following:

1. An inability to build or maintain *satisfactory* interpersonal relationships.
2. Behaviors *inappropriate* to the circumstances, such as general or pervasive mood of depression or the development of physical symptoms or irrational fears.

A psychiatric evaluation may also be required. But the magic trick occurs in the words "satisfactory" and "inappropriate." The first is arbitrary, biased in favor of the person making the judgment. The latter is ironic. "Inappropriate." Behavior that is not considered suitable for the situation—a pervasive mood or depression, physical symptoms, irrational fears. Inappropriate? The experience of being in school for many such kids is depressing and scary. They go on automatic pilot, shut down whenever they encounter authorities, and often describe their everyday experiences as humiliating. So by doing their best to survive this humiliation, they are viewed as emotionally disturbed.

In 1986, "ED" kids made up the third largest group of New Jersey's handicapped youth population, after the "perceptually" and then the "neurologically" impaired. By 1989, there was a rapper named Special Ed, he had an album out.

There is still no official definition of what an emotional disturbance is, and no consensus on what programs would be effective in treating it. There are no standardized or even reliable instruments with which a valid definition of this condition could be derived, operationalized, measured, and evaluated. The state of being "emotionally disturbed" is subjectively determined on a case-by-case basis across localities, regions, and states. As such it is quantifiable only at the lowest level, since nobody even agrees on what the behaviors are or how to measure them. Yet this condition is often reported as if it is empirically evident across the population. In addition, many of the "symptoms" of emotional disturbance are transient in nature and found, in varying degrees, among all young people.

At a loss for even the most crude methodological tools, those who attempt to diagnose the emotionally disturbed are urged to try everything: intelligence testing, projective tests, achievement tests, observation, interviewing, and neurological exams. Of all these, observation is the most widely used. It allows for more subjective, arbitrary interpretations. Even if the observer is sympathetic to the kid, likes the kid, the prerequisites of the bureaucratic empire may prevail. Everyone knows that if a program needs kids, kids will appear to need that program. Normal kids will end up needing special services.

In the 1980s, when social intolerance was high *and* the population of America's children was low, *and* very few resources were available for social welfare and educational programs for kids, *and* parents were hard pressed to keep up with bills, or to make time for their kids, special education for "emotionally disturbed" kids was a quick way of soothing guilt-ridden, overworked parents.

Special education functions as a dump site for troublemakers; but also, the threat of being labeled and sent to the "rubber room" (resource room) with "the retards" exerts a powerful pressure on all kids to do everything possible to please the teacher. It has a chilling effect on creativity, individuality, and spontaneity. It encourages rigid conformity. Kids who do not develop on cue, or jump hoops to the norm, can easily catch a diagnosis of some sort. Some critics fear it can ultimately lead to a totalitarian state.

The desire to turn nonconforming behavior into a disabling condition is first expressed in a language game. This is how it works: A kid who is bored and can't sit still in a lifeless classroom with a punitive teacher is "hyperactive." The child is thus controlled by being identified as having a disabling condition. This condition is treated by medication, and then by sequestering the child in an even more controlled environment, like the Rock.

Special-education practitioners and bureaucrats will admit that of all their classifications, "emotionally disturbed" is the most vague. Passed off as a clinical diagnosis, it is sometimes referred to as a "conduct disorder" or "behavioral disorder." Plainly stated, the kids don't cooperate with the teacher. They express their feelings and they have to be removed because this is disruptive.

"We're emotionally disturbed!" This "acting bad," being a juvenile delinquent because you were emotionally disturbed, was what the boys sang to Officer Krupke in *West Side Story*. Today, this condition reappears in special education as a medical and psychological "disability." Almost every definition offered for the emotionally disturbed student of the 1980s matches those once outlined for juvenile delinquents of the 1950s.

Special education. Life at the Rock. This was the worst of all worlds. Not so bad that you could be hip in teen jail like the baddest of bad—the brothers (blacks). And not quite crazy enough to be in a fancy mental hospital cooling off and partying with more affluent burnouts for a month or two. You were stuck at the Rock. Some kids have been stuck in special education with bogus diagnostic tags since they were in the third grade. Nobody you knew stayed in jail or the psycho ward that long!

Yet nobody was doing magazine and television exposés about how fucked up it was that you were being labeled and warehoused by these amateur scientists. Or that your school seemed to be in collusion with special educators to scam resources that kids who really did have special needs deserved. And your parents were sure the experts knew better, what was *in your best interests.* If they failed to go along with the plans made on your behalf, maybe your parents weren't doing their job very well. Maybe that's why you were "emotionally disturbed."

Now in the state of New Jersey, the classification dealing with bad boys can be "emotionally disturbed" or "socially maladjusted." A socially maladjusted youth has problems with authority to the point of having an arrest record. It is a practical, objective definition. In effect, the socially maladjusted youth violates the laws of the state. The "emotionally disturbed" kid violates the social order of the public school.

Every boy I know in special education who has been diagnosed as "ED" got that label from fighting. Maybe fighting like that shows he was "socially maladjusted"—he should learn to act properly around people, talk to them about his feelings, not act them out. But kids labeled socially maladjusted ("SM") can't get federal funding for special education. They are specifically excluded. So where possible kids will be labeled "ED" by altruistic school personnel, because that way more program options will be available for that kid.

Welcome, my son, welcome to the machine: Kids are silent because they fear getting sent to "retard" school (stigma worse than death). Observer reads this as repressed anxiety. "That kid is ready to blow up at any moment." Kid fidgets? This proves poor impulse control. Everything is suspect, any act can incriminate. It is not difficult to see how these "specialists" not only invent but often facilitate the pathologies they need to observe in order to classify and compile the body count that keeps the machine moving smoothly.

Over the last ten years, several books have been written about the dangerous "side effects" of special education. Parents with kids caught in this morass have successfully organized self-advocacy groups. Anger at the misuse of education for the handicapped—as a way to coerce, control, and warehouse uncooperative kids—may not be news. But it's still coming down hard on lots of hapless kids every day and it is destroying many of them.

II

It took me a really long time to figure out how Nicky, Joe, and Randy got involved in education for the handicapped. What were three such street-smart boys with long histories of fighting doing here, at a facility for children with extraordinary needs, and not simply in some juvenile detention as delinquents? What was the leap of logic used to justify this particular strategy?

Well, it seems that shortly after their invention, learning disabilities, minimal brain dysfunction, and hyperactivity were linked to the idea of "predelinquency." And known offenders' histories were probed to prove that they had a "history" of school failure, that they were, in fact, "learning disabled" students.

The traits of the predelinquent child could include anything even remotely eccentric, irregular, or deviant. Emotional disturbance was to be expected. Such conditions usually came in pairs, multiplicities of disorder. Since these "diseases" did not exist before the 1970s, the linking of them to prevention, deterrence, and diversion was brilliant. If they could fix Nicky's handicapping condition—presumably, his very bad temper and his poor attitude—he could be saved from a life of crime.

Joe's story was the most upsetting. When I met him he was a good-looking guy, muscular, well-groomed. But he says when he was young he was very funny-looking. He was short and he walked weird. He says he didn't develop exactly like other people. The teachers had it in for him.

He wonders if maybe it was because his mother wasn't too articulate and his father was always drunk. Maybe the teachers couldn't
get a straight answer about Joe's situation. Maybe they just figured
he was such a mess, why bother with him?

But, he says, the school didn't like it that he was so slow. They
thought he was stupid. They put him in with the "retards." He
couldn't take it. The dicks finally made him take some tests and it
turned out he wasn't retarded. He was normal. He was even smart.
But by now they had fucked with him so many times that he finally
hit his teacher. That was wrong, he admits.

It almost sounded like they drove him crazy so they could say he
was disturbed. And by now he probably was. Then they certified
him so they could get rid of him.

Nicky, in a Motley Crue T-shirt, tells the story of how he got sent
to the Rock. "You're a psycho," Joe laughs. (Because of the fight he
got into with the kid who was bothering his sister.) Randy laughs
proudly, reiterating the rap on Nicky. "Yeah, attempted manslaughter. He bashed the guy's head in." Nicky nods solemnly and goes on
with the story. Nicky's sister told him the guy was "bothering" her.
So Nicky decided to straighten it out. "Look, it got out of hand." He
pounded the guy's head into the cement. Nicky says the kid almost
died. "Look, he tried to rape my sister." Not one of us doubts his
sincerity. This was a few years ago, Nicky says, around the time his
girlfriend moved away.

Pretty much every guy I'd met on the streets in north Jersey has
gotten into trouble for fighting. They had gotten in trouble for a
number of things. They were troublemakers. What highly trained
mental health professionals viewed as pathological rage, psychotic
or "borderline" tendencies, meant something very different to these
guys. Within the context where traditional values of male toughness,
street-smartness, and not taking any shit count, they were heroes.

Like many boys with prole roots before them, the socially maladjusted boys lived in one world while they were expected to be part
of another. And they were confused themselves about where they
really belonged. In this other world their healthy desires for thrills
and adventure, their loyalty to the group, and their independence
from adult authority did not cut it.

Traditions like hanging out, unstructured street-based recreation, and creativity in "staying out of trouble" have never impressed authorities. From the beginning, early on in the twentieth century, as child labor laws and mandatory schooling were implemented, the newly sequestered working-class kids' "shop floor culture" carried over to the school. These practices were part of their heritage, prole survival strategies developed over time. Assembly-line sabotage took the form of "pranks"—stealing the chalk. Workplace solidarity became loyalty to one's friends, not the institution. After-hours and break-time fraternizing became "smokin' in the boys room." But middle-class school caretakers interpreted these activities as sure signs of moral depravity. By the 1980s, such moves were being read as indications of possible mental illness, future criminality, and maybe even brain damage!

So Nicky and Joe and Randy were stuck. Sometimes feeling angry for reasons they never put into words, feeling proud for being bad and strong, they also felt worthless. Low self-esteem. Did it come from your father kicking you around the house telling you that you were a scumbag? Or from your teachers suggesting that you were mentally ill, retarded, and maladjusted? They weren't poor, and they were white. Wasn't life in the suburbs supposed to be different? Weren't they in "good schools" and from "good homes"?

When they didn't feel like they were street gods—in the adventure of the moment—they felt like shit. And when things didn't seem to be going their way, they started thinking maybe they really were losers, hopeless cases, emotionally disturbed, like everybody said.

It was hard to figure out who to be angry at. There were no "gangs" or clear lines of class or ethnic difference to focus your rage. So you struck out directly—at the teachers and principals who treated you like shit. At the dickhead who bothered your sister, disrespected your family, baited you to prove yourself. At anyone who bothered you—the "dothead" who owned the card shop in Foster Village, the "queers" walking together on the streets of the towns you were cruising, looking for something, anything, to make you feel okay. You defended everything you had and everything you were with a fierce passion. If you couldn't stick up for your family, your friends, what were you?

"I have a mean streak," Nicky declares. His teachers have convinced him of this. They said he was mean. "Yeah, I'm a problem child." Nicky laughs as he rattles off a string of language that sounds cut-and-pasted from the *Diagnostic Statistical Manual.* All Nicky really gathered from his encounters following the "attempted manslaughter" was that he was "emotionally disturbed."

Here is all this professional jargon coming out of Nicky's face. He rattles it off like the lines to some stupid poem your English teacher makes you memorize. His eyes are blank, blinking at words he thinks might mean ugly things. Then he lights a cigarette and fiddles with the bass and treble dials on my car stereo. When he doesn't numb out about it or laugh it off, he seems to accept it as an essential truth about himself.

But what he isn't doing is making any connections between what he did to the kid who bothered his little sister and how his father disciplines him: the beatings, the names he sometimes calls Nicky "for his own good," and all the trouble at school. No, Nicky just keeps his mouth shut.

Fighting on behalf of family honor is something his friends understand. Nicky prides himself on being righteous. "My friends know me. Ask any of them. I'm loyal to the end. I've proved it." Nothing else really matters.

Nicky says he wants to graduate for no other reason than to show his dad he isn't "a dummy." His father often baits him, puts him down. But Nicky understands this as a challenge. Nicky's father figures his son has to learn things the hard way, the way he did when he was growing up. Dom—Nicky's father—works in an auto body shop. For a hobby he rebuilds muscle cars. Years ago he raced them. He was pretty good, Nicky likes to boast. Nicky says Dad comes home every night after work, eats dinner, blows a joint, and listens to Floyd before he goes to sleep. Nicky's mother is younger than I am. She had Nicky very young.

Randy volunteers some collective case histories. "Our parents are just like us!" He goes round-robin among his friends. "Ex-alcoholic, ex-junkie . . ."

Randy, Nicky, and Joe saw themselves as the seventh sons of seventh sons—bad seed, black sheep. They acknowledged their burnout roots as genetic, not social. They respected their parents, and they feared them. They loved and hated them as all children do. Randy's father went to Woodstock, he says, and of this Randy was especially proud.

Joe's father seemed unusually abusive, especially while he was actively drinking. He'd calmed down a lot since he'd been in A.A., but he was still a pretty nasty guy. Joe couldn't win, but Nicky was trying real hard to be a good boy. And sometimes Randy and Joe gave him shit about it. But Nicky knew that his father was behind him no matter what. He believed this absolutely, and that was Nicky's strength.

Your friends, and your family. That was the main thing, the three agreed. The rest was just strategy: Let the dicks play their stupid games. You tell them what they want to hear, and then put it behind you.

The State of New Jersey claims to offer lots of counseling services for emotionally disturbed kids like Nicky. But for all the obscure language used to describe Nicky's frame of mind, and his implied mental illness, he wasn't getting any treatment. And if he was, he didn't know about it.

The Rock is a campus that hosts students with a variety of special needs. Nicky's school day lasts from nine in the morning until two-thirty in the afternoon. Nicky says he hates taking the special-services buses, they are the same buses that transport the physically handicapped kids—"the retards." But it's not so bad. There's a residential drug-treatment program at the Rock and so it's fairly easy to get drugs, meet girls.

But basically, they say, the Rock is a dump. No heat in the winter, so you freeze your ass off walking through the corridors. Nicky says there was a big thing at the Rock a few years ago. Asbestos falling from the ceilings was all over their desks. Nicky says the asbestos was so bad they had to sweep it out themselves. He says the dicks lied their way out of it. For Nicky, the asbestos scandal proves what scumbags the administration is. People could get cancer, and look at the way they covered it up. Any proof of falsehood on the part of the administration empowers Nicky. It vindicates him, at least for the moment.

"The niggers are another big problem," Nicky says. The school is racially polarized and Nicky thinks the dicks use it to their advantage. There are always fights. Sometimes they stage them down at the gym. Nicky figures the dicks want them to let off steam—to beat the shit out of each other so they'll leave the teachers alone.

Nicky thinks that's really dumb. "You'd think that we're all here getting fucked around, we'd stick together, but we don't. The whites don't go near the blacks." Joe laughs. "It's the same way in prison."

The rest of it at the Rock is pretty boring. Nicky says you are locked into your classroom the entire day. You sit there all day doing nothing but waiting for cigarette break. I ask what courses there are. Any that they like? They like art. That's it. Sometimes Nicky writes lyrics, or else letters to his old girlfriend. Since I know they are very interested in music I ask about that. Nicky plays drums. What about music class? Forget it, Nicky says. The teacher's a wimp. Randy and Joe confirm: "The guy makes you listen to Beethoven!"

One thing that really bothers Nicky is the environment he's exposed to at the Rock. All the filthy language the kids use. "Motherfucking this, fucking that. First thing in the morning. That's how my day begins?! This is supposed to help me? Hearing that kind of talk—is that how I'm supposed to start my day?" Nicky says, "The only reason I'm human is because I went to a normal district high school for three years. I went to a normal school, I had normal friends."

The campus that hosts their program looks very pleasant—set in an open area, lots of greenery and fresh air for the boys. The buildings are spread out and it does look like a small community college. We pass the drug program, which looks like a church. Some of the people in the program live there, but Nicky thinks it's a big joke. The concentration of people at the Rock interested in getting high makes life much easier in Bergen County. People no longer have to make drug runs into New York City.

Strolling along on the campus at Rockleigh, the "special" boys show me the woods behind their building. You can easily sneak off to fool around or get high. "There's the shed." Randy was recently caught sneaking off toward the shed and had to serve all-day detention. Another crucial spot is up on the roof. They point to a chair some ten feet overhead. You can hang up there and take a break, smoke a joint, watch the fights.

This whole special-education thing seemed so male, I wondered if there were any "special" girls. Nicky says the Rock is coed. "There's two girls here and they get the shit fucked out of them cause they're the only ones." Real whores; Nicky wants no part of them. "You want somebody you can be proud of. Those girls will go with anybody. Who wants a slut?"

I ask Nicky about "therapy" for the "emotionally disturbed" boys of the Rock. Was he getting any help? Was there anyone there he could talk to? He laughs. "No, man, if I'm fucked up enough to get to the Rock, forget it. They've given up on me."

Disposable Heroes

We must try to get rid of it. We've tried to look after it and to put up with it as far as is humanly possible, and I don't think anyone could reproach us in the slightest.

—From Franz Kafka,
The Metamorphosis

I

There was Bergenfield High School, there was the Rock, and then there was the vocational high school. By now I understood from several of my street companions that a better life could be had at Bergen Vo-Tech. Dirtbags, burnouts, metalheads, and thrashers alike could find pride and purpose in Bergen County's trade schools. Here, as in other suburban towns, the local vocational and technical school is usually called "heavy metal high school" because of all the metalheads who attend.

Vocational high school may be viewed by academically oriented educators as a convenient dump site for troublemakers with low test scores. But for the kids who end up there, it's often a pretty cool scene. Especially here in Bergen County, where every dirtbag shuttled over to a vocational school has the additional prestige of knowing S.O.D.'s lead singer went to one. Wherever I went in Bergen County, if music was seriously discussed, people made sure to tell me that S.O.D.'s powerful front man, Billy Milano, was from Bergen County. So what if the jocks were winning state competitions—the dirts had Billy and S.O.D. for their regional pride.

Meanwhile, there were guys like Roy. I had met him on the Ave one night, talking to Jeanne and Nicole. Roy rarely hung out anymore, now that he was learning to labor on the cars of America. It was a great career choice, and it seems to have happened quite by chance. It's a familiar story, though.

This is how it goes: The teacher calls you down to talk about your record. Or maybe it's the guidance counselor. "So, Roy, what do you see yourself doing five years from now?" And Roy is thinking what did I do wrong, what does she want me to say, what is going to come down on me now? And then the guidance counselor will say something about Roy's lack of spectacular grades—"not on any teams or in any clubs, are you, Roy?" And Roy starts feeling stupid and maybe he fiddles with himself nervously, and says the first thing that comes to his head, like how much he enjoys working on his car. Like she shouldn't think he's a total loser. And that's that! He's never really given much thought before now, but today, the future is laid out before him and now Roy's going to vocational high school and he's going to learn about cars.

He's so relieved that he's not in trouble, and that this adult hasn't figured out that he really hasn't got a clue about what he's going to do with his life because nobody ever asked him about it. Or impressed upon him that what he wants might be important. Until today, most of what Roy has been concerned with has been keeping out of trouble, keeping out of his teachers' way. So Roy is satisfied because now he has a future, and with it, an identity and plans. Maybe he'll do well at it. His foster mother is proud of him. He's almost grown, and now he's got a direction.

In the suburban high schools of America the greasers have always been found hanging around outside "shop." There are many "hoody"-looking types who have good academic grades, who are book-smart, but that's not the stereotype. Working-class males smoking cigarettes and bonding around labor. Girls gathered around small office machines and hair-setting apparatus. This territory is now the domain of America's metalheads. Dirtbags, metalheads, thrashers, burnouts. Black and Hispanic kids are part of this too.

Bergen County's Vocational Technical School, where Roy was now enrolled, was in Hackensack. When I mentioned this to some guy I met at Hav-A-Pizza in the Foster Village Shopping Center, he said, "Oh yeah, that's a real burnout school." The school has a great street rep. So I drove out to Roy's school that afternoon, to find out what this school was doing right.

The campus is situated near Roy Rogers, which is right away a good spot for a school. In the parking lot an unidentifiable thrash band's snarecore drumroll propels two long-haired dudes deep into the engine of an old light-green Chevy Nova. Many of the grand bombs of the Ave will have been resurrected here. Engines and bodies and hoods and fenders and hair. Here, the celebration of car culture becomes a legitimate practice, and it's okay to be yourself. You learn what you like to learn. That's why you're here.

There are greenhouses, and clusters of girls in smocks. Before I introduce myself to the authorities I meander through the halls. The school is clean and cheerful, although clearly "not for kids." Serious business is conducted here. On display are the successful liaisons of youth and industry, career ladders in various trades, union wage schedules. I am stopped by a man who is a teacher. We chat comfortably. This is far from Bergenfield and he is delighted that I am interested in the school.

For more information he suggests the guidance counselor's offices, and directs me there. I am told that someone can see me in about twenty minutes, as a door shuts behind a middle-aged woman with dark hair and a young girl. Meantime, would I mind waiting in the library?

I walk by a room filled with computers. A few moments later I am seated near some kids doing library time, working on a report, relaxing and quietly talking. I pick from a table of magazines: *Psychology Today, BYTE, Horticulture, The Conservationist, Parents, New Jersey Outdoors, Family Computing, Gourmet.* Something for everyone.

A glamorous teenage girl shows off an earring someone made for her in shop. It's delicate metal sculpture, something nice enough to wear to a show. A boy in a concert polo shirt teases her, all the while viewing the librarian for sanctions. The librarian glares once or twice, but goes on to other business. The students seem more physically relaxed than their counterparts in regular schools. They're more stylish too, from a street point of view. That makes sense; these are specialized programs for kids interested in food preparation, cosmetology, carpentry, commercial art, and the interest in grooming and styling is strong. Also, they will be working with the public in some of these fields, so personal appearance is important.

The time passes quickly in this sunlit airy room. I am greeted by the dark-haired guidance counselor, Dolores Bentivegna. We sit down in her office and I ask her, simply, why kids seem to like this school so much. By now I understand the basic breakdown: Kids with behavior problems are sent to special services—emotionally disturbed kids, school phobics, and disabled kids. And kids with low grades are often encouraged to come here, dumped into vocational education. That way teachers can spread scarce resources efficiently, focus on the more intellectually responsive kids, the college material. Keep the school looking good, the test scores robust, all so their "brighter" kids have a better chance.

I also understand from the kids that getting farmed out to the vocational high school involves some degree of coercion. But once they get here, they like it, they are happy. So I ask this guidance counselor what is the secret of this school's success.

Mrs. B. explains that this school has the longest school day in the district, no study hall, a short lunch break. Half the day is academic, half is for work in one's chosen field. The program is highly structured. Not all the kids can handle it. That makes sense, I say, since a number of kids who have been encouraged to come here say they have no real interest in vocational training.

I am offered a general overview of the school system in Bergen County. Mrs. Bentivegna also hands me a leaflet with a phone number for help. Kids can call from anywhere in the county and hook in through this number. Mrs. B. tells me that the school deals with suicide prevention in two ways: directly, through talking about it with the students, and indirectly, by building self-esteem, giving kids attention. Kids get support in structuring their lives, setting real goals and meeting them. Mrs. B. pulls out a wad of program materials, group-counseling modules based on values clarification, reality therapy, failure and success orientations, self-image. She had prepared most of it herself.

I remembered Roy telling me he felt his new school was more personalized—his teachers actually talked to him like he was "a person." At first, Mrs. B., like all school personnel, seemed very formal. But she was very helpful and after a while I really liked her.

The most striking thing about this environment is its basic assumptions about how kids should be schooled. There is a difference between its supportive, structured program and the authoritarian humiliation academically uninclined kids usually experience in regular public high schools. Here, the kids seem to respond to the formal discipline because the rules and orders have measurable goals. Knowledge has a discernible, practical application. There are reasons for doing what you are told.

Mrs. B. is firm and clear in her opinions. She obviously believes in the kids. But she says she worries about young people today. She's a mother. The problem, she feels, is too much permissiveness. There's no discipline, the family isn't what it used to be, morality, values have been lost. Kids are scared by society, drugs and alcohol are everywhere, and violence too. For many kids it's a no-win situation. They ask for help, they get labeled. They say nothing and don't get help.

After the suicide pact, Mrs. B. explains, everybody worked overtime, calling families of kids who lived in Bergenfield, meeting and talking it out. She thinks there are a lot of good people at Bergenfield High School—teachers, counselors—who got a bad rap from the media. Some of the kids had said that too, but they begged me not to go speak to these people, fearing it could get them in trouble. It didn't matter if one or two people were nice to you there, it was still school, and that meant you had to watch it.

Following a good hour of her time, Mrs. B. gives me her card, and I thank her.

That night it occurs to me that most of the guys I knew from Metal 24, guys in my neighborhood, were "B.O.C.E.S." graduates —New York State's version of Bergen Vo-Tech. The Board of Co-operative Educational Services of Nassau County was famous for many things. Some kids were sent there for vocational training or for programs in the arts, and they spoke lovingly of their high school experiences. Some programs were directly related to Long Island's aerospace and technology industries.

Other kids were "special," like Nicky and Joe and Randy, too "emotionally disturbed" for the mainstream classroom. These guys were sent to the school in Baldwin Harbor because they were even too rowdy for the "rubber rooms" in their own districts. They just took it in stride: the label, the Ritalin, the warehousing.

Then there was "B.O.C.E.S. for chicks"—that's what the guys call the traditionally feminine fields of cosmetology, flower arranging, data processing, food preparation, and dental assisting. I live near Nassau Tech, a major B.O.C.E.S. site that is known for its low-cost, high-quality lunch cafeteria. The kids do the cooking and the public gets a great deal on a meal.

My "research consultants" at the convenience store, Eddie and Cliff, also agreed that life in vocational courses had a lot more dignity than life in regular high school. Eddie says he was coming to his school drunk every day, so they steered him over to B.O.C.E.S. When asked what he wanted to study, Eddie figured food preparation, because this was where all the pretty girls hung out and he wanted to meet them. So he embarked upon a career in "food prep." This eventually landed him a job baking donuts, then making sandwiches at a deli.

Of course Eddie couldn't support himself on five dollars an hour, so, like many local entrepreneurs, he began moonlighting in the underground youth economy. This illicit activity got him sent up for two years. In prison, he had the opportunity to take some college courses. Eddie says he would like to complete his B.S. degree some day, but he's got no money for tuition. Besides, he says, he's not in any rush for school right now. So he's just working at the convenience store and playing in a local band.

Cliff studied graphic arts and printing, but had also worked in a deli. He hoped to buy one of his own but needed a chunk of cash to do it. His parents died before he was twenty-one; there really wasn't anyone to help him out. At one point he was going to go in on a limo partnership, hoping to drive and work for himself. But he needed to put up heavy cash for it. So for now he's working at Metal 24. Late at night it's arts-and-crafts time at Metal 24. Eddie will be writing lyrics, Cliff setting up designs for future tattoos. Sid and a few of the other guys will be playing video games and Cliff's girlfriend, Ann, and I are probably discussing horoscopes.

Sid is another B.O.C.E.S. alum who studied auto body. He offers to do a light compounding on my car. He did an impressive piece of work on his Boxcar; he won't take any money from me because we're friends. He works at the parts counter at Auto Barn.

The "disposable" heroes in my neighborhood are all working in fields related to the training they got at B.O.C.E.S. Ann works in hair, and she sweeps the floors of a local beauty parlor. The other girls have babies now, so they don't hang out anymore. A few hold jobs as cashiers or hostesses and you rarely see them. One girl goes to Nassau Community College at night and works in a video store during the day.

Meanwhile Cliff dreams of being a bass player, Eddie is writing lyrics, Sid plays drums, Ann wants to have a family. Friends from the neighborhood who are my age hung out at Metal 24 when it was a drive-in hamburger stand. Many people here live the same lives, ten years after, with some of the same dreams.

In the scheme of things average American kids who don't have rich or well-connected parents have had these choices: Play the game and try to get ahead. Do what your parents did—work yourself to death at a menial job and find solace in beer, God, or family. Or take risks, cut deals, or break the law. The Reagan years made it hard for kids to "put their noses to the grindstone" as their parents had. Like everyone, these people hoped for better lives. But they lived in an age of inflated expectations and diminishing returns. Big and fast money was everywhere, and ever out of reach. America now had an economy that worked sort of like a cocaine high—propped up by hot air and big debt. The substance was absent. People's lives were like that too, and at times they were crashing hard.

In the meantime, wherever you were, you could still dream of becoming spectacular. A special talent could be your ticket out. Long Island kids had role models in bands like the Crumbsuckers, Ludichrist, Twisted Sister, Steve Vai, and Pat Benatar. North Jersey was full of sports celebrities and rock millionaires—you grew up hoping you'd end up like Mike Tyson or Jon Bon Jovi. Or like Keith Richards, whose father worked in a factory; or Ozzy, who also came from a grim English factory town, a hero who escaped the drudge because he was spectacular. This was the hip version of the American dream.

Kids who go for the prize now understand there are only two choices—rise to the top or crash to the bottom. Many openly admit that they would rather end it all now than end up losers. The nine-to-five world, corporate grunt life, working at the same job for thirty years, that's not for them. They'd prefer to hold out until the last possibility and then just piss on it all. The big easy or the bottomless pit, but never the everyday drone. And as long as there are local heroes and stories, you can still believe you have a chance to emerge from the mass as something larger than life. You can still play the great lottery and dream.

Schools urge kids to make these choices as early as possible, in a variety of ways. In the terse words of the San Francisco hardcore band MDC, "There's no such thing as cheating in a loser's game." Many kids who start out as nobody from nowhere with nothing will end up that way. Nevertheless, everyone pretends that everything is possible if you give it your best shot. We actually believe it. While educators hope to be as efficient as possible in figuring out where unspectacular students can plug into the work force, kids try to play at being one in a million, some way of shining, even if it's just for a while.

A few years playing ball, or in a band, and then you get a job. My boyfriend K. had a father employed as a mechanic at Grumman Aerospace. His father offered to get him a job in management there, since K. was "quick with the words." But K. had other plans. He got a part-time job in shipping at the age of seventeen. He kept it after high school, and held on to it for ten years while he played in the Grinders and other bands. The music was always his first priority. Over the years, he's picked up some more hours, and he's glad to have good Teamsters benefits.

But during those years he also got to play at CBGB's and Max's Kansas City, and he cut a few albums. Periodically there was champagne and limousines, and so once in a while K. got to be spectacular.

Girls get slightly different choices. They may hope to become spectacular by virtue of their talents and their beauty. Being the girlfriend of a guy in a band means you might get to live in his mansion someday if you stick it out with him during the lean years. You might just end up like Jon Bon Jovi's high school sweetheart, or married to someone like Cinderella's lead singer—he married his hometown girlfriend and helped set her up in her own business. These are suburban fairy tales.

Around here, some girls who are beautiful and talented hope to become stars too, like Long Island's local products Debbie Gibson and Taylor Dayne. Some hope to be like actress Heather Locklear and marry someone really hot like Motley Crue's drummer, Tommy Lee. If you could just get to the right place at the right time.

But most people from New Jersey and Long Island or anywhere else in America don't end up rich and famous. They have some fun trying, though, and for a while life isn't bad at all.

Yet, if you are unspectacular—not too book-smart, of average looks and moderate creative ability—there have always been places for you. Much of your teacher's efforts will be devoted to your more promising peers, and so will your nation's resources. But your parents will explain to you that this is the way it is, and early on, you will know to expect very little from school.

There are still a few enclaves, reservations. The shop and crafting culture of your parents' class of origin is one pocket of refuge. In the vocational high school, your interests are rewarded, once you have allowed yourself to be dumped there. And if the skills you gather there don't really lead to anything much, there's always the military.

Even though half the kids in America today will never go to college, the country still acts as if they will. At least, most schools seem to be set up to prepare you for college. And if it's not what you can or want to do, their attitude is tough shit, it's your problem.

And your most devoted teachers at vocational high school will never tell you that the training you will get from them is barely enough to get your foot in the door. You picture yourself getting into something with a future only to find that your skills are obsolete, superficial, and the boss prefers people with more training, more experience, more promise. So you are stuck in dead-end "youth employment jobs," and now what?

According to the William T. Grant Commission on Work, Family and Citizenship, twenty million people between the ages of sixteen and twenty-four are not likely to go to college. The "forgotten half," as youth advocates call them, will find jobs in service and retail. But the money is bad, only half that of typical manufacturing jobs. The good, stable jobs that don't require advanced training have been disappearing rapidly. From 1979 to 1985 the U.S.A. suffered a net loss of 1.7 million manufacturing jobs. What's left?

In my neighborhood, the shipping and warehousing jobs that guys like the Grinders took, hedging their bets against rock stardom, are now seen as "good jobs" by the younger guys at Metal 24. I am regularly asked to petition K. to "find out if they're hiring" down at his shipping company. Dead-end kids around here who aren't working with family are working "shit jobs."

The skills used in a typical "shit job" like the ones Cliff and Eddie have involve slapping rancid butter on stale hard rolls, mopping the floor, selling Lotto tickets, making sure shelves and refrigerators are clean, sorting and stacking magazines, taking delivery on newspapers, and signing out videos. They are also advised to look out for shoplifters, to protect the register, and to be sure that the surveillance camera is running. Like most kids in shit jobs, they are most skilled at getting over on the boss and in developing strategies to ward off boredom. It is not unusual to see kids at the supermarket cash register or the mall clothing shop standing around with a glazed look in their eyes. And you will often hear them complain of boredom, tiredness, or whine, "I can't wait to get out of here." Usually, in shit jobs this is where it begins and ends. There aren't many alternatives.

Everywhere, such kids find getting into a union or having access to supervisory or managerial tracts hard to come by. Some forms of disinvestment are more obvious than others. In a company town, you will be somewhat clear about what is going on. At the end of the 1980s, the defense industry of Long Island seemed threatened; people feared that their lives would soon be devastated.

But the effect of a changing economic order on most kids only translates into scrambling for a new safety zone. It is mostly expressed as resentment against entrepreneurial foreigners (nonwhites) and as anomie—a vague sense of loss, then confusion about where they might fit in.

Through the 1980s, people articulated their sense of loss in songs. Springsteen's Jersey was a suicide rap, a death trap. The Pretenders' Chrissie Hynde found that her industrial city, her Ohio, was gone, turned into shopping malls. Billy Joel's "Allentown" mourned for the steelworkers of Pennsylvania who had lost their America. To those of us who relate to music nonlyrically, the middle 1980s "industrial noise" bands, the postpunks, and the death-metal merchants were saying the same thing: when old ways die out, before new ones are firmly established, all that remains is a vacuum, a black hole.

For example, on Long Island, the ripple effect of peripheral industries had forced layoffs at Grumman and the death of Fairchild. It opened up questions about the future of jobs with large corporations like Hazeltine and Unisys. The engineering networks set up to support these industries were now on shaky ground. Small-job shops that produced specific parts for highly sophisticated defense contracts began dying out; universities and specialized technical schools would have to reorient themselves or fold. There would be jobs lost, and then declining property values.

Things were changing everywhere, but it was still too soon to determine the final outcome. Meantime, the social chaos kept seeping in. In *Rusted Dreams*, their book about the devastation in Chicago's Southeast Side following the closing of two steel mills in 1980, David Bensman and Roberta Lynch noted the increase in juvenile crime. Local youth workers attributed the delinquency to "the malaise that has afflicted teenagers since the mills began to decline. It has always been taken for granted that there would be jobs waiting for these kids—decent jobs that required little in the way of prior experience, skills, or education." The authors described aimlessness, hopelessness. There had been a lot of "untimely deaths" among youths, drinking, car accidents, violence. The dropout rate had gone up too, since the kids didn't see the point of going to school when it didn't lead to anything.

By the end of the 1980s many of the unaffluent turnpike towns across America had already felt some degree of devastation. Most parents work locally, and so kids understood that something was going on when their parents began talking about relocating from Long Island to Florida or Pennsylvania because Grumman might shut them out and then they couldn't afford to live here anymore.

In such situations, the immediate chaos is metabolized as a profound insecurity, a panic, loss of place. Like animals before an earthquake, the kids sense trouble ahead, feel desperate.

So where are we going? Some people fear we are polarizing into a two-class nation, rich and poor. More precisely, a privileged knowledge-producing class and a low-paid, low-status service class. It is in the public high school that this division of labor for an emergent postindustrial local economy is first articulated. At the top are the kids who will hold jobs in a highly competitive technological economic order, who will advance and be respected if they cooperate and excel.

At the bottom are kids with poor basic skills, short attention spans, limited emotional investment in the future. Also poor housing, poor nutrition, bad schooling, bad lives. And in their bad jobs they will face careers of unsatisfying part-time work, low pay, no benefits, and no opportunity for advancement.

There are the few possibilities offered by a relative—a coveted place in a union, a chance to join a small family business in a service trade, a spot in a small shop. In my neighborhood, kids dream of making a good score on the cop tests, working up from hostess to waitress. Most hang out in limbo hoping to get called for a job in the sheriff's department, or the parks, or sanitation. They're on all the lists, although they know the odds for getting called are slim. The lists are frozen, the screening process is endless.

Meantime they hold jobs for a few months here and there, or they work off the books, or at two bad jobs at once. They live at home, in a finished basement. If they get pregnant, they still remain with their parents. Nobody has health insurance. Unless they are sucked in by car salesmen who urge them to buy on credit and are paying off heavy car loans, they drive old cars.

And they don't marry. Some think it's hopeless because of the inevitability of divorce. But many girls have told me marriage is their dream, since it is their one shot at a home of their own. In 1985, only 43 percent of high school dropouts had incomes high enough to support a three-person family above the poverty level. That's a decline of 60 percent since 1973. In 1985, 3.1 million family households headed by youth under twenty-five had incomes below the poverty level, nearly double the rate of the early 1970s. If we disengage the romanticism normally ascribed to "adolescence," these are simply poor people with few options and no understanding of the social relations that permit adults to keep young Americans poor, disenfranchised, and without skills. Young people are poor people without rights, poor and powerless even without any added burdens of region, class, race, and sex. In the absence of a "youth" movement of magnitude or any memory of intergeneration politics, many kids are simply stuck.

In *Learning to Labor*, a study of British working-class kids, Paul Willis argued that by messing up at school, kids tricked themselves into reproducing their parents' bad lives. Willis was writing in the middle 1970s. By now, his "lads" and my "kids" don't even have those same bad options, since so many working-class jobs are disappearing. Today, dropping out of school in a society that is curtailing production and moving toward technical knowledge is the kiss of death.

Working-class kids have learned patterns of coping with an educational system originally designed by middle-class reformers to elevate the masses. It is generally agreed that the values and "cultural capital" needed to survive and thrive in this environment have given middle-class kids a bigger advantage. Traditionally, working-class kids had a number of strategies mentioned earlier, shop strategies adapted from the parent culture (sabotage, workplace solidarity, after-hours fraternizing). But if the parent culture itself is dying out, the strategies learned from it have no value. They won't lead to reproducing one's parents' lives in industrial labor. They'll lead to nowhere.

Kids who bomb out at school, who express their outrage and defy the regime by ignoring it, will now pay a worse price than ever before. They have higher expectations because of the inflated rhetoric of the Reagan years, and lower life chances because of global transformations in the economy that most people cannot even comprehend. Older guys I know who are struggling to keep their jobs in American companies say we should be more organized, be like the Japanese. Labor blames management and management blames labor. The public buys American out of loyalty and then curses the shitty product. Beyond that, nobody has a clue.

Responsibility for containing young people, for prolonging their entry into the work force, is now shared among families, school, the military, and juvenile jails. Meanwhile, life outside, in the real world, has changed drastically.

So if kids fuck off in school, they have nothing to fall back on. They are tracked, early on, for life. According to the Grant Commission, kids with math and reading scores in the bottom fifth as compared with their peers in the top half were almost nine times more likely to leave without a diploma, have a child out of wedlock, almost five times more likely to have incomes below the poverty line, and twice as likely to have been arrested the previous year.

In 1986, high school dropouts between the ages of twenty and twenty-four earned 42 percent less than similar kids did in 1973. In 1984, 12 percent of them had no earnings at all. So kids who make up the forgotten half and are unspectacular are now learning to labor at the bottom of the economy. These undereducated and underemployed kids will be tracked into low-paid, futureless jobs. The dropout rates, all the invisible kids bombing out to nowhere, foreshadows the career possibilities available to whole classes of Americans.

Unspectacular children of the baby bust—*Los Olvidados*. And these will become America's invisible classes. They will remain as unseen and unheard as the legions of young people who now serve the baby boom and others, in fancy eateries, video stores, and supermarkets. Adult employers regularly complain that such kids have "poor work habits," are unreliable, "tardy," and perform badly at whatever they're told to do. The kids today lack "basic skills." Half the time they don't even show up for work. The impression is that for most kids, work is a low priority. They lack the discipline. They just don't seem to care about anything except having a good time.

Before I knew better, I asked Nicky what he was planning to do after he graduated. Was he going to college? He had decent grades. He could study music. Nicky was annoyed that I would even suggest something so idiotic. He laughed right in my face. "Yeah, right. I'll go to college for four years, be bored to death, and come out owing all this money and then I can get a job that pays less than what some guy pumping gas is making." For him, school is a joke. He wants the diploma but beyond that, education serves no purpose.

For Nicky, there also doesn't seem to be any desire to try to live differently from his parents. Nicky has dreams; he'd like to make it someday as a drummer. This is his shot at becoming spectacular. He was practicing, he said. Maybe he'd get in a band. Meanwhile Nicky was planning to put in some applications. Maybe get a job as a stock boy at Rickel's, a huge home-improvement chain.

After school he'd go right to work. If he didn't leave north Jersey he would probably look for a place around here. Or stay home and save money. I asked him if he wanted to get out of here, leave the area for good. Maybe; he might like to move to California someday. Maybe he'd move there with his old girlfriend. But Nicky also told me he didn't want to leave his friends or his family. He was always saying, "This place sucks." He was always complaining about how boring it was. But when it came down to making a move, he doubted there was any place else he'd rather live. It would be hard to get started where you didn't have people you knew. His friends agreed.

But even for kids who finish school, have good records, and obey the rules, there is no guarantee they'll make it into productive careers. The American dream won't work for them, and nobody has bothered to explain why. So they find their concentrated effort and motivation only lead to an extra dollar an hour. At best, they'll earn a promotion to another boring job.

Stuck without hope, dreaming of jobs that no longer exist, with the myths of better days further convincing them of their individual fate as "losers," kids today are earning almost one-third less, in constant dollars, than comparable groups in 1973. For white kids, the drop in income is almost 25 percent; for black kids, it's 44 percent. The scars of race discrimination run deep, and minority youth feel hopeless because they get the message that this nation does not value its nonwhite citizens.

White kids have scars too, but with no attending socioeconomic explanation, they personalize their plights. They are "losers" because they are shit as people. They are failures because they are worthless. Either way, it hurts.

The understanding of how class works in "classless America" eludes everyone. Parents can teach kids what to expect, help shape attitudes toward their "lot in life." If your parents are losers, it's because their parents were. It's just that way.

In nonaffluent white suburbia, all this is hidden. The big picture isn't there. You're middle-class, you think. You believe that this country works for you. You do what you are told. It doesn't work, even though you're sure you made all the right moves. So who's fault is it? Yours. You have shit for brains and you'll never be anybody. This feeling becomes part of you.

II

Almost half of American high school seniors now work. Not in the skilled trades or factory settings of a generation ago, but in service jobs. The jobs are low-paying, demanding little discipline or skill. For most kids, cash is hoarded for partying, and to subsidize teen-status commodity-consumption patterns that many kids adhere to. While adults feel working is good, teaches you a sense of responsibility, even kids who do well in school learn very little about responsibility in most job settings. By the time they are seniors, over two-thirds of America's employed youth will spend fifteen hours or more a week at their workplace. Eighty percent of American kids will have held a job during the school year at some point during their high school careers.

Actually, suburban communities offer the most favorable opportunities for youth employment. In my neighborhood a tour up and down the turnpike in the middle of the afternoon allows me to drop in on people working at the deli, card store, record store, hardware store, several supermarkets. And then there are friends working at restaurants and mall shops, driving taxis. The abuse and boredom suffered in a shit job can be compensated for by sticky fingers—nobody buys records, beer, cigarettes, or car parts anymore. Not when your friends can get them for you free.

Income from these jobs rarely contributes to "the future." Maybe car payments, abortions in extreme cases, apartments, and school. But usually movies, leathers, fast foods, videos, shows, and memorable overnight trips upstate.

Not only does the youth labor force dominate turnpike commerce, but adults rarely enter into things. The boss becomes a little like the narc. At Metal 24, we had a code: the Sun was rising, if the owner, Mr. Sun, was due in; setting, if he was leaving soon and we should hang around and wait so we could watch horror movies or rock videos on the surveillance camera VCR. Eddie's technological prowess came to the fore as soon as the Sun set.

It's fun, but ultimately self-defeating. There is very little opportunity on such jobs for kids to learn anything from adult employers. They are generally supervised by a more experienced peer; they rarely interact with the boss. The virtues of self-management, co-operation, autonomy, initiative, and personal and social responsibility are learned by default, after a blunder. Up to the point of getting fired. This is how the discipline of labor is learned.

Everything Eddie and Cliff have learned at Metal 24 they already knew. Mr. Sun took Eddie under his wing, recognizing that he was smart. He even posted the bail when Eddie was arrested for outstanding warrants. Mr. Sun thinks American kids are fucked up. He's amazed at the lack of discipline, the "laziness." It just doesn't seem worth it to go out of your way for them, since they don't seem to want to help themselves. Mr. Sun is an immigrant from mainland China. He thinks like my father. If you work, you get somewhere. But most kids just don't see it that way.

"No job is worth cutting your hair for. No matter how much money they'll offer." This articulates a tenet of faith that is central to the metal orthodoxy. When Eddie got fired from the convenience store for sneaking free beers to his friends, he was busy looking for a new job. The only criterion he had was not having to cut his hair.

Two weeks after he lost his job, he couldn't pay his rent and he was living on the street. His car had been stolen a few months earlier and he had cut his ties to his family. He had no resources and his only marketable skills were in food preparation and dealing. He had worked in delis and restaurants but that wasn't the kind of work he wanted anymore. Eddie was determined to make it straight. But he would resort to crime—he laughs—rather than cut his hair.

At first I laughed with him but he was serious. "No metalhead would ever cut his hair. First of all, that would be the end of my leather jacket. I mean how could I wear my leathers with a guido haircut? Can you imagine that?" Besides, he's in a band—he'd have to quit! Eddie also knows his girlfriend of two years would break up with him if he ever got a haircut; "she told me so." What could there be left to live for, he asks, if Metallica toured and he had short hair? No way!

For kids tracked into dead-end jobs, cutting your hair is a political issue, a statement even more radical than smoking cigarettes was in the eighties high school. People felt that way in the 1960s and 1970s, and maybe they suffered the ridicule of "straight" society. But in the 1980s the stakes are much higher.

This time it's for real. If you get thrown out on your ass, if you're an outcast, you're *really* out. Eddie says he's a rebel. Undisciplined, messy, and wild, he would rather freeze and starve than give in. This isn't as romantic as it once seemed. Eddie cannot fathom the absurdity of having to cut his hair to "make it" economically. "Can you imagine me cutting my hair to get a job at Burger King?" He probably could walk right into a management position in food preparation. But it just wasn't worth selling yourself for that. It would drive him crazy. He would die, he says.

Still, the kids have tried to carve out some honor, and so alternative "underground" economies have sprung up to tide them over. If small-time dealing and petty crimes were once helpful in the transition from the poverty of adolescence to the self-sufficiency of early adulthood, now they are crucial. So the Italian-American kids in Bensonhurst who can't get coveted jobs in the dying construction industry, or with city sanitation, find small-time careers as local "wiseguys." They spend their time running small scams, regulating turf, and acting as neighborhood border guards. Living off the economic organizations developed by immigrant fathers and grandfathers. Girls work, hoping to marry soon.

In urban settings there are even fewer "youth employment" jobs to go around. One alternative economy that is highly developed among low-income urban youth is the drug industry run by "cocaine kids." Black and Latino street gangs have organized themselves into local drug-dealing cartels. There isn't any better economic opportunity to be had, adult community representatives have lamented.

Meanwhile, suburban white kids are not so organized. They have failed to nurture such flourishing alternatives to blocked mobility. And so they look up to minority kids, city kids, for their superior economic organization on the street.

Where I live, all the white people are ethnic—Greek, Jewish, Italian, Irish—and most are members of the "third-generation nation." Their parents and grandparents got jobs, made connections, and organized opportunities for their sons and daughters to follow. In my neighborhood there are second and third generations of same-trade families: cops, carpenters, bartenders. Kids with families who can set them up with something do well. Everyone else improvises.

I know a guy named Jackie. I met him up at the Pathmark, where he works in the dairy section. He also works as a nonunion bricklayer when he can. We became friends initially because of Jackie's tattoos. He has several dedicated to his favorite band, Metallica. One is a tombstone with a bass slung over it, a testimony to Cliff Burton. Cliff died in a bus accident while Metallica was on tour. Jackie has another one that says "Damage Inc." Jackie is twenty-two. Sometimes I see him at Slayer shows. In the summer he conducts business down at the beach. You can always find him there. It's his "third job."

He describes his customers: "All these people do is hang out. They're all alcoholics. They can't hold jobs. Some of them never worked more than three days here or there, never really worked in their lives. They don't know how to keep from getting fired. I know what to do to keep from getting fired but these people, they get busted, they go into rehab, they come out, and before long they're back, doing more coke. It doesn't take much for it to start again."

Jackie says a lot of kids scam off their parents, deal, fuck up, get busted. That's it. Jackie doesn't know why they're so fucked up. "They just don't give a shit." Partying becomes the main thing, the only thing. Besides that, there is burglary, assault, car theft, criminal mischief (vandalism, trespass, menacing, disorderly conduct). This is how people express their desire to create, how they use their smarts. Street life in suburbia is disorganized in this way.

In Bergenfield Lenny and Ray were two street innovators I sometimes ran into. They could usually be found hanging around by the archway that leads from the garden apartments to the Foster Village Shopping Center. This was prime, since from here they could easily duck into the complex to conduct business, or to reduce their visibility on the Ave. Ray and Lenny didn't go to school anywhere. They were full-time street soldiers, from a very different crowd than Joe and Randy. Some overlapping friends, maybe even a past party episode, but Ray and Lenny had a different look, musical interests —another scene, basically. They weren't metalheads or thrashers, just your basic American dirts. Ray and Lenny went for the older bands, Cream, the Who, Blind Faith, and of course, Led Zep, now playing a street-side concerto off Lenny's box.

While they wait around for something to come down they usually pass the time hustling people passing by to buy them beers; they're well under twenty-one. Ray's folks let him have a few at home but that's no fun. Lenny lives with his mom and his two uncles. One goes to A.A. and the other was in Vietnam.

At eighteen, Ray knows the score. "I'm old enough to go into the Army, to kill, but not mature enough to drink in a bar!" Ray looks a lot like Robert Plant. He dropped out of Bergenfield High School two months ago. He hated school; they got all this "drug money," so they tried to get him to go in to see one of their "drug counselors." Lenny laughs. "And Ray doesn't even get high!"

Lenny goes by bus, then subway, to Washington Square Park to buy pot. He laughs about the enforcement of New Jersey's drinking age of twenty-one. "I can get any drug I want in five minutes but I can't buy a few beers, pretty stupid, isn't it?"

As usual, there is nothing going on. But Ray has a better attitude these days. He has recently decided to go into the Army. A month from now he is leaving Bergenfield for good. "I can't get a job around here except one that pays $3.50 an hour." And then he'd have to cut his hair, he says, work real shitty hours, give up his free time, and for what? Ray really wants to buy a Harley. His cousin is in the Army, making big money "black market" and living well. "He has a house, a bike, a truck . . . he's doing something besides getting hassled by the cops and sponging off his folks." Ray is ashamed of living this way, but he's glad it's only temporary. I figure he'll be sorry to see the hair go. But no, it won't be so bad, at least he can keep the earring. That's why he went Army. "They'll let you keep your earring." That's what his cousin said.

Both of these guys look imported from the late sixties: the flannel shirts, faded concert T-shirts, ragged-bottom jeans, an earring, and a bandanna. But there's a hard-metal overlay, an assertive edge, little details in their clothing that pin them to the late eighties.

Lenny looks to the economic side of situations. The Army and Navy recruiters want their commission. The school needs to keep enrollment for tax monies. There have been budget cuts in education. The shrinks just take your money. They need kids to justify drug money from the government. So they like to call you down to see "drug counselors" at school. Everything is a scam. At fifteen, Lenny is jaded. Lenny's alienated, populist intellect naturally gravitates to the bottom line. The doctrine behind the veil—adults getting rich off kids, pretending they give a shit. Kids snaking around the rules, and throwing it in their faces. Then there are the police.

As usual, the afternoon is structured around drama after drama. The police car across the parking lot, a guy they owe money to, a relative, some girls, drugs, food. Then the police again. "Yeah, they'll confiscate our beers and drive behind an abandoned building and get wasted themselves!" Lenny and Ray are further convinced that the police are in on burglaries, on the take. And then there are stories of beatings.

I ask about the jocks. "They get pretty wasted too, they're real party animals." Lenny says he doesn't hate jocks, just the inequality of how they are treated. He says, "If they get busted for beer, the cops look the other way because they know the kid from the station bench press, from sports. Me, I'll end up getting nailed." Why give a good kid a record, mess up his chances for the future? Kids like Lenny are somewhat more expendable. Like everyone else, Lenny and Ray speculate about what might have driven their four friends to suicide. "They just couldn't take it anymore." "Take what?" I ask. "This town!"

Lenny and Ray were archetypical teenage toxic waste that people here didn't want to know about. While the bad boys they could label as mentally disabled were safely tucked away in special education, and the less promising students were farmed out to Bergen Vo-Tech, *these* guys were the lumpenscum of the town. They were the reminders of how bad it could be if any footing was lost. Suburbia's white-trash, hard-core losers. Lenny and Ray were everyday eyesores. They were like old bedding that has been discarded but hasn't yet been carted off, just sitting there, for weeks, soiled by rain and then more trash, rotting right in your face. People just wanted them to go away, they didn't care how.

I look at Lenny. On the surface he's a mess. Bad teeth, dirty clothes, just hanging around. But he's curious, articulate, sharp. And at fifteen, he's a de facto high school dropout, waiting to be old enough to sign out legally, waiting another year after that until he can go for his equivalency diploma. He laughs at the hustle he has going at the school. He just comes in and signs his name so the school has him on the books. They'll look the other way while he disappears. A nice symbiotic setup. Kid gets to blow off school while school keeps the statistics nice and puffy. They don't want too many dropouts, Lenny says. They probably figure they're doing him a favor. And he's sure he's getting over.

Lenny wants confirmation—"You went to school," he asks me, "I mean, you understand . . ." Very little was ever said about what was going on here; it was understood. But sometimes we did get into more formal discussions. I went to school, so Lenny figures I can validate his view of things. So we start talking about the difference between schooling and education. Lenny reads a lot, Ray tells me. Ray respects him for that. Lenny reads whatever his uncle has around the house. Both guys listen heavily to old Frank Zappa music. "He's cool, he stuck up for us." Lenny was referring to rock censorship debates. Zappa was very strong on kids' knowing their civil rights. He was definitely someone they respected.

Knowledge is power, true, but school had nothing to do with that, did it? Lenny's mother said he might as well drop out because she was tired of the school bugging her. He agreed he should at least get the equivalency, though.

Lenny and Ray did what they could to keep moving forward, but they were somewhat confused about the direction. First step, recoil from the mainstream. Recognize it's them, not you, who's crazy. You drop out and stay out of their sight whenever possible. Finally, you had to develop economic alternatives.

There were few satisfying legitimate avenues open to them; Lenny and Ray acknowledged that they were being manipulated, exploited, and fucked over. They tacitly understood that adults were the perpetrators.

They also understood that they were identified losers. Lenny and Ray were much more alienated than guys like Joe, who were viewed essentially as poseurs. It was too late and they were too hip for all the empty promises. Why hustle for the limited, dreary options open to them? Lenny was a street philosopher of the highest order. In one mid-afternoon dialogue he posited Lenin's rhetorical "What is to be done?" How can people extricate themselves from this shitty little game?

Lenny and Ray were also not racist; they extended their friendship on universal grounds of righteousness. Lenny had friends who played sports, were smart, or nonwhite. And it was no problem to understand how some mainstream kids' hatred of dirts and burnouts paralleled the collective hatred of newly arrived "dotheads" and "gooks."

We are stuck looking for a well-traveled answer, like "brotherhood" or "revolution," or even "looking out for number one." Truth to borrow for the moment. An explanatory scheme to tuck this all away. Something to hold on to beyond goodwill.

So I figure maybe I should give personal advice. Tell Lenny to just hang in for the new situation. Don't get depressed; be patient. The world is changing. Things will come around; they always do. It's the darkness before the dawn. I try to explain their personal hell in terms of ruptures and transformations in monopoly capitalism. History has motion, and lately everybody is reeling.

But it starts to sound really stupid. Imagine, "Well dudes, it's a real bummer, but your class of origin is now obsolete. Too bad. Your country won't be needing your labor anymore. America is a scrap yard of rusty metal. Production is over. Bon voyage, baby." But these guys are way too hip for a Springsteen whine. That's for college kids.

Maybe I could get high-toned and postmodern. "Hey, guys, welcome to the simulacrum. There's nothing to believe in here, but don't worry, Lenny, there never was. It was always . . . pretty vacant. There's nothing to hold on to and there never was.

"Look," I could say, with sincerity, "the world is changing and nobody really understands it. I don't get it. Your parents don't have a clue either. And forget about your teachers. They're doing their best just to keep the lid on. The shrinks and the police are there to scrape you off the walls if needed. We love you, but we mostly hope you'll withdraw, stay numb, and keep out of the way till we figure out what we're doing and where we can fit you in."

Words of encouragement—"So what if it's the end of the world as you know it. You'll find a new place, eventually. Meantime, have you thought about the service sector? I hear they have lovely jobs! Why not put in an application *today*. Meanwhile, even though the world around you is falling to bits gloriously, please say no to drugs and don't forget to use condoms."

I do say that sometimes, when we get confused, we seem to think it's the end of the world. Yet we always seem to survive: the Cuban missile crisis, Great Depression, world wars, industrialization. But it gets hard to say anything, so I just try to make sweet promises to them from the heart that life will go on, no matter how bad it seems. It *has* to.

Hendrix spanks a chord along the watchtower as a beer possibility walks by, ending our conversation.

The only solution as far as Ray was concerned was signing himself into the service. By now, there were formal organizations dedicated to trying to talk dead-end American kids out of being disposed of in that way. Veterans went around to schools telling kids what it was really like in the military. Not the grand promises of recruiters, or the Green Berets, or Delta force. No, actually, it was pretty beat, they said. It was sort of like how vocational education doesn't really give you the skills you need. The military promised a lot more than it delivered. But from the strip of turf Ray was standing on right now, the Army really didn't look like such a bad idea.

The relationship between military service and the rocker's imagination is long and strong. Biker culture came right out of World War II, and its most famous right-wing boho organization, the Hell's Angels, has a place in every suburban rocker's heart. Then there was Elvis. He went to Germany to serve his country, and married a serviceman's pretty daughter. Maybe the Army was your only option, but after Elvis, you could enlist in style. Soldier boys from the rock and roll war in Vietnam offered even more attractive images for guys like Ray. And, finally, Jimi Hendrix himself left high school early to join Army Airborne. What could top that?

But Ray had practical reasons for joining the Army—economic

opportunity, schooling, a ticket out of here and into the world out there. The Marines had the macho image, the Navy was "for fags." Army has always been rocker's haven. Because of Elvis and Hendrix and because they let you keep your earring, I guess.

For those shipwrecked in the dead-end towns of suburbia, the recruiting station looms as an island of possibility. It is also easy to imagine the glamorous life in military service several times a day. Bad day at Bergenfield High School, you're walking up to 7-Eleven, and there's the Marines. Once up at 7-Eleven the Navy posters are in your face as you gaze out on the Ave of despair. As we spoke, Lenny and Ray were facing the Army station, adjacent to that Amoco station where some months earlier for three dollars their four dear friends bought the express ticket out, one-way.

It's the same everywhere, with the recruiters. On Long Island there are two crucial spots to buy hardcore and heavy-metal music. In the white ethnic prole town of Valley Stream, Slipped Disc is situated right next to the recruiting station—you buy some records and a T-shirt, why not drop in, select from among the branches of our Armed Forces. Shopping is shopping, even for the right military experience, so in Levittown, the recruiting station is a few doors down from Uncle Phil's, the best hardcore/thrash/skin/metal record store on the island. And since the recruiting station is also directly across from the Tri-County Flea Market, it is situated in the heavy-metal fashion capital of Nassau County.

The military now advertises on the radio, in the leading rock magazines, on MTV. They are ever-present in the rocker community. You always know somebody who is going, or is in. So the idea of joining is always there, in the back of your mind.

The recruitment officers are a cross between Jesus freaks and car salesmen. They offer deliverance for the down-and-out, promise honor to the common man. The various service branches of the Department of Defense practice a heavy-duty outreach program, even for reserve components. And according to guys in my neighborhood, they start in on you pretty early. They come to the high school, talk with you about your "future."

If you even cue them a bit that you're interested, the recruiters will follow right up on it. Call you up at home, hound you for months about what you're doing with your life. Are you happy? Where are you going to be six months from now? They promise you high-technology skills, a place to belong, dignity you've never had, free college, weapons, and groovy uniforms. Girls are invited to join up too. Many people look to it as a public trust fund. Money for school, training and credentials.

Ray didn't have too much to say about his encounters with the recruiters. It went down pretty simple, he said. But now he felt his future was secured. Unfortunately, the military doesn't always work out to be the promised land. My neighborhood is full of disposable heroes who had spent a year or so in the service and were now back on the streets. Again working low-paying jobs, they were a few years older with one less option in their back pockets. One guy, who works in the car wash near me, left the Navy because "they said they'd send me to school, teach me about radar. I ended up stacking trays."

One guy I know returned to Long Island from service having seen recent combat action. But even a decoration for bravery did little to overturn his rep as a loser in his hometown. He got some respect for a while, but as with the person fresh out of detox, it was easy to just slip back into the old routine. Most people like having been in the service; it makes for good stories.

These days, recruiters are nice guys, people you can identify with. The baby boom's image of the 1960s R.O.T.C. Nazi action man isn't happening here. And the average dirtbag metalhead is a heavy patriot, even after Vietnam. Many are willing to die for their country. Most have a Hollywood view of what military life is like. Ultra-heroic, righteous, rewarding. "Kill! Vietnam! Rambo!!"

Anarchistic types won't have any part of it. These are the guys who do not register for selective service and drive their cars illegally. They ask their employers to pay them in cash; they don't open bank accounts or pay taxes. That way they figure The State will have no record of them. But they are the exceptions. Despite subversive antiwar lyrics targeted at America's disposable heroes by their most beloved bands, Metallica and Megadeth, and the influence of hard-core's radical take on things, most suburban metalheads do not question America's claim on them.

Like their older brothers and uncles who wanted to go to Vietnam, most people were behind the invasion of Grenada, and were very impressed by Bush after Panama. "Fuck the Ayatollah" T-shirts were also very popular in my town, and if anybody was ever seen burning a flag here they would definitely get stomped on.

I decided to drop in on the Army recruiters across from Foster Village. In Bergenfield the recruiters seem to moonlight as big brothers, offering a macho drop-in center hang. The recruiters come from all over the country; they make impressive role models to guys and, more recently, to girls. If the bumper sticker you see pasted onto the garbage can next to the burnouts' smoke line at Bergenfield High School convinces you to "Be All You Can Be," the recruiters will do their best to help you out.

I introduce myself to Sergeant Mixon, a Southern gentleman who laughs heartily when I tell him my dad was a "Calvados Commando." I explain my purpose in Bergenfield, that I wanted to see the town from the bottom up. The kids liked the recruiters. But I soon learned they had taken some flack after the suicides for "pressuring" the kids with a hard sell. People were trying to blame the recruiters, along with Satan and AC/DC and Ozzy. Then one of the recruiters had talked to some reporter from the local *Twin-Boro News* and everything he said got twisted. The recruiter had gotten into deep shit with the higher-ups. So once again, I'm sworn not to use real names.

These recruiters feel they have worn out their welcome in the town of Bergenfield. They are only too happy that this particular office is moving to another town, a better location, in the next few months.

Sergeant Mixon explains that he volunteered to be a recruiter because he likes talking to people. He likes the kids who drop in, but he's uncomfortable with the idea of thirteen-year-olds on drugs, all the peer pressure, the fast life of the Northeast. He's waiting for the big rush, when the school year ends and the dropout population has to face the fact of no future. But the Army prefers the kid who stays in school, will not accept the equivalency diploma. He feels this hurts the educational system. Kids should stay in school, he tells me.

I ask him about their big commissions that Lenny is so convinced is the motive force here. Sergeant Mixon gets involved in a complicated system of points and quotas he makes each month and I drift off but tune back in when he explains that after the Grenada invasion, the volunteer Army got a hot boost; Libya helped too. Now he doesn't have to recruit as hard. We get into a little discussion about who the real hero was in *Platoon*. "The pot smokers screwed everything up," he says. "They lost us the war, in fact. Then they turned around and blamed it on the juicers!"

"Hanoi" Jane Fonda is mentioned. Then Hollywood. "The kids think that war was just one big party." We agree that the romanticized version of the war is good for Sergeant Mixon's business, even if it isn't an accurate point of view.

The Sergeant hands me some brochures. You can get a Certificate of Completion of Apprenticeship from the Department of Labor, which supposedly can help you get a job. Lots of vocational preparation in electronics, repair work, welding, machinist and mechanics training. You can learn radio and TV repair, aircraft mechanics, cooking, and photography. These apprenticeships are hard to milk for anything once you've returned to civilian life, but it's better than having no training at all.

The real enticer here is the college tuition. Higher education is far beyond the reach of many more kids than ever before. Without rich parents or perfect grades, forget it—you're lucky if you can get through the local community college. But the Army offers the New G.I. Bill Plus the New Army College Fund deal, and this means you can accumulate big bucks.

It was a slow day and there were a few officers on hand, so I ended up staying for a long time. A few teens came in, a young Hispanic male getting a practice test, a young lady who had just signed up and "really wanted to jump," two giggling boys trying to be cool. They come in almost every day. Sergeant Mixon teases the twelve-year-olds—"Ready to sign up?" Sergeant Mixon remembers Tommy Rizzo, "the big guy" who came in a few times to talk, but he remembers the kid never did sign up with the Army. It isn't so easy anymore. Army won't take everyone. I mention an old high school beau who went into the Army to shorten his sentence in reform school. "Oh no, Army's not like that anymore."

In 1987 the volunteer Army could afford to be much more selective. With limited employment options for non–college grads and no war on the horizon, entry to the armed forces had become more competitive. Throughout the 1980s, the Army could pick from a larger and "better" pool of potential recruits.

Sergeant Mixon pulls out a huge code book of regulations. The Army is willing to help you out if you are a high school dropout. Just score a fifty on the test. The recruiters will help you study for the test, work with you until you pass. They'll give you every chance.

Except if you've been in serious trouble. Forget about it. No psychiatric, drug, alcohol, or serious law violations. He reads 'em off: grand theft auto, arson, murder, breaking and entering, two charges of controlled substances. He says they lose most of the kids on the law violations, but the drugs are a big problem too. If the kid has a record of being in detox, it counts against him. The Army's not looking for problems, Sergeant Mixon explains. The volunteer Army is professional. "In wartime, that's different, we'll lower the standards."

But for now, small-town losers weren't getting any free rides. Sergeant Mixon was emphatic in his belief that the Army should not be a substitute for a family or for schooling. Yet a "join the Army if you fail" sentiment was still being impressed upon the kids from the other end. A residual body count remained after dumping kids into special education and vocational education. This left some surplus youth unaccounted for, so the military was still an invaluable last resort for Bergenfield's unspectacular youth, and it *was* often substituting for family and school.

One of the recruiters pointed out that the test scores from Bergenfield High School students were "not West Point material." And he was surprised at how many kids were already alcoholics. "Typical story the other day, a decent kid, wants to join the Army to get away from an abusive home life. Says his father beats him, the father is an alcoholic, the kid drinks too, goes and gets help, cleans up his act, and now he has a record. So now the kid can't get into the service." That meant the kid's last ticket out was null and void.

For the most part, the recruiters are as jaded as Lenny and I are about the local scene. They understand the status hierarchy very clearly. Like the media, the recruiters have been banned from the school, scapegoated for the suicide pact, accused of agitating the kids. They feel the police are the only real allies the "burnouts" have. There's the whole outlaw posturing, the cop-watching, but ironically it is the cops, knowing some of the family situations, who will put a wasted youth in the squad car, take him up to Dunkin' Donuts, buy him coffee, drive him home, and look the other way. Some of the kids had told me that too.

Sergeant Mixon picks up the local paper. "Before the suicides all you read about was the sports, the teams. Now they have all these services . . . it's just a whitewash. That's all it is. There is something evil in the air . . . I don't know . . . people in this town just don't respect each other. The way they talk to each other, real mean like."

It was obvious. Waste-disposal problems in Bergenfield were getting worse. For as long as anyone can remember, the armed forces were the last shot. But for some kids, even that was moving out of reach. On the edge of town, where the colored people live, garage #74 had served as the last available dump site in Bergenfield—the final solution to the town's teenage waste-disposal problem. A place for expendable youth.

This Is Religion I

. . . Anyone who has felt the drive to self-destruction welling up inside him knows with what weary negligence he might one day happen to kill the organizers of his boredom.

—From Raoul Vaneigem,
The Revolution of Everyday Life

I

My father said recently, "Music is the kids' religion." I asked him to explain. He said, "Look, their parents are all screwed up, the politicians in this country are a bunch of liars, and organized religion has become a joke . . . a big business. What else do the kids have to hang on to?"

He was right. The kids have a hard time putting faith in any of the things they are supposed to believe in. Basically, religion offers empowerment—gives you courage, faith, tells you how to live, how to feel about yourself and the people around you. It gives you the sense of something greater than yourself, of some higher power or purpose. Religion also explains the unexplainable and it comforts you—it helps you get through this life. So it's important to understand some things about the kids' religion and where it comes from.

This is how it works. Early on, people develop "special relationships" with their music. They may embrace Jimi Hendrix, Elvis Presley, Elvis Costello, the Rolling Stones, Lou Reed, Alice Cooper, Black Sabbath, David Bowie, Van Halen, and on and on through the years. But this is not a linear process. If you hit puberty and your older sister listens to Led Zeppelin, even if it's 1981 and the band isn't together anymore, this could change the course of your entire life.

All you have to do to find out someone's "religion" is to ask what band they think is the greatest band of all time. And you'll find that most of their friends agree about who rules their rock and roll universe. In the Rockaways, by the end of the 1960s, we lived in our private world with the Mothers of Invention, Bob Dylan, Cream, Big Brother and the Holding Company, Jefferson Airplane, the Doors, Country Joe and the Fish, the Grateful Dead. In those days people argued over guitar heroes. Who was king? Eric Clapton? Jimi Hendrix? Jimmy Page? We were freaks playing the liturgy in the basements and bedrooms of suburbia.

Our conversations were incomprehensible to outsiders. Lyric strings were woven into the most mundane situations: in front of straight people, at school, in English class, especially in the princi-

pal's office. In the profane world, the lyrics and regalia armed us
against the bullshit. There were a lot of great bands to get involved
with. But it was Jimi Hendrix who stood above all others. Zen master
of the Stratocaster. Ruler of haircuts and dress codes, now as in the
hour of our deaths. Undisputed King of our rock and roll universe.

Some people I know who are three or four years younger were
baptized by the glitter bands. They worshiped Bowie, Alice Cooper,
T-Rex, Aerosmith, New York Dolls. They took different drugs, used
different language codes, and they *dressed*. Guys played with themes
of gender-fuck; they wore gaudy baubles, black eyeliner, and
platform shoes to high school. People streaked their hair with food
coloring. Girls got a high-powered slut look going and had boy
dolls to play with. Ten years after, styles, moods, and taste still reflect the age of glitter. And these trends cross, retread, and regroup
into new forms—like glam metal and some of the pop "haircut"
bands.

Each new band takes something old and transforms it into something new. Then the fans get it, and push it forward, turn it into
something else. Where it comes from is impossible to trace. It's a
convoluted, chronic flux of cultural production. Origins are passionately argued—is punk American or British? Did it come down to us
in the middle of the 1970s after glitter via ex–New York Doll cum
Heartbreaker Johnny Thunders? From the Ramones? Richard Hell?
Or was it handed down to us from the London boys—the Clash, Sex
Pistols? These are fine points of theology, street scholarship.

We know that Hendrix, unrecognized in the United States, went
off to England, then returned to conquer America. Dismissed as
shlock masters in their native land, Led Zeppelin crossed the Atlan-
tic Ocean and sealed it in blood forever with American kids. This is
generally acknowledged as the first wave of heavy metal. It came
down around 1969, specifically in "Whole Lotta Love." By the 1980s
there was another wave, and a new generation of Zep fans. Young
suburban mall kids. Mostly prole teens, usually boys, living in the
turnpike towns of suburbia—the children of ZOSO. For them, no
question, Led Zeppelin was the beginning of creation.

Those of us baptized in Hendrix will usually carry on about the
guitar licks, the raw power of shrieking feedback. And of course *we*
think heavy metal was born in 1967, in "Purple Haze," marking

Hendrix as Metal Messiah. Obviously, children of ZOSO do not see things this way. But hey, who has ever agreed about God?

If you ask them what it is about Led Zeppelin that matters most, they will say the songs. Not the chords, not the words. The songs.

Majestic tales of olden days. Electric gasps of Celtic glory. Alchemy of the first world's decline. The mixture of hard and pretty, of ballistic missiles and tender sentiments. "ZOSO" was the common-law title of Led Zeppelin's untitled fourth and most revered album. It is the name fans gave to the 1971 masterpiece with "Stairway to Heaven" on it. ZOSO was the first of four mystical symbols printed on the record label. Each represented one of the four members of the band.

Lead guitarist Jimmy Page asked each band member to design a self-referential symbol. ZOSO was Page's personal sign. It isn't exactly those four letters of the alphabet, it's some ancient thing. But that's the way it's read by people. Page was always vague about what it meant, or where it came from. Some people associate it with the gemstone amber. The high vibratory rate of amber purifies as it emits a strong magnetic flow. When used in healing, amber stones help reestablish the power of the sun center—the solar plexus, the power source.

Page the mystic junkie, dabbler in the black arts, was a self-styled disciple of Aleister Crowley. Supposedly, Led Zeppelin had a pact with the devil. Except for the bass player, John Paul Jones, they sold their souls for rock and roll success. Some people believed Page's spells killed people—drummer John Bonham, Plant's son Karac.

Far more mysterious and darker than the theatrical Black Sabbath or Deep Purple, Led Zep was followed by a trail of destruction through its years. These tragedies are as easily explained by the "too much too soon" fate of legendary rock and roll bands as by satanic lore. But from the beginning, Led Zeppelin carried an irreversible overtone of evil. By all accounts, the band was particularly rowdy, vulgar, sadistic, and wild—as repulsive to adults then as the youth-generated subcult sounds of hardcore, metal, and rap are today.

Even in a time when most rock bands were pretty raunchy and many intimidated adults, Led Zeppelin always did it better. Jim

Morrison was the Warlock, but he was really a poet. And the Stones could get witchy, but everyone knew that Mick was just a businessman at heart—he had attended the London School of Economics. Zep scared the shit out of everybody, including the rock press.

Zep's handsome lead singer, Robert Plant, lovingly referred to his fans as "my people." But it was Jimmy Page who really spoke to them, though he rarely uttered a word on stage—Page, the introvert, the skinny, creepy only child with more creative power than he could possibly handle; the magician whose effect on his audience William S. Burroughs compared to that of the trance musicians of Morocco. Burroughs likened rock stars to priests. After seeing the band live, Burroughs, patron saint of punk, noted, "In the Led Zeppelin concert, the result aimed at would seem to be the creation of energy in the performers and the audience. For such magic to succeed, it must tap the sources of magical energy, and this can be dangerous." It was. These are the elementary forms of religious life.

Through esoteric signs and appropriated symbols, Led Zeppelin created a secret society that excluded the adult world of parents, teachers, rock critics, and everyone else. If Page procured loyalty through his musical sex magick, Robert Plant wanted to encourage a spirit of unity, friendship, and peace. Wearing golden locks and satin, sex bomb Plant told the children romantic tales of ancient times.

With each new Led Zeppelin album, a trip to the mall record store could end at King Arthur's court. Kids felt the pride of warriors and fair maidens on their stereo turntables. The white-race music of the empire. Grace restored to bleak suburban landscapes. And this music was sexy. With volume and elixir, you were transported into the orgasmatron.

And it was fun! In the definitive biography of the band, *Hammer of the Gods*, Stephen Davis pins Led Zep's aesthetic as somewhere between Marvel comics and *Beowulf*. That's pretty much the foundation of heavy metal—folklore as anthem, comic book theatrics, fast video-game action, and horror-movie pop thrills.

To date, Plant's legions of fans have never wavered, they remain steadfast and faithful. Now as in their hour of glory, Zep is adored. Even in the late 1970s, when Robert Plant was cast out, humiliated by the punks as a dinosaur, his people stayed true.

Like Led Zeppelin's original fans, children of ZOSO are kids who just don't believe that mass culture is all that disappointing. They aren't urban trendies. They don't intellectualize their pleasures. They could care less that their scene is dismissed and devalued as "commercial." They are unconcerned about things like the "political correctness" of music, it's "socially redeeming value." No, this stuff is spiritual, tribal.

It was these primarily male white suburban teenagers that kept the faith during the years when American xenophobia turned much of our attention to the rich subversive subculture of England's punks and away from our own. Here they were, through the late 1970s and early 1980s, getting bashed for uninformed commercial tastes, yet resisting the trendy "new wave" imports, adhering instead to local traditions of class and community. And when the great Zep revival of the summer of 1988 spread across the land, and Led Zeppelin was formally, finally anointed as god—the forefathers of heavy metal— their fans were vindicated at last.

Because heavy metal is a mutant strain from out of the belly of Zep, the vulgate of classic rock, it also nauseated rock critics and other hip knowledge workers. But heavy metal is white suburban soul music. In England, the children of ZOSO hang around the fish-and-chip stores of the Britburbs wearing their concert T-shirts and their painted denim jackets. Here they're at 7-Elevens from Bergenfield to Bakersfield. When I got to know him better, Bobby told me he was going to get ZOSO tattooed on his arm. It's the mark.

By the middle of the 1970s, ZOSO had become a unifying symbol for America's suburban adolescents. In the eighties, there would be other contenders, second and third waves of metal bands. And people would tattoo themselves with the esoteric symbols of newer bands. But loyalty to Zep remained unchanged.

In the seventies it meant having long hair when everyone else went disco. *Hair* against punk spikes and bare skinheads. In the eighties it meant shags in the face of a hip-hop crossover. Some promises are for life. *Hair* out of respect because in its prime, Led Zeppelin was the loudest, rudest, heaviest band ever.

When I told the children of ZOSO that I had seen Led Zeppelin live, it was as if I had touched heaven, could walk on water. I carried reverberated charisma. But when pressed for details, it was always hard to remember those days. Cause if you did it right, you had usually passed out by the fourth song.

Stephen Davis notes the chronic bad blood between Led Zep and the press. Critics hated the band. They missed the point. Barbarians. And this repulsion extended to their audience as well. Davis quotes various instances of audience bashing, concluding that to the press, "Led Zeppelin appealed to Seconal gobblers and Boone's Farmers. To field hippies and speed freaks. Led Zeppelin was déclassé, low-rent, sleazy cock-rock with no redeeming social values." Only their fans understood. If anything, critics' failure to get the point of Zep delegitimated them early on. Just some college twits.

The barbarian hordes knew Led Zeppelin was the ruling band of the 1970s. The band that carried the torch of the 1960s idealism and youth rebellion long after the dream was over and so many soldiers were fried, down in flames and burned out.

By 1975, ZOSO was painted or carved on every static thing kids could find. By then the Stones were mainstream, respectable. The Stones always had a more diverse audience. Stephen Davis notes that Led Zeppelin eventually outsold the Stones at arena shows. Yet, Led Zeppelin remained a cult. And it wasn't restricted to Northeastern suburban development towns, either. It was everywhere.

Faith in Led Zeppelin helped a lot of kids get through everyday life in The Garrison State of Adolescence. Everyone has their stories of how teen life was made bearable through Zep. My friend Anthony went to high school in a small town about thirty miles south of the Alabama border. He says the big thrill in 1975 was to cruise by the Assembly of God Church with his friends piled into his 1968 green Chevy Impala, drinking Boone's Farm apple wine and blasting Led Zep on his eight-track tape deck.

Anthony says that if you wore a Led Zep T-shirt to high school, you were making a statement—"I smoke reefer." Good kids didn't listen to Zep. You would be damned to "vocational ed" for life. Forget about going to college. In this conservative Christian town, you were through! In the Bible Belt, long hair and a Led Zep T-shirt was the best way to X yourself out. And that music! Parents hated the volume and complained, "You can't understand the lyrics." This was a very good thing!

To embrace Led Zeppelin with all the trimmings was a declaration that you would have *no part of it*. Your place in your town was set in stone. You flirted with evil, you were dangerous. So the cult of Led Zeppelin helped kids carve out some space, communion. Zep was a liberation theology in vinyl.

Everybody I spent my time talking to outside the 7-Eleven in Bergenfield understood this very well. Because Bergenfield, I learned, was a very religious town. Take Nicky. He's a Deadhead. Like some kids, he respects the old bands, trusts them more than the newer ones: "Back then, they really meant it." Led Zep, Frank Zappa, the Dead, Neil Young, Keith Richards, there are a variety of great religious figures who could always be counted on never to betray the faith. Some still defend rocker honor openly and passionately—Neil Young's scathing "This Note's for You."

Any indication of selling out is a sign of betrayal. It's okay to become millionaires, or even, as Guns N' Roses singer Axl Rose advises, to take business courses so that when you become a rich rock star they can't fuck you over on the contracts. Nobody here would have any problem being rich and famous, living in mansions, getting lots of hot dates, touring the world by jet, and driving killer cars. Self-effacing hippie downward mobility has been cut from the script here. Selling out means you became an asshole, betrayed the rebel soul of rock and roll, sold your outlaw heart.

Then there are the Grateful Dead. You see Deadheads coast-to-coast in tie-dyed shirts, long hippie hair, beads and cloth bags, patchouli oil, crocheted caps, long skirts on the girls. They have the same things to say that they did twenty years ago. About Jerry, about their trip, about the road.

The Dead have a roving ministry, a network of kids linked together through the spirituality encouraged and demonstrated in the band's music. Books have been written about the Dead and their legions, and it's still St. Stephen with a rose. But now, it's a garden with an overlay of hard grease. Suburbia is filled with second-generation Deadheads, twenty wack years after. Violence at Grateful Dead shows is expected, bad drugs too, even with all the good cheer the Dead continue to impart. Diehards claim it's the work of the newly converted—the guys who drink too much, get into fights, come there to destroy. The girls, as young as twelve, hit the road and end up getting pregnant on tour. It's a mess, a good thing gone hairy. But then the orthodox of any scene will usually say that about the newly converted.

Deadheads and metalheads are cozy but they are very different. The Dead's ties to bikers add to their credibility among metalheads. Here, as in my town, Deadheads and metalheads usually hang out. Metalheads are more likely to get tagged as dirtbags while Deadheads are viewed as burnouts, space cadets. It changes from town to town, but in Bergenfield, a guy like Nicky is not unusual with his Harley and Dead regalia, a mix of patches and decals in his life.

Yes, music is the kids' religion; a belief system organized around guitar gods, sacred bands, outspoken rock heroes. But then there are the deacons of the church—bikers, Satan, Charles Manson. The deacons are crucial to a kids' psychic survival. For example, the Hell's Angels are big role models because they are an international brotherhood of rebels who command respect. Bikers get through life just being who they are, and their friends are there to back them up. Serious suburban rockers have never been shy about demonstrating reverence for all things biker: the look, the bikes, the life, and above all, the spirit. In turnpike suburbia, heavy-metal thunder is heavy metal thunder.

Whether or not the kid is a lapsed Christian, another long-standing ally for the suburban outcast is Satan. There are many types of satanic practice in this country. Some are practiced through established groups like Temple of Set or the Church of Satan. These are formal organizations, hierarchical, with rules. This is really adult Satanism, although a lot of kids do read the *Satanic Bible*, which is published through the Church of Satan.

Founded by Anton LaVey in the 1960s, the Church of Satan was primarily a "human potential" movement with colorful rituals and a strong antipuritanical orientation. Members are mainly concerned with "getting" and "having" whatever it is they want. LaVey, it seems, was disgusted by the hypocrisy of the Christian church and the abuses against humanity carried out in the name of "god." LaVey's *Satanic Bible* is required reading among alienated teenage rockers, but that's about as far as it goes. Most kids like the hedonistic philosophy which condones doing what you want. This is something minors are rarely encouraged to do.

Other forms of satanic worship in the United States involve small cliques, dabblers, self-styled cults, or loners. Sometimes the unaffiliated devil worshiper comes to our attention because of the racy satanic iconography surrounding a grisly murder or heavy drug situation. There are the infamous crime stories involving satanic worship, weird sexual and drug activity that make the headlines—the Manson family, the Matamoros murders in Mexico, Sean Sellers, who wiped out his parents for Satan, Tommy Sullivan, who killed his mom and then himself for the God Below; David Berkowitz, and then Daniel Rakowitz. Most of these people were marginal, social outcasts. If nobody else would have them, well, Satan would.

Satanic worship is also suspect in recent child pornography and institutional sexual-abuse cases. From the Inquisition to the Salem witch trials, anywhere there is social evil or fear over upheaval, religious fanatics will persecute "non-believers" and, most likely, Satan will be invoked. It is a convenient way to avoid facing harsh social issues. If there were no Satan, American politics would be a lot more coherent and probably more volatile.

Over the last twenty years or so, in addition to Satan, we have also had Charles Manson to hold up as our mirror emblem of absolute evil. But to rebel kids, Charlie's people proved that social outcasts can get their revenge. Manson is the first prophet of Armageddon. Every day, elements of the race wars he predicted in his paranoid messianic vision of Helter Skelter are played out across America. Regardless of his demented social program, some kids admire Manson, they think he's cool, that a lot of what he said made sense.

Manson was just this little guy, nobody from nowhere with nothing. His fascination with and possession of profound personal power over other people made him a role model for many disenfranchised, lonely suburban teens. And his ability to instill fear in straight America made him heroic to "losers" everywhere. Manson-as-myth is now the deposit box for adults' projected fear and hatred of young people. Over the years Charles Manson has become the archetype for every parent's nightmare. Some kids find that helpful.

Interestingly, the Manson family was always concerned with America's waste, with its garbage. They ate out of dumpsters, surviving on the nation's surplus. Charlie was simultaneously adored as Christ and Satan—Christ because he said he loved America's throwaway children, Satan because he was the Destroyer. He gave aimless, worthless drifters a place to belong, a family to be part of. Kids identify with that, but mostly they envy his power.

"Satanteens" make up the rest of Satan "worship" in America today. Lucifer is an old friend of the youth culture. Like sex and drugs and rock and roll, "Satan" is part of a long tradition. Rock and roll began as outlaw music, forbidden, frightening to good white Christian adults who feared its implicit call to sexual and racial mingling. Satan and sin made this scary social force simpler for adults to comprehend, and a lot more dangerous for kids to embrace. If partying was sinful, the flesh, the drink, the desire to be fully human could only be expressed by embracing the very evil you were condemned to. And if you were a kid, with no power and no voice in the social world that regulated you, Satan could help. For years, kids have beseeched favors, invoking his power, asking him to intervene on their behalf.

Such activity may often retain some of the rituals associated with paganism. The earliest religion, dating back to the Upper Ice Age, pagan practice came into play as humans moved from hunting and gathering to farming. Pagan activities were actually cause-and-effect techniques used to control nature, an ends-means approach to solving concrete tasks, like the way we might use science and technology today. Approximations of pagan rites are often part of "Satanteen" repertoire. But they are usually more performance-oriented, lacking the knowledge and discipline occult activity requires.

The term "pagan" was actually invented ages ago by early Jews and Christians to designate people who were unaffiliated with either religion. Literally, "pagan" means "hick," a person who lived in the countryside. But Satan came later. In the early Old Testament, Satan literally meant "adversary." This adversary is first personified in the Book of Job as a tempter of God. Two centuries before Christ, during the period of Apocalyptic Judaism, Satan began to take on a new importance. And with the fall of the Temple, the idea of Satan, of a personified evil, became very strong in Jewish thought.

Christianity, which began with Apocalyptic Judaism, picked up on this notion, and Satan became a central part of religious doctrine. In order to fully practice Catholicism, one must believe in the existence of Satan. So for lapsed Catholics, or bad kids from religious homes that have inculcated a fear of damnation, Satan is a tempting way to go. For kids who feel the squeeze, Satan may be the last resort, the only way left to control reality, through a rational ends-means calculation. And the woods of suburbia, the "countryside" that remains undeveloped and uncontrolled, offers a perfect spawning ground for such exotic activity.

Many kids say they fear the end of the world—they listen to the news, they read about Armageddon in the Bible and in the predictions of Nostradamus. So they look for God and salvation. But all the good things they used to trust have betrayed them. Wherever they have been taught to look for good, they find evil. Families are falling apart, and the papers are full of atrocities perpetrated by adults on kids. You can't trust anyone. The school bus driver, your pastor, the babysitter, even your dad could rape you or beat you or lock you up and no one would even care!

So kids start to look in all the places adults tell them are evil. They figure maybe what adults say is evil is really good. Rock lore is full of martyrs, losers who are really saints, legends. I noticed that "Only the Good Die Young" was sprayed all over the turf of suburbia during the 1980s.

Actually, kids turn to Satan for all sorts of things. I remember in the Rockaways, when I was about fifteen, there was a dorky guy who used to tell people he was Satan. It was basically his way of scaring girls into respecting him. He had no money, he wasn't good-looking, and he wasn't very smart. But we were all a little afraid of him. He didn't have a car but he would get all these girls to drive him around, meet him at all hours, do whatever he said. So in a sense, Satan did empower him because everyone would have ignored him without the "presence" of the devil. He actually got a lot of girls to go out with him too; they found him "fascinating."

Satan, the occult, and pop mysticism have been a part of rock and roll from the beginning. The relationship dates back to the pre-historic ages of rock, before the Beatles, even before Dion! References to the devil appear in the 1930s in the songs of Delta blues king Robert Johnson. His music is widely acknowledged as primordial: the root of all rock and roll. Some rock mythologists claim Robert Johnson cut a deal with Satan to secure his massive talents, taking literally such lyrics as "Me and the Devil was walking side by side." And what were Led Zeppelin, anyway, but a bunch of white guys, *Englishmen*, attempting to play the blues? They fucked it up —and that's what we call heavy metal. So by now it would be impossible to purge Satan lore from any serious rocker's life. A few volumes by Aleister Crowley, a copy of *Helter Skelter*, some candles, *The Necronomicon*, a pack of Tarot cards, and books about the famous Satanteens who've killed their parents are part of every orthodox rocker household. This is pop wicca, up there with wearing tight jeans and leather, styling your hair, eating junk food, piercing your ears, getting inked, and having fast cars.

But for any kid needing evidence of the intellectual impoverishment and cultural ignorance of the adult mind, Denver talk show host Bob Larson's book *Satanism—The Seduction of America's Youth* is a wealth of proof. With a rigid "Christian" agenda which he hopes to impose on our misguided and seduced kids, and in the absence of any understanding of context or referent, Larson reviews everything from horror movies to board games—everything that's fun—and tries to figure out how these things are destroying our kids.

Then he examines the most crucial bands, the "black metal music" of everyone from Zep to Slayer, and frets over the gruesome ways kids might interpret the stuff. While most kids view this stuff like carnival amusement, as art, as a means of expressing profound anxiety and the frustrations of living, adults take it seriously, undermining whatever confidence kids would have had in their abilities to make sense of an overwhelming world. Larson underestimates the average teenage music consumer. Kids regulate their market very closely. Larson simply has no respect for kids' intellectual or aesthetic sensibilities.

At least aware of the fact that kids often turn to Satan when all else fails, and that a lot has failed recently for kids, Larson tries to help parents understand what their kids are doing. But he offers no legitimate alternative to the powerlessness and hopelessness that affect kids.

For most kids, black metal is fun, entertainment, culture. If science fiction and horror are traditionally vehicles for playing out societal anxieties in a dramatic form, the best death-metal bands do this too. Much of their imagery is appropriated from movies and comics to begin with. But when Ozzy says nuclear war is the ulti-mate sin, Larson isn't satisfied. He thinks he should go further; he complains that Ozzy is missing the kids' need for a religiously based morality. Adults have failed to impart this morality across the cul-ture, but Larson wants it in metal!

Larson thinks rock stars like Ozzy and Slayer are evil because they make money off kids (not unlike the church that bleeds poor people for every dime). Larson the moralist is pissed that kids go for Satan to get the big easy. He's missing the point that most people use religion to "get" something: comfort, hope, understanding, grace. He seems to think kids have a problem delaying gratification and that's why they turn to Satan.

Larson probably means well. Unfortunately, a lot of loving par-ents will probably take him seriously. In his hysteria, Larson finds Satan lurking behind almost anything interesting. So concerned par-ents will read his book and get all torn up about anything their kids do. Then these parents will say things to their kids that alienate them even more.

People turn to religion in times of defeat and despair. Likewise, "Satan" offers kids a stockpile of personal empowerment. Scratch the surface and everybody has an excellent, if now embarrassing, Satanteen experience to share. In high school, I spent several months cranked on "crystal meth." I used to sit in my room all night stringing these little beaded necklaces. At one point, I had an enemy. A girl I hung around with started seeing my ex-boyfriend. I hated her for this. I had a picture of her, so I burned the face off it. For a few hours I chanted and twirled frantically around my room, singing to Cream, obsessing over her destruction, asking the forces of evil to serve justice on my enemy. While my parents slept, I worked myself into a frenzy. Then I smoked a joint and forgot about it.

Two days later the object of my spells and incantations got ar-rested for heroin possession. She spent the next year in a drug program, where she gained a good forty pounds. Nothing could have satisfied me more. I had taken my rival down, with the help of . . . a friend. I had avenged my honor, I had the power.

But then the girl's mother died. And after that she was diagnosed with some really weird blood disease. It had gone too far. I prayed for her, and felt so guilty about "causing" this with my magical thinking that I went to see her. I confessed everything to her. She understood that I was angry, and apologized for having gone out with the boyfriend. I felt so horrible that I decided then to devote the rest of my life to "white" magick and always to be very good. Like many Satanteens, I learned a hard lesson—as Charles Manson once said, "What goes around, comes around."

Most everyone I know who has had such a "satanic experience" is still not too sure if the outcome of their experiments was "real" or "just coincidence." With the rise of heavy metal, this tradition flourished. More recent than my own "dabbling" was a story Cliff told me one night up at Metal 24. He thinks he was probably inspired by the legend of "Say You Love Satan" Ricky Kasso, the dude from nearby E. Northport who adults say killed Gary Lauwers for Satan. Everyone knows the killing was the result of Ricky's getting beat on some angel dust. But Cliff says at the time it seemed really cool, so Cliff and company went to the mall on Sunrise Highway in Valley Stream and bought copies of the *Satanic Bible* by Anton LaVey. Picked up a copy of *The Necronomicon*, too.

Cliff explains, "The *Satanic Bible* is based on excess and freedom. And Satan always represents vengeance. So we were looking at the spells and stuff that you could do, and there was this real easy spell, that you had to take something of somebody's, you had to take a rope and tie it in seven knots and each time you tied a knot you had to say the person's name. That was cool, and you had to hide it on something that belonged to the person. So we took this rope and we said this kid's name . . . this black kid in print shop . . . seven times for each knot and we hid it in his notebook. And he came to school for four or five periods and he was like deathly ill. It was the coolest thing. Me and two of my friends."

I asked Cliff if he was really into Satan worship in high school. He smiles. "We thought we were." This was in 1983, and I know Cliff has been a hardcore heavy-metal fan since before he hit puberty. I asked if he got into Satan from rock and roll, from Maiden or Ozzy. "No," Cliff said. "That had nothing to do with it. The two were separate from each other." So I asked Cliff, "Why do people think Ozzy makes kids worship Satan?" He says what all the kids say—"Because they have to blame someone for all the bad shit that's going on."

But then how else are adults to make sense of 666 and the pentagrams and all the animal sacrifices attributed to Satanteens? Were they really satanic or just some sick kids with the devil as veneer? Cliff said he had a friend who used to go to the graveyard and dig up heads, boil the flesh off them, and then sell the skulls. A few years later the guy was arrested for murder. He wasn't into Satan, but people thought he was, given his previous preoccupation with cemeteries.

There are kids who regularly torture animals. They take their feelings of powerlessness, their aggressions, out on them, and ritualize it. Dressed up in all the pseudo-Satanic trappings, such motivations are easily overshadowed. Animal experimenters refer to the animals they discard after lab use as "sacrificed." Nobody thinks they mean Satan, since this is always done in the name of "science."

Regalia is a big part of rock and roll. Posing is too. And suburban kids like the "ancient texts" by Aleister Crowley (1875–1947) and H. P. Lovecraft's *The Necronomicon* because they are mystical and exotic in a world of bland, prefabricated, mass-produced artifacts.

Satanteenism is also very high among kids with born-again or religious parents. If you are so bad that you are going to hell anyway, you might as well get in good with the guy in charge. In families where good and evil are expressed in black-and-white terms, and where kids are maimed by gross contradictions and hypocrisies, these old, contrary knowledges can be helpful. For kids, American citizens in their minority, it is clear that invoking the Lord of Darkness serves a purpose. And what better way to rile your misguided Judeo-Christian mom and dad?

Yet when Eddie from the convenience store invited me home to meet his mom, he admonished me, "Look, whatever you do, don't mention Satan . . . she's a Christian. She'll have me in church all week if she thinks . . ." It was bad enough that Eddie was already going to burn in hell for his sins, but mentioning Satan would hammer the nails into his coffin. Eddie never took religion seriously anyway; he was too busy running away from home to avoid punishment. Now he's an atheist, into science fiction.

The kids' religion has always been misunderstood, but after a while, the stupidity of adults became annoying. They wanted to "protect" kids by keeping them imprisoned in some idyllic 1950s vision of "family life." But this just is not the real world anymore.

Adults worried about protecting kids' "morals" but were completely unconcerned that the minimum wage hadn't gone up once during the whole decade. Since the 1960s kids have lost power in leaps and bounds; but when they turned to "Satan" or to other youth culture traditions for help, for comfort, for support, adults complained that kids were being seduced by evil.

Everything kids did to empower or protect themselves in recent years, any refuge they created from adult indifference and brutality, was turned around and used against them. We should have been proud of them. Proud that the kids' religion gave them so much courage to fight back.

A leading yearbook entry by the end of the 1980s was a line from a Grateful Dead song: "We will get by, We will survive . . ." It was a prayer.

This Is Religion II

Creating a new culture does not only mean one's own "original" discoveries. It also and most particularly means the diffusion in a critical form of truths already discovered, their socialization . . . and even making them the basis of vital action, an element of co-ordination and intellectual and moral order.

—From Antonio Gramsci,
Prison Notebooks

I

The best thing about the kids' religion was that it offered a worldview that made sense when nothing else did. Parents, the school, the town—they all had their version of things. But the kids could learn most everything they needed to know about the meaning of life from their friends, their scene, and, most important, their bands. As far as the kids were concerned during the 1980s, hardcore, metal, and thrash carried the Truth. A few crucial bands offered the kids a viable philosophical system which they could use to understand life. Often these bands were referred to as *crucial*. S.O.D. was such a band.

S.O.D. (Stormtroopers of Death) had a strong hardcore skinhead-thrasher following and had been around for a while. I had bought and played out their now-classic album, *Speak English or Die*, long before I'd heard of Bergenfield. Billy Milano had been a face in the New York City hardcore scene for years. But he was also a famous organic intellectual of Bergen County. Kids here were proud that one of their own had made it. This was much closer to home than Jon Bon Jovi, and a lot more hip. Basically people admired Billy because he was the powerful front man of a great, loud, assertive band, and he was also one of them.

By the time I met Billy, S.O.D. had broken up. In the beginning, S.O.D. was made up of four guys: Billy, Charlie, Scott, and Danny. Any time their subsequent bands are written up in the rock press, this glorious history is recounted: When S.O.D. broke up, guitarist Scott Ian and drummer Charlie Benante devoted themselves to Anthrax. Danny Lilker, the bass player, went on to organize Nuclear Assault. The third great band to emerge from the ashes of S.O.D. was Billy's band, M.O.D. (Method of Destruction).

Now, Bergenfield's burnouts were aptly identified by the outside world as thrashers. Thrash is a hybrid from when the heavy-metal and hardcore scenes were forced, for various reasons, to share space. As venues for organized performance dried up or fell to gentrifiers, many great bands were born, and new fashions were innovated. That, at least, is a local reading of what happened.

To the college/radio-trained ear looking for socially progressive rock product, heavy metal has always meant bad politics. Lyrics were considered stupid, with no redeeming social value. At best it was dismissed as mindless schlock; at worst it was vulgar, spandex rock, white, male, mass, suburban corp-rock. Bread and circuses for turnpike trash.

But hardcore was different. The kids looked rude and dirty, angry and psychotic, but they were ultimately positive. This was a highly factionalized scene, split among Nazi skins, surf punks, trash cross-overs, peace punks, some rads, antiracist skins, and much more. In hardcore, as in every other major scene of the decade, males dominated. But a few females did get their voices in, and by the end of the decade all the scenes included some women: lady rappers, all-girl metal bands, and hardcore's female bass players.

Some hardcore factions were vehemently antidrug, anticorporate, local, grassroots, and self-sufficient. If hip hop is now understood as the home-grown self-educational emancipatory tool of alienated African-American youth, hardcore scenes served a similar purpose in urban and suburban bohemian enclaves.

While the dirts and burnouts, and metal itself, had a strong 1960s lineage, the hardcore kids' roots were England's 1970s skins and punks. Much of the 1970s punk and antihippie sentiments carried over, which meant hardcore kids and metalheads were natural antagonists.

During the 1980s, hardcore scenes festered in clubs that opened and closed by the week. Beer and antihistamines were the drugs of choice in some settings, and fighting was often part of a night out. Dancing was violent and wild, yet clear boundaries of behavior existed. Strict rules of order were observed in the pit.

Participation in the scene was made possible only by word of mouth. Fliers, occasional street sheets, were the only clue. "Xerox art" and mimeographed copies advertised bands and temporary music venues. The general idea was to do it yourself, to create immediate rupture, quick community, in a place you could call your own.

Sometimes 1960s-based radical rock critics saw the promise of social revolution in this scene. This was misguided. For the most part the hardcore kids were as suspicious of the left as they were of the right. Some of this carried over from the punks, who were puritanical, rigidly ethical, socially critical, and anti-excess. Resentful of the world they inherited, the punks hated the hippies for their street naïveté and bogus idealism.

The idea of a generation of spoiled, pampered hippies becoming self-involved yuppie consumers came as no surprise. To them, the opportunistic Jerry Rubin represented the *Geist* of the Woodstock generation.

Deeply alienated but forward-moving, hardcore kids believe in taking action, seizing control—excluding adults by the sheer power of signs, symbols, and attitudes. At the very least, hardcore kids view themselves as politically minded; radically anticorporate and anticommercial, often ecologically oriented. Fuck the multideath corporations. Do it yourself. Meat is murder. Know your rights. Create an alternative economic base for cultural production: squats, fanzines, warehouse scenes with local bands. No adults. Though there is no organized movement, hardcore ethics borrow from several radical and anarchist traditions, and many kids are active in social movements: Greenpeace, People for the Ethical Treatment of Animals (P.E.T.A.), and abortion rights.

The hardcore imagination retains the punks' rapid antibureaucratic sentiment, and the desire to disrupt order. Yet there remains strong suspicion of formal programs and dogmas. Idealism isn't dead here, but cynicism runs rampant.

The ministry of information for this scene did not come on vinyl alone. For years, it came in the form of publications known as "fanzines." *MaximumRocknroll (MRR)*, among the most consistently published of the lot, first came out in 1982. One of the most widely distributed fanzines—in 1987 circulation was over 13,000—*MRR* runs between forty and fifty pages and covers local subcults from all the states, Europe, and Asia. Readers are encouraged to interview their own bands, to develop and write about their local scenes. *MRR* is popular for its six or seven pages of letters to the editor. The magazine offers an arena for kids to debate all types of social issues. It is a place for kids to share experiences, ask for help, comment, whine, and brag. Every social and personal issue faced can find a forum here.

The editor, Tim Yohannan, has been involved in cultural politics since the late sixties, in and around Berkeley. Nonaffiliated but committed to alternative youth culture, Yohannan has often been targeted in the commercial and indie rock press for being a yippie, a politico co-opting the kids' culture, and a self-righteous dogmatist.

Like any social stage, fanzines offer an opportunity for backbiting, backstabbing, and competition for primacy of place.

From our conversations and his many editorials, Yohannan articulates a long-term view of youth. He says that in the sixties, the youth culture routinized within three years. Punk/hardcore was uglier, less conducive to marketing, and so it gave the alternative industry time to develop its economic base and sphere of influence (radio, warehouses for bands, and performance, fanzines, squats, etc.). Yohannan views the social base of the hardcore "movement" as largely white, largely middle-class, arty and pretentious at the upper range, and trickling down into proletariat at the lower.

Although many fanzines subscribe to a youth internationalism, there is some antagonism toward European bands, whom American kids resent for being supported in the production of arts by their governments. The European bands can be more radical and political because they have long-term alternatives to the star-power circuit American youth fear they must yield to at some point.

During the 1980s, alternative record companies, press, and other independent situations evolved. The "indie" bands worried endlessly about their commitment to staying free of the corporate world, and fretted over selling out by becoming too commercial, too mass. But many also realized the inevitability of that happening. Two things mattered as far as this scene was concerned: that you were honest, in it for love of craft; and that you were doing it first.

Hardcore was essentially home-grown—unlike the metal or hip-hop scene, hardcore kids did have some aversion to the notion of rock-star-as-millionaire. Of course a lot of people in the hardcore scene saw through this posture of purity, and there were groupies, entrepreneurs, hucksters, vultures, and wanna-be's, here, as anywhere.

As cultural artifacts, fanzines offered a forum for discussion and strategy. They also provided a temporary respite from youth isolation, atomization, and basic disenfranchisement. The traditional form is unpretty and intentionally unglossy. In addition to information and community, fanzines offered art, book, film, band, and record reviews, as well as advertisements for indie culture industry. There were usually interviews with local bands; instructions on how to avoid registering for selective service; and extended discussions on Bill of Rights censorship, animal liberation, sexism, nuclear war, police, school and family violence, rape, and teenage suicide.

All text is written by "fans" and anything else is seriously suspect. Some fanzines solicit scholarly contributions. One issue of MRR, or example, might include interviews with Noam Chomsky or transcripts of "important issue" radio show discussions.

As a form, fanzines date back twenty years or more. They began simply as fan club sheets for film and rock stars. But in the eighties, fanzines became central to the creation of alternative, autonomous, dissenting youth subcults. They came from everywhere anyone could produce and distribute them using primitive production techniques and, ideally, scamming free supplies, reproduction, and postage at school or work.

Over the years fanzine topics have grown to include not only the creative arts, but technology as well. The geographic and topical range remains vast, the titles deep—*Murder Can Be Fun*, from San Francisco; *Violent Noize* from College Point, New York; *No Answer*, in Twin Falls, Idaho. This is networking for youth. You can meet friends for crashing, locate pen pals, exchange tapes of local bands, organize letter-writing campaigns.

Some fanzines are now also tied to an "electronic underground" of message boards, where computer-literate outlaws share pilfered credit card numbers, bust security codes, and infiltrate the credit infrastructure. These rebel hacker boards are highly esoteric and secretive.

Although I didn't come across any during my time in north Jersey, fanzines are especially big in suburbia. Almost everyone has a friend who puts out a 'zine. For example, *Smash Apathy* came out of Fair Lawn, New Jersey. It began in 1981 as a "one-page street sheet" to inform local kids of goings-on. The fanzine was started by a guy named Estraven and three of his friends. By 1987 the 'zine had grown to forty pages and only Estraven was left holding the rag. Estraven says he started the 'zine "as a way to communicate with people worldwide to bring ideas into one publication and distribute them to other people."

Smash Apathy came to my attention through *MRR*. I remember reading a lengthy debate initiated by Estraven, spanning two or three issues, over the appropriation of the hardcore scene by Chris Williamson, a New York City rock entrepreneur. Estraven and some friends leafleted and boycotted the Ritz, a downtown Manhattan commercial rock club, where Williamson, a promoter, was presenting shows through his "Rock Hotel." There were fights, threats, and ultimatums. All this caused a flurry of letters and endless discussion about the workings of rock economy, the fate of the "scene," and the intrusion of "heavy metalists."

Wherever hardcore kids and metalheads congregated, the scene became an instantly contested terrain. Girls were pushed back, metalheads were stomped on or smashed. If you were not white, but people knew you, or you were obviously part of the scene, no trouble. Otherwise, death. Sexual politics weren't any better among hardcore kids than elsewhere. For most girls, it was virtually impossible to see a band at a hardcore show because the front of the stage was dominated, always, by muscular, lean, sweaty boys stage-diving and slamming around. A few girls took a dive now and then, but most were relegated to the sides, watching the boys. Still, it was a place to belong, something to do, a way of defining yourself—it was your scene.

By 1982, as gentrification and the high costs of running clubs limited the number of arenas for such scenes, the constricted space forced confrontations. In the end, everybody had experienced the great crossover.

This is how it worked that fateful night in my life. Some years ago, a band called Saint Vitus opened for Black Flag at Irving Plaza, a New York City club known for hosting hardcore shows throughout the 1980s. I had lived in California in the beginning of the eighties. I had seen a lot of hardcore bands there and I still kept up with some of them. In those days the idea of heavy-metal fans and hardcore fans under the same roof was unthinkable.

But on this particular night I noticed things changing. The audience was half headbanger and half slammer. Longhairs versus skins, spikes, painted Harley jackets. Mohawks, Motorhead patches, Maiden T-shirts up against Doc Martens. But Henry Rollins, Flag's shaman poet-singer, seemed determined to bring us together. The West Coast scene had been merging for a while, hardcore and metal welded into thrash. Speed metal, death metal, biker metal, rap metal. Scene integration meant slam, headbang, and mosh!

Saint Vitus, a biker-looking speed-metal band, came on, and all the metalheads went crazy. But the punks were pissed off. United forces? Fuck off! No way. Of course some people were willing, and a few went crazy.

The situation remained less than friendly. Hardcore kids resented the metal fans at their shows. They were polluting the scene. By day the high school was a war zone; at night, the dance floors became battlegrounds. For years, the fanzines were filled with bitch-and-moan manifestos about the dreaded alloy invasion. Meanwhile metal kids started pushing their own 'zines in hardcore territories, and a few thrasher labels found their way into the hardcore record bins. This was a new scene for headbangers.

But there was friction. The classical heavy-metal legacy of spandex and dick-oriented lyrics remained associated with corporate rock in sexist, capitalist America. Left-leaning hardcore kids hate metalheads for their bad politics; right-leaning skins hate them because of their passivity and drug abuse and political ignorance. All the things the punks hated the hippies for, and some of the things the hippies hated the greasers for. Basically, metalheads just want to have a good time, and as we move into the 1990s they are still beating the shit out of each other.

Beyond contempt for some of the values the metal kids' scene was founded upon, the hardcore kids had another reason for resenting them: the marketplace compliance of suburban metalheads pissed them off. Because metalheads are willing to spend upwards of twenty dollars on a ticket to an arena show, and then another twenty dollars on a concert T-shirt, and everyone out to fleece kids today knows it, the intrusion of metalheads on the hardcore scene was viewed as a severe threat to the local economy.

Hardcore fans feared that once rock entrepreneurs knew kids were willing to be exploited at those prices, there would go the whole scene, back to the corporate parasites. The space squeeze ultimately defeated many of these scenes, as kids have never been able to get around the problem of adult control of private property and public space, except by temporarily appropriating empty buildings and parking lots. So everyone knew that once their scene was organized by adults, there would be police, fire marshals, bouncer brutalities, beer searches, weapons frisking, and the kids would be as pushed around here as they were at home, at school, and on the streets of America. They would have nothing at all to call their own.

However disjointed, the hardcore scene, in its various incarnations, maintains an alert political orientation. Metal and hardcore music were both strong on the death-and-destruction themes, but hardcore offered solutions. If the world was going to hell, hardcore music was angry and active, fighting for a better world before it was too late. Metal, on the other hand, was romantic, lamenting, sadly resigned to its fate. This was a familiar debate. In the face of death, we have these choices: commit to a project or have a real good time. These are the choices pondered by both "social crisis" theorists and American youth.

The metal scene came out of the mainstream, a warp in the hardrock center. It was the vulgar legacy of Led Zep *et al.* It was hedonistic, grandiose, strong on pleasure, and committed to the ethics of sex, drugs, and rock and roll. Drink beer and get real loose. Wave your fist in the air, wear your pride band on your back. Get through the week, and when it's over, party down! Whether you were waiting for Armageddon or Monday and a shit-for-wage job, you could at least feel good tonight.

The idea of the world ending, or "Armageddon," had been a principal theme in music since the punks. Different subcults expressed it in their various traditions. The more culturally conservative metalheads projected their fears through symbols their parents had taught them—evil, the devil, hell. The hardcore kids, on the other hand, projected their fears onto social ills. The names of bands, song titles, and lyrics were focused on the social porn of the day. Thrash bands borrowed from all of the above.

When kids in America learned anything about right and wrong in the brutal 1980s, they learned it from their bands. If they were able to express themselves openly and honestly at any time, it was in their scenes. Of course there were people who exploited themes as trends, but those bands didn't last. They were dismissed as poseurs, teenybopper bands.

In the Great Crossover there was above all a cultural exchange. You had bands like Metallica hanging out with the Misfits, and after a while everyone started writing songs about the real things that threatened kids: drug pushers, Army recruiters, spiritual isolation, nuclear holocaust, child sexual abuse, mental hospitals.

The metal influence relaxed the cranky puritanical punk roots of hardcore. In 1983 Metallica released their first album, *Kill Em All*, on Megaforce Records. When the album placed number thirty-five in the top one hundred albums of the 1980s *Rolling Stone* said, "Metallica rose up from the heavy-metal underground to establish a vital new sub-genre known as speed metal or thrash metal." Some Metallica fans insist their band transcends such banal category structures. Metallica's music was fast, brutal, crucial, hard, loud. Lyrics were serious, loving, critical, angry and hurt. The thrash bands took the best guitar leads from metal but left the trivial ideological pursuits behind, a contradictory fusing of hardcore's abrasive spirit of anarchy and metal's heart-and-soul romanticism.

Emotionally and intellectually provocative, thrash was a harsh, healthy combination of social outrage and personal remorse. By exposing, lyrically and musically, how society ate people up alive, thrash ultimately brought people together from traditionally oppositional class cultures. It illuminated as it relieved, accomplishing this across traditional aesthetic categories. Saint Vitus led me to Motorhead and that prepared me for Metallica. Because of thrash, new friendships were born and new musics were experienced.

Once I was open to it, Joe and Randy were able to share their metal heritage with me. So I was ready to *hear* Ozzy, Motley Crue, and Iron Maiden. In the absence of the Great Crossover, I might have dismissed these bands as "spandex goons," or approached them simply as "data," missing the telos. In turn, I did get some people interested in my psychotic industrial noise bands. Tapes were exchanged, fashion ideas and attitudes were shared.

Thrash is so fast it actually calms you down; it's relaxing, like Ritalin. But in Metallica, many emotional conflicts can also be resolved. For example, for a long time, nobody was really talking about suicide. It was a sin, taboo, yet kids kept doing it. Metallica decided to deal with that.

One night, I remember Randy and Joe talking about "Fade to

Black," one of the most beautiful of Metallica's songs. "I had to take it off the turntable, it made me feel like doing it," Joe explains, and Randy agrees. You have to be selective. But to help me understand the recent suicides, Randy recommends the album *Ride the Lightning*. "It's got good suicide stuff on it." Randy says he prefers the later *Master of Puppets*, but for text on suicide, "definitely" Randy advises, "check out *Ride the Lightning*."

Following his lead, I start listening to it. First it makes me sick, I cry. It's tender, hurtful. I start playing "Fade to Black" almost every day. This is such a beautiful song, so morbid, insidious. The hour-of-darkness lamentations of a dying human soul. Alone, defeated, depleted, hopeless and stranded but for one last exit. Fade to black and kill the pain. "Death greets me warm, now I will just say goodbye. . . ."

I listen to it some more and it makes me think of the time a close friend tried to blow his brains out, but failed. We were so close, yet for years I was never able to ask him why he wanted to do it. "Fade to Black" makes me imagine what he felt like holding the gun, sitting there with a hangover on a rainy Friday morning. After a while, though, when I play the song, in the last minute, after almost six minutes of morphine agony, the rescue guitars come in. This song goes to the bottom, but comes back up. It gives you the will to power, to triumph; it's cathartic, it's killer.

Of course, the song has been blamed in more than one teenage suicide. Kids just laugh about adult cultural retardation, like how they worry about satanic "backward masking" of messages in songs, and take the poetics of songs literally. That's all part of the glorious history of rock. While most kids view Ozzy as a great entertainer, a rocker's Halloween, and experts have reassured them, adults still worry that he encourages them to worship Satan and to commit suicide. It's sort of like how Helter Skelter made Manson orchestrate killing sprees, not rage built up over years of institutional abuse and social disregard. Like the "Paul Is Dead" myths that surrounded the Beatles. Or how people are convinced "Elvis Lives." Superstition and adult paranoia aside, if you're too high, and your life is shit, some kids figure "Jingle Bells" could probably do you in too.

Rock critic Chuck Eddy once said Metallica was "the Led Zeppelin of the 80s." Thrash reflected the world eighties kids lived in.

Unlike Led Zep, this is not sexy music. It's deeply emotional, powerful, and pummeling. Metaphorically, death replaces sex as resolution. Bands are critical of the world. But it's neither preachy nor contrived, nothing at all like the sloganeering U2. "Political" music à la Tracy Chapman, Sting, David Byrne, and the rest of the "consciousness brigade" is viewed with suspicion, "for yuppies."

Now as it turned out, M.O.D. had an album coming out just around the time I got to Bergen County. Since everyone I spoke to in Bergen County went on about how Billy Milano came from the area, I felt it was important to get his view of things. So I called his management company.

It's all set. Billy Milano will meet me at Megaforce Worldwide, a small record company responsible for much of the decade's best thrash. It's a mom-and-pop store run by Jon and Marsha Zazula. Over the years, these folks have handled Metallica, Ace Frehley, Overkill, Testament, and Raven. Headquarters had recently been moved to a suburban home in East Brunswick. I had located Billy through my S.O.D. album. The appointment was set up for him by Metal Maria.

I get to the place and Billy's running late, so I sit in a room looking at posters, talking to Maria about the recent Anthrax tour of Japan. Maria tells me Billy is afraid I'll hate him (his public image as a racist, sexist scumbag). She says he's a pretty sweet guy, actually. Then we talk about our haircuts, the Cro-Mags, and the future of bands like Sisters of Mercy and Mission. Finally, Billy arrives.

Before the interview formally convenes, Billy says he's pissed off about something—a recent TV feature on *20/20* about teenage suicide and heavy-metal music. This was the most recent in a series of media specials aiming at understanding the loony cultural activities of American youth. The show, "The Children of Heavy Metal," explored the social bond among metal audience members. In retrospect, this seems like one of TV's best efforts of the decade, since the kids were presented in their own context, in their own words. Yet even with the best of intentions, it was obvious that adults *still didn't get it*. While this was obvious to Billy, Maria, and myself and it only took us a few words to establish what went wrong, it's worth taking some time here to explain.

The clip opens with discussion of recent violence at an Iron Maiden show. There had been a rock riot in New Jersey, three dozen arrests, injuries to fans and police. The music is described by a concerned commentator, Stone Phillips, as "screeching guitars, flamboyant bands, lyrics obsessed with sex, Satanism, and even suicide." A kid, obviously a fan, is asked what this music's about. He's fifteen. He says, "Togetherness man, we got to stick together and fight." For what? "Fight for our right, man, to listen to our music, to party, man."

Serious politicos have always gotten annoyed by the idea that kids see their "right to party" as a crucial issue. How can American kids be preoccupied with such trivial issues? But the kids understand their right to party as their right to create, express, and commune. It is a crucial political question for young people. The right to produce and to express yourself through culture is essentially a First Amendment issue; it is no less sacred than the freedom of speech, the press, or to assemble peaceably—rights most young people do not fully enjoy. The "right to party" means more than the freedom to get high. It is, in effect, an expression of the right to the free exercise of religion.

But this is not the interviewer's focus, and so the kid just comes off looking cute, if stupid. Critics, the viewer learns, are concerned with the destructive potential of metal music, that it may have contributed to a number of teenage suicides, "like the one in Bergenfield, New Jersey, on March 11. Four young people died in a suicide pact. A heavy-metal cassette box was found at the scene." Then the camera turns to the brother of Nancy Grannan, who died in a suicide pact with her best friend the day after the Bergenfield, an apparent copycat. According to her brother, the Alsip, Illinois, teen was "obsessed with the lyrics of the band Metallica" and she wrote down the lyrics to "Fade to Black" before taking her own life.

Then the lyrics of Ozzy Osborne's notorious "Suicide Solution" flashed across the screen. It has been linked to more than one teen suicide, but every Ozzy fan knows the song is an antialcohol eulogy for Bon Scott of AC/DC. Bon Scott was Ozzy's friend. But adults disregard the lyrics "wine is fine, whisky's quicker." Ozzy isn't the most articulate or coherent person to explain, as he has done in interview after interview, that this is a serious anti-drinking song.

20/20's reaction to his song is enough to cue kids watching this particular segment that the show is bogus.

Like most "inside kids today" shows, this is primarily a dialogue between adults about kids. *Not between kids and adults about life.* And this particular show aired at the height of the heavy-metal witch trials. It hadn't been that long since the infamous Ozzy song was the subject of pickets, record burning, and the relentless interference of the censorship police: Christian groups and self-appointed morality squad, the PMRC (Parents' Music Resource Center). PMRC spokeswoman Tipper Gore is a woman about my age with young children and not a clue about how music works in kids' lives. Parents turn to people like this to help them understand their kids. Then parents ask their kids questions about the music that are so embarrassing that the kids know never to expect their parents to understand anything.

So Tipper Gore is interviewed once again, to remind us how bad it is that kids are exposed to extreme violence, graphic sex, and suicide in lyrics, and how they have to be protected. Bruce Dickinson, lead singer for Iron Maiden, is produced to combat her argument. He is very annoyed. "I wish people would get a sense of proportion about what's right and wrong, and who are the real people poisoning people's minds, and why they're doing it." He feels his band says things that mean something to kids, something they can relate to. Never the critics' darlings, Iron Maiden is a band that has had little airplay yet notoriously loyal fans—even behind the Iron Curtain *before* it fell.

The band has always made a point of showing appreciation, treating fans with respect as well as concern. Maiden is famous for opening shows with a humane plea of some sort, like asking the kids to take care of themselves, not to drink too much, not to commit suicide or get into fights, not to be self-destructive.

Acknowledging that secret societies are regularly formed in huge, commercial rock arenas, commentator Stone Phillips decides to check it out firsthand, to find out what the kids are up to. He's going to take us there, to see Iron Maiden.

To set this up, Phillips locates some Iron Maiden fans to act as informants. He will hang with them first at their high school, and then check out their scene at an upcoming Maiden show. Now live from New Jersey, Phillips says, "This is the high school in Teaneck, New Jersey, a school with a reputation for academic excellence. But like just about every other high school in America, Teaneck High has its own group of so-called tough kids, hoods or burnouts—some into drinking or drugs, others who aren't into too much of anything at all except heavy-metal music." He introduces us to four metalheads blasting an S.O.D. tune.

Phillips asks the kids dumb adult question number one: "S.O.D. . . . Stormtroopers of Death, now what does that *mean?*" The kid looks at him. This is a child of signs, not symbols, so he just says the music calms him down. "It's like, you know, if anything's on my mind, I just go and sit in my room and play some music, and just sit down and think." Phillips twists this around to say that the music helps the kid shut out the world.

Such music is used as a legal stimulant by kids in boring lives everywhere. It gives them an edge, attitude, and courage. But Phillips misses this. At one point, Phillips actually reprimands the kids for playing their noise box during the interview, and asks one kid in a condescending tone to turn it down!

Face to the camera, Phillips explains, "For the most part these kids are not star athletes or straight-A students. Most don't belong to any high school clubs or hang out with the popular crowd. Often they feel like outcasts, like they don't fit in, especially in the classroom." He asks the metal kids what they want to do with their lives. After a Twisted Sister anthem the kids bleat off, "I Wanna Rock!" A happy-looking fourteen-year-old says he's not going to college; he figures he's spent enough time in school. He can't see spending any more time there.

The kids start talking about nuclear war, inspired by a Megadeth song. "You talk about the future and everything and like, there might not be a future 'cause they're still makin' all these weapons and everything, and I think about peace a lot." They don't talk about these things in school, so most such serious thought is provoked by the music adults hope to censor. It's a sad irony—because the only place where taboo subjects like sex, death, suicide, loneliness, and terror are discussed is in their music.

The Teaneck metalheads talking to Phillips explain that they don't just buy whatever is out there, though; they make informed choices. "If you don't like the lyrics, you just avoid them." That's a solution offered by Melissa, sixteen, who finds some of Motley Crue's lyrics a little too sexist for her taste. Then there is suicide to consider. The kids here are still shocked by the Bergenfield suicide pact, it is still fresh in their minds. But they agree it is wrong to blame the music. They point out that they listen to the same stuff, and *they* didn't commit suicide. Millions of American kids' lives are deeply invested in metal. Besides, suicide isn't for burnouts only; plenty of kids with mainstream music taste do it. So, they wonder, where is the connection?

The kids defend the S.O.D. song "Kill Yourself" by saying it's just a song: "You're not gonna go out and do it unless you got real bad problems and everything, you know?" "It's not the music that's going to kill you, it's yourself." Actually the lyrics are a goof, and the sound of the song is so powerful you are more likely to feel relaxed and satisfied after it than like "doing it." The kids tell Phillips that they think the problem is adults overreacting to their music and therefore missing the point.

The camera cuts to Charles Young, a music journalist who defends metal as a healthy outlet for the kids. "Heavy metal speaks to the anger and despair of teenagers today, the way the blues used to speak to the despair and anger of black people in the South. Without heavy metal, there would be—there would probably be a lot more suicides, because metal and certain other forms of rock give teenagers something to believe in that they get noplace else."

Another interpretation is offered to parents—that the metal scene may be providing the kids a deeper form of socialization and bonding then ever before experienced in rock shows. According to rock promoter John Scher, these concerts have a communal, tribal atmosphere. But this point is easily swallowed up over and over again, when protective adults read ulterior motives into Scher's interpretation of scenes: "Sure, he stands to make a fortune off of this music. What does he care if it screws them up?"

The show ends explaining how some adult groups are now giving parents instructions on how to "de-metal" their kids, to impose dress codes, to forbid black, spikes, leather, and key symbols of metal. They are instructed to tear down posters and turn off their stereos.

"The Children of Heavy Metal" concludes that "the kids who listen to heavy metal may be telling us something, that they feel pushed down and shoved out. That it helps them cope with the pressures." This was apparently the point of the show.

According to one of its producers, the program was intended to show the kids' side of things, based on the assumption that the kids today were "not being heard." But the "both sides" approach of the show, though well reasoned, actually muffled the young voices. Some kids who saw it felt it was cool simply because they got to see and hear about S.O.D., Maiden, Ozzy, and Metallica on mainstream TV! That was a real thrill. By now they knew what to expect from anything produced by adults for kids. Even the best stuff would come across as weird once an adult point of view was interjected. A number of metal fans I know were also pretty annoyed about the *20/20* show.

Like I said, Billy Milano had his opinions too. "One-sided . . . I mean it's basically one-sided, the kids that spoke their opinion on it got some sort of opinion in there but it was always re-questioned by the people reporting it. I mean you can always make an answer a question, it depends on how you react to it . . . just like that Phil Donahue thing with the punks on it . . . that was a joke, a circus, it only hurt what everybody was trying to stand up for, some kids got through it without getting chopped down, but most of the kids got chopped down . . . it was just a joke." It had to be in kid talk or not at all. Otherwise, they had you.

Now Billy Milano is not a metalhead. He's a skin, he says. He also says he doesn't hang out anymore much. The skinheads in America are fashioned after white working-class English factory town youth, but here they are often suburban, generally not poor, and sometimes ethnic—Asian, African, Latino, Jewish, and Italian American, depending on the region. They are by no means mono- lithic: some are racist, white supremacist, with ties to Aryan sepa- ratist groups; others are vehemently antiracist, for world peace. Some are simply "fashion skins" who just go in for the look. There were no visible skins in Bergenfield when I was there, although Joe seemed to be moving in that direction.

I was glad to meet Billy Milano in person and I apologized for placing this burden of speaking for others upon him. But he was close to the situation and known to be a man of strong opinions.

Billy felt he understood what was going on with the suicides. "It's a bad situation to begin with, people on TV just make it worse, turn it into an epidemic . . . the suicide pact had nothing to do with the music in the first place. I mean I see no connection between people listening to music and trying to kill themselves. Some kids killed themselves and [the adults] blamed it on Ozzy Osborne. So if I go home and watch the President's speech on TV and I go out and kill sixty-five people with a rifle at McDonald's . . . then I gotta blame the President because I listened to his speech and he made me freak out??"

Billy had written a song about suicide for his new album. He was in the hospital once and a girl came in at 7:00 a.m. who had cut her wrists with razor blades; she wanted to kill herself, for what reason Billy does not know. It was a horrible thing, he says, to see this girl with her wrists split open, blood all over the place. He was also angry about the Bergenfield suicide pact, which added some elements to his song "Your Beat."

The song mocks people for giving up on life before they start it, for selling themselves out. He believes it's better to be dead than to be someone you are not just to please your parents—that's *worse* than suicide. But by committing suicide you are ultimately betraying yourself anyway. Taking other people's bad opinions of you too seriously could be your downfall. By killing yourself, you're actually giving in to your parents' demands. If they are saying, "You are a disgrace to humankind, you're not my child, you're not what I thought a child would be," you're letting them get to you. Billy figures, why let your parents kill you when you can go forward?

Billy says, "If you went to your parents and told them you were thinking about committing suicide they'd say shut up, you're a stupid fuck, you're an ignorant asshole, go to your room, whatever. That's the main reason they do it, because none of their mothers will talk to them about it. Everybody thinks about it, I'm not ashamed to admit I've thought about it . . . but it seems ridiculous. I just think about other things. I mean this is a sick thing to say, but dying is expensive—I mean funerals can cost $10,000. That's why they have life insurance policies, so your parents can afford to bury you when you die!" We are laughing. "A plot in the ground, a gravestone, you're talking a lot of money. It's expensive. Some families have to go out and get a mortgage on their house just to bury their kids, it's a fuckin' joke."

Billy Milano thinks parents should stop blaming music and blame themselves. "They don't listen, don't try to understand, no matter if the kid is into disco, metal, if he's smart or dumb. Nothing hurts a parent more than watching a kid repeat the same mistakes he's made. Then again, making the same mistakes as parents is growing up. You can't grow up if you don't make mistakes."

The lyrics on the S.O.D. album had addressed some of the issues of everyday life among the young and alienated, so I wanted his opinion. Like the song "Kill Yourself." Billy explains that the whole purpose of the album was to show that there is a lighter side to everything. "I mean you've gotta take it on the light side every day or you'll just go crazy and you'll end up like those four kids in the car . . . People who take everything very serious without a chuckle here and there . . . wind up self-destructive.

"You know, my brother Michael committed suicide . . . and it's something that everybody has to deal with." I didn't know this about his brother. I tell him I am sorry about it. I apologize for asking him about it. But Billy says "No, why? I mean it's something you have to deal with."

But the Bergenfield suicide pact upsets him. "I'd like to see the whole thing just end, let the kids at least have one thing left, their dignity."

Billy talks about something that was a real "kick in the ass" for him. He says, "In the last year and a half . . . my whole life my father told me how much he didn't like my music . . . and I said, but I like doing it, is there anything wrong with liking what you do?" But Billy's father said since he was playing bass, why didn't he take lessons? Billy says, "I said I don't want to take lessons, I just like playing. I'll get better with practice. And he never liked what I played. And he was ill for a while, and on his deathbed he said to my brothers, out of everyone in the family he was most proud of me because I got to do my dream. I wish I was there, that was the kick in the ass, not to be there to hear him say that. It rips your heart out, all along you think he's a bastard and he turns out to be your best friend."

"This album is dedicated to my dad. I miss you and I love you." In a photo on the record sleeve of *U.S.A. for M.O.D.* Billy stands with his arm around his father. Billy was lucky. He had managed to get something in life that few kids have. It was what Nicky dreamed of—his father finally admitting to *his face that he was worth something, that he was proud of him, that he loved him.*

Billy says his father's love was the foundation for forming his new band, M.O.D. Without that love, he says, he couldn't have done it. That's how discouraged he was over the breakup of S.O.D. But he was really happy with M.O.D. "It's all kids, seventeen-year-olds from Lodi and Garfield." This was extremely cool, to have very young, local kids in your band.

Now twenty-three, Billy was an alum of a vocational high school, although not Bergen Vo-Tech, as everyone who went there claimed. One of the guys in M.O.D. apparently had been a student there. Mrs. Bentivegna said they had tried to counsel him against dropping out of school so he could go on tour with his band. But she was very careful not to tell me who the kid was, since that was confidential.

Billy and I discuss the healing power of music. It's violent, kids getting their aggressions out, a release. Billy talks about life in the pit. "What music basically becomes is a filter for them. They filter everything out into this and it doesn't come back into them when they leave, so everything is left in this big empty room with sweat all over the place and cups of water all over the place. Just echoes of pain; it's over with and they go home and they feel great."

He continues. "I remember getting into arguments with my parents all the time, sixteen years old, taking buses into the city to see a hardcore show until 6:00 a.m. and then catching a bus home. And then I'd do the same thing again . . . every chance I'd get I'd go . . . even if it was just to hang out on the corner . . . there was this club, A7, the big skin hangout. It closed and I was lost! I had no place to go crazy in . . . it was like our club, it was like something we owned. Everybody just went there to vent, and when you vented in that place forget it, it just got crazy. Just like these kids, they need music, it's like something they own, they relate to it."

Billy's life had found a positive direction because of his involvement in the scene. I say, "I think this is all kids have anymore." He agrees. "That's it, the suicide rate would be higher if kids didn't have music.

"I mean the biggest thing now going in this music is Metallica. Now think about how some sixteen-year-old kid feels opening up a magazine and seeing a picture of like, say, James Hetfield just standing there, in his ripped jeans, hanging out, having a beer, instead of some dick-fucking heavy-metal guy like DIO, with leather all over the place with a dragon and a fucking whip. I mean who would you better relate to, for somebody who's just hangin' out?" But Billy says that for Metallica, it's really just a look—"That's not what they look like really"—and he points to an early 1980s poster of Metallica on the wall, in *spandex*!

In addition to everything else, this interview with Billy Milano was my chance to get a skin's view on certain long-standing points of contention within the hardcore scene. Like many habitués, I was annoyed at the recent violence in the clubs, particularly the clashes between skinheads and thrashers. There were constant fights. The intrusion of metalheads had been bad enough. But the skinhead situation was such a big problem in the hardcore scene that page after page of letters to editors of major fanzines were now devoted to whining about scene fracture at the hands of violent skins. I kept reading and hearing about how bitter rivalries were destroying scene after scene: club owners just didn't want to deal with it anymore. Insurance costs, police, who needed it?

Together, kids had to fight adults. Apart, they fought each other; eventually they lost control and forfeited space. By 1987, the dream of scene was long gone. The clubs were now slime pits of broken bones, vomit, and rudeness. Slamming (or moshing, dancing) was once a serious male-bonding ritual, a communal statement of solidarity. You dove off the stage into the arms of your comrades. There was nothing to fear. If you were falling, your friends, peers, scene brothers, your *generation*, would be there to catch you, pick you up, and push you forward. It was the strongest statement of intragenerational solidarity ever, thrilling to watch. But sometimes if people were too drunk or didn't know the rules, it simply got psychotic. People got hurt. After a while it was impossible to distinguish a fight from a dance. Skins blamed drunken thrashers; thrashers blamed fascistic skins, and on and on. It seemed only fair that I ask Billy his opinion of it. I had my biases too.

Billy describes the skin's scene as having once been very unified. "You saw a skin, you didn't just see one person, you saw a hundred, or a thousand." I wonder what they were unified around. "Unified against the outside world. What you wanted to do was to lock out the world from the time you walked into the door to see the band till the time you left to go home. That was your world. It was like having an antechamber. You scream into the chamber and you lock it and your scream is in there. And you open it up and it comes out no more pressure and that's where you're locked, and that's where you come back into the world. The skins basically said to everybody keep out, this is our world. We don't want you in it."

The boundaries of eighties scenes worked very much like those of the neighborhood. Subcult styles, sounds, and attitudes worked toward a politics of exclusion. Like religions, people either belonged or they did not. If they did not, they had to be kept at a distance. By force, if need be.

Billy and I move naturally to a discussion of race relations in America today. "People say S.O.D. is racist and fascist. The country is racist, everyone is racist by nature, look at Boston—it's got a white area, a black area, an Irish area, Italian, Jewish . . . I walked into a black area there and ten black kids walked me out of the neighborhood. They were nice enough to say we don't want you here, get out or we're going to beat you up. This is a racist country." I add, "It's a racist world."

Festering throughout the eighties, by the end of the decade, racist youth and racially biased crime were big news. Billy explains, "There's nothing wrong with being racist, you just have to know when to start and where to stop. I can have a black guy come up and say something to me and I can say, Look, I don't want to talk to you. Or I can say, get out of here nigger, before I shoot you. I mean that is bad, but the first expression . . . isn't that bad. I mean there's an extreme to everything. There is a fire and there's an inferno.

"I'm not racist to begin with, I'm just very outspoken. Now in one of my new songs I have a line, 'Let the niggers starve' [song title is "Are You Hungry"]. I don't mean the Ethiopians—the album is *U.S.A. for M.O.D.*—I mean everybody—everybody who doesn't want to get up and help themselves deserves nothing more than what they can get . . . and I don't mean by stealing, I mean by working. I've paid for things myself by working, I mean working is the positive attitude, you live, you work, you die. You don't work, you starve. Don't expect handouts, that's what I'm trying to say, because if you expect handouts then the next guy is going to say, Well, where's mine? You gave him a dollar, give me a dollar . . . you gave him an apartment, I want an apartment. I mean I know someone who works with me, makes thirty thousand a year and he's got a brand-new apartment, five bedrooms, two baths, and he's paying fifty a month. Why? Because he's black.

"If I make a hundred dollars a week I would never get that, because I'm white. Free college because they're black, because they're too stupid to want to go out and earn it. And what does that do?

"What I'm saying is why are we worrying about these other countries, about people who don't want to help themselves? We have an economy that needs to be strengthened, we have a fucking drug problem that needs to be fucking cured, we have so much shit going on, ghettos, murder, rape, I mean the list is so long . . . fucking endless, and so why should we worry about some fucking people who are never gonna get what we're trying to give them, never—I mean you're talking eighty million dollars, to do something . . ." Billy soon begins to sound a little like my dad, like everyone's dad. Like everyone who loves the country, thinks we're losing it, and blames everyone around them for it.

Billy Milano is an American kid whose dream came true. He was validated and powerful on his own terms. In some circles, he remains a legend. And if he retired today and went to work with his brothers in the family's business, he would still be *Billy Milano*, and that means something.

When *U.S.A. for M.O.D.* was released, some people were pissed off about all the racist stuff. He got a lot of shit about it, especially in the rock press. Even some of his fans thought he had gone too far. Others thought it was cool. My friend Cliff admired Billy for being so honest, "for saying what most people feel but don't have the balls to admit."

Some time later, in interviews I'd read, Billy seemed to have changed. He explained how angry he was after his father died, how he was full of hate. That's why the album was so harsh. A few of his more jaded fans thought Billy was just saying that to get a better record deal.

But I believed him. Some people will turn deep loss against themselves, others will turn it outward at the world. Billy had recovered and he had moved forward. His next album was a lot more fun.

Wild in the 'Burbs

But Zion said: "The Lord has
forsaken me,
my Lord has forgotten me."
Can a woman forget her infant, be without
tenderness for the child of her womb?

Even should she forget,
I will never forget you.
See, I have carved your name on the palms of my hands.

—Isaiah 49:14

I

It is true that the best street adventures transpire spontaneously. Nothing is planned for tonight. It's cold, so everyone is in their leathers and feeling fine. I can tell tonight will be an endless party—the energy level is high, it's the weekend, and the world is for taking.

The single guys want to pick up chicks. Joe decides they'll just say I'm his cousin from the Bronx. As we go from town to town, nothing looks familiar. Joe's box is bleating Metallica's "Master of Puppets," Randy is hyper, maybe even dangerous. Joe is cheerful, hopeful maybe he'll find a lady tonight. I'm talking about my visit with Billy Milano. Nicky feigns interest but is distracted every thirty seconds by something smart he thinks of to howl at passing cars. Wild in the 'burbs we clam a passing "old man's car." I get involved in this long-range target-spitting too.

Cruising north Jersey en route to another town, we giggle, guys snatch butts and make fun of people. "Fags!" We pass by a deserted-looking place, a gay bar, the guys tell me. Annoyed, I ask, "What are you, homophobic or something?" No reply. This is Axl Rose country. My hosts do not have "good politics," and they don't care. They take abuse, they dish it out, and that's the way it is.

We are now curbside, down for the kill. Two unsuspecting, sweet-looking girls are cajoled into the car. "Want to go to a party?" One is dark, pretty, rock and roll, wearing a flowing black cloak. The other is short, blond, with a baby face, in blue leggings and an oversized tie-dyed T-shirt. They look about sixteen and they seem interested. They take their time, check out the guys. Cute, good ratio, more than enough to go around. They are two frisky girls with nothing much to do.

Everything is set to go when two much foxier-looking ladies pull up in a shiny white Camaro. The possibility the guys have just forfeited is devastating. They lament what might have been but they can't, they don't have the heart to ditch the first two. Monogamy and monotheism. Metallica is blasting, and it's on into the night. Joe lets Randy drive. That way he can talk to the one with the darker hair. I am thinking they look sweet together.

Oh my God, Randy's at the wheel! He gives it one of his demented jerky turns. I'm in the back, Heather is in the "death seat" place of honor so she can be near Randy. The road is empty. Joe is oblivious, he's with Ruthie in the back. Next to them Nicky and I giggle as Randy takes us down "the highway to hell"! Heather screams, "Stop! We'll all get killed!" Randy responds with a bland "So what?" Snare corps drumrolls in triplicate, a chant in unison, from the front seat to the back, "Ta Ta Ta Ta Ta Ta Ta Ta Ta! Method of destruction!!! Ta Ta Ta Ta Ta Ta Suicide Pact!!! Ta Ta Ta Ta Ta Ta!

Onward to Paramus where the scene outside the RKO Tenplex theater arcade is hopping. Bikes, wheelies, skateboards. Inside, couples my age go to the movies, kids buy junk food, play video games, and flirt. It's like the Rink without the surveillance and with a carnival street scene in the parking lot so you can move freely in and out of situations. We came here to pick up Mingo.

Introduced formally by Joe, I remember I had met Mingo once, at Hav-a-Pizza, near Foster Village. Mingo is a black thrasher, a metalhead who likes the dirtbags more than the brothers in his school, and who takes abuse from both sides. All night long there will be comments about "Buckwheat" and blackness. After a while it's just like the comments about the funny-looking seams on my pants. But I ask Mingo if he thinks his friends are racists. He says, "No, they're okay."

As usual, Mingo's wearing his Metallica colors. He's in a really good mood too—"Kill! Vietnam!" It's all set up. He's taking the Army test next week. He can't wait to go. Can't wait to get a gun. Joe is wearing his best paramilitary look tonight. It's thrasher deluxe and very macho. He's got a new haircut but it's working out okay. Ruthie likes him, I can tell. She flirts, pulls his earring. Joe puts together some cash and goes to get a case of Buds. The girls decide to take a walk.

Change in plans from a slow night to one more promising: Ruthie leaves the car to make a phone call, ostensibly to her mom. Meanwhile, smoking furiously, the guys conspire to figure out who should go with whom. Nicky has it all mapped out. Ruthie should go with Mingo, because she's black. But I think she might be mulatto. She might even be Greek, Jewish, or Sicilian. "But who cares," I implore them in the name of the Ronnettes, "Ruthie likes Joe! Can't you see that?!"

I urge Nicky, "Just let it alone. Joe *needs* a girlfriend." I remind Nicky that he doesn't, he has Denise. "Yeah right. She stood me up!" (Nicky and Denise had missed their planned rendezvous at 7-Eleven earlier in the evening. Just past the appointed hour, the cops banished everyone from the area. We'd circled the block a few times, trying to find her in the shuffle, but it became too risky, so we had to give up.)

"Come on," I say, "I am sure that wasn't the case. She probably had to work late and couldn't get in touch." Randy agrees. We know what kind of night it will be if Nicky is allowed to remain feeling rejected and sorry for himself. But that's history, this is strategy. Nicky is a comprehensive rational planner and these things have to be worked out now.

Okay, so Heather is obviously hot for Randy. But Nicky just broke up with Doreen, got burned by Denise, and so he wants Heather. That overrides emotion. He's whining and moaning how it's not fair because Randy already has a girlfriend. "Yeah? Her mother called the cops on me the other day." Again? This was every three days. Randy nods in disgust. "What do you think."

Heather was a cute, short teenage girl who was about forty pounds overweight. She was a fat girl. Randy admitted he wasn't that into it, but if she was, why not. Now this was not a serious mating ritual for Nicky either, just a game he felt he wanted to win. And he persisted throughout the evening. He wanted to get Heather. He didn't like her, the way Joe liked Ruthie, or the way Heather liked Randy. It was something else, and he was determined.

After half an hour Heather approaches me surreptitiously. "Can I talk to you?" She tells me that a sly Nicky told her I was Randy's girlfriend. This is absurd, almost obscene. If I had gotten pregnant in high school, Randy could be my kid. But this is protocol. Heather is a good girl checking out the rights of territory. She assures me if what Nicky says is true, she definitely won't go with Randy, she means it. But I explain no, I'm not Randy's girlfriend. I have a boyfriend, in the Bronx, where I live. I'm just hanging out in Bergen County for the weekend visiting my cousin Joe.

In Nicky's logic, this ploy left Heather with the choice of either him or Mingo. Since Mingo was black, and he was white . . . he'd get the girl! Four guys and three girls and since Randy and Joe had already set up Heather and Ruthie for the night, that left Mingo and Nicky hung, since it was Joe's car and there wasn't anything else to do tonight. But we did have that case of Buds.

Prepared to party on into the night, we leave for the Building. Mingo is in a festive mood, screaming, "Sex and drugs and rock and roll!" to everyone we pass.

But the adventure is almost aborted when Joe's car runs out of gas a few blocks from our destination. "No big deal," says Joe, and the guys push it half a mile to the Building. To get to the Building you basically have to jump a wall, walk through swamps and woods and over barbed wire. The approach to the Building on foot, at night, is in itself a whole social situation. During the day you can drive right into the place, if the gate is open and you're sure there isn't anybody around. But after dark you become swamp foxes on military maneuvers.

Joe takes the lead. He's showing the troops how to balance the planks of cheap lumber to avoid falling into the Jersey shithole we are now crossing. "Snakes, rats, be careful." The terrain is muddy and wet. There is talk of toxic waste. Grasping for trees and hopeful of the strength of fragile vines, we slip and slide up and down the poisonous little hills. At the edge of what promises to be a black hole, Randy lends me a hand.

Through the barbed-wire fence and over the parking lot's concrete plains, and you're there. The Building has no lights, no electricity, only endless protruding wires, metal rods, plastic stripping, and exposed pipes. Styrofoam and glass are everywhere. Truly industrial, it's beyond the architectural imagining of any rock and roll club I've seen. It's grand apocalypse art.

Deep inside are the private rooms the kids have decorated for comfort—mattresses, a make-out pillow, a radiator which they refer to as a coffin. It's scary, and the chronic hysteria generated over cops is supplanted by a mystical feeling that "someone is there." As the night and the moods get more ripped, this hide-and-seek becomes high-level drama, kicks and thrills.

Heather is in a position of power tonight. So she plays with Nicky, kisses him but decides nah, she'll have Randy, thank you. "Fat piece of shit," says Nicky under his breath, getting progressively hostile. But he forgets about it while Heather disappears for a tour with Randy and Ruthie.

As yet uncommitted, Joe kneels down where I am sitting with Nicky and it starts getting weird. He says he wants to talk to me. "Look, in the beginning, when you started hanging out here, it was just a goof, we were just playing with you and shit . . . but . . . I really like you." I figure out what is coming down and I am pissed off because at this late date, this move is really off the wall. Terse, I tell Joe, "I'm flattered but gimme a break, dude." What the fuck is his problem, I wonder, feeling betrayed.

But then Mingo comes back in from the front of the Building where he has been out on patrol and I figure what's going on here. I say, "Joe, you know Ruthie didn't go with Mingo, Mingo is right here. She went somewhere with Heather and Randy." He is much relieved. It would have been a bad, hard night if she had blown him off. Nicky was just being proud, competitive. But Joe was different. He really liked Ruthie. On this, his aim was true. He needed her.

Resigned for now to celibacy, Nicky tries to explain to Joe and Mingo, who has now moved in on me-as-prey, that I'm not really a girl. I'm like a mascot, a spirit. Mingo's move wasn't sexual, though, it wasn't even personal. Simply expected behavior in the Building: divide the beers, the bodies, and the butts.

Ruthie soon returned with Heather and Randy from their patrol in the bowels of the Building, and the couples went off into the back rooms. There were pillows and makeshift "beds" there, and above all Styrofoam. Endless empty beer cans and extraneous debris. Nicky kept drinking. Eventually, he, Mingo, and I got restless, and decided to go prowling. First in the room with the coffin. It was a radiator cover I could barely make out. "Lisa!" says Nicky. It is surreal; I am thinking maybe he thinks the ghosts of the four kids from the suicide pact are now living here.

Point-blank I ask if there is really an ongoing teenage suicide pact here in Bergenfield, like the adults said. Nicky and Joe were the only people I could do this with, get away with direct questioning. "No!" Nicky answers emphatically, angry, contemptuous. Like how could I say something so lame? This strikes him as almost disrespectful. It's like I insulted his intelligence.

Yet Nicky and his friends were extremely intent upon having me portray them correctly. I remember an earlier trip to the Building, with the *Village Voice* photographer. The kids made the rules clear, up-front: no face shots would be allowed, not even a body shot. Just enough to give people a sense of what their scene was about. Of course this would have to be very colorful.

On the night of the big shoot a small group of us made our way down to what must have been the cafeteria for employees of *Parents Magazine*. Somebody produces a flashlight and Randy pulls out a large knife, a skinning knife, he informs us proudly. He proceeds to carve 666 on the wall, next to OZZY and a Motley Crue pentagram. "Don't put that shit there," Nicky says, really annoyed. Joe agrees. They know what will happen if adults photograph the Number of the Beast in suburbia. Everyone will think they are Satanteens. Then all their problems, the suicides, everything will be blamed on teenage satanic cult activity. Everyone will just dismiss them as fucked-up metalheads into devil worship.

It was really important not to let adults get the wrong impression. 666 might be cool, but people would associate it with Ricky Kasso and Sean Sellers and drugs. It was important not to confuse adults. Be perfectly clear that kids' lives were shit *because of adults*, not Satan, not Ozzy, and not "666." Must not feed into adult/media hysteria over "Satan." The politics of teenage life in Bergen County could easily get lost. People shouldn't be confused about what that "something evil in the air" really was.

But maybe even worse than that, regional pride was at stake. "Satan metal" was getting pretty played out by now. Maybe a band like Danzig could get away with it because they treated it intellectually, as an esoteric knowledge, sort of like the way we might have explored "Eastern religions" or Marxism in suburbia twenty years ago. And death metal really was another scene. But most people weren't into the Satan stuff anymore. Even the Slaybags (Slayer) seemed to be moving on. So they had to be careful, they didn't want other kids to get the wrong impression of their town—it would be embarrassing.

Yet tonight, sitting here in the parlor—the front room of the Building—it was spooky, it could look evil. Long wires and things hanging from rafters, layers of decaying fast food, old clothing, garbage, rot and ruin. No industrial noise band alive could invoke such grand imagery.

Periodically the guys who got lucky come back, there are sighs and whispers, progress reports. Blow job? Randy's shirt is off. We go outside, prompted by Mingo, who is convinced that he has found a dead body and it's buried right in front of the building.

Nicky is more interested in spying on the couples from the windows outside. He's disgusted with everything. Complains about how he had to pay for an abortion, twenty dollars a month for a really long time. What a pain. "I mean she's the one who put out." He says he always uses rubbers these days.

Jumping up into the window where he thinks she is with Randy, Nicky insults Heather. "You fat slut." He is told to shut up. At one point Nicky actually picks a fight with Randy. But they end up just laughing. The next day there will be severe teasing, threats to tell Randy's girlfriend Susie that he fucked around on her. "Oh shit!" Heather left a big purple hickey.

Heather comes over and asks me, "What's his name, the one I like?" We laugh at the boys, Heather feels in control and satisfied. Randy is gorgeous, we agree. She wonders where Ruthie is, and we smile.

Joe will be the one to stay sober enough to drive the car. Periodically the guys watch the clock for curfew. Nicky has to be home by 1:00, Randy by 12:30. Randy cannot fuck up again; he's still on probation. Nicky doesn't need probation. His father is probation. Whenever Joe appears, he monitors the beer intake. "You're drunk, that's it." He gives Nicky one final Bud. Everyone pools resources. Chain smoke 'boros and soak up the life force, music.

Nicky bangs his head against the wall to "Leper Messiah." The Metallica tape *Master of Puppets* must have played sixteen times and still we are moved. Nicky, by now, is bombed on a six-pack of Buds. He's totally wasted. The songs make the guys with girls more bold. The guys alone tonight cry over the one they loved and lost.

Tonight Metallica rules the rock and roll universe. Metallica Alcohollica, One Nation Under Alloy. Nicky sings the lyrics to "Disposable Heroes"—"I was born for dying"—a grunt's antiwar song. Nicky and Mingo joke around. "This music kills kids! Listen to the lyrics!" Then they confess they'd die without it.

I'm sitting with Nicky against the wall of the front room of the Building. It starts getting late. Nicky feels hopeless, depressed. He's on a misery roll now. He'll never get her back. Who, Denise? "No!" he says, impatiently. "Doreen?" I ask. "No—that slut?" (Turns out she recently ditched him for another guy.) He's talking about the one who moved away, the one he went out with for five years.

From here it just gets worse. He's thinks he's fat, he hates his hair. Come on, we remind him that Jon Bon Jovi's dad is a hair-dresser. Doesn't he perm and strip Jon's hair? "Grow it in and have your sister do it." Pump some iron, I suggest, as I pull my own stomach roll to show that no one is perfect. But everyone knows drunken cries can be dangerous. Nicky himself has said that being really high could push you over, this is what he thinks happens a lot in suicides. "Slit your wrists, the blood is your release." It would set you free. At this hour, if you were really wasted, it could start to sound attractive. It wouldn't take too much.

But right away four guys erupt into a wall bashing. *Master of Puppets* is cranking and they are literally bouncing off the walls of the Building. This lasts a good five minutes. It's a mosh against whatever is left standing after last week's bash. Joe draws blood and turns to the spectators. "Whoa . . . dude . . . look!" He turns around, walks over, and slowly wipes the blood on my hand.

Relaxed, everyone walks outside. Randy and Joe go off with their dates for one last kiss. Nicky is in a much better mood now, he's back to his old self. He points to Ruthie. "Take-out food . . . sushi." This is what he calls the one-night stand of the moment. The rest of us go out again to look at a mound of debris that Mingo is convinced is a dead body. By now we are digging it up under the moon. Then there are sounds. Blades come out. Knives, Army surplus. The guys are certain that someone is living in the Building. We run in to stalk the ghost. We creep around looking for the resident. We avoid the windows and carry sticks through the halls. Someone has a lighter. Mingo grabs it and goes pyro on the hanging styrofoam, now coming down in gobs, drips of flame. Nicky's commentary: "See, this is how teenagers die!"

The "take-out" girls pull me aside to ask how they are supposed to get home. Ruthie has a midnight curfew. Will they be stranded? They are fourteen years old (lied, said they were sixteen, look it too).

I reassure them that Joe is decent, he would never fuck them over. But his car is out of gas! Don't worry, I say, they'll be fine. I have my car down by 7-Eleven. Worst case, we get hung, we walk to my car, we can do it, it's not that far. I promise myself as a backup.

In this moment the transhistorical bond among adventurous girls has been activated. I would never allow young women to be left hung anywhere by guys. Fuck my "research," real life preempts. Solidarity with the take-out girls has already been reinforced by the exceptional kindness shown to me by Ruthie and Heather during our approach to the Building. At one point I had been abandoned by the boys, left to slip and slide in the toxic trenches. But the girls patiently helped me across the treacherous terrain. That made us friends for life.

A fight suddenly breaks out. A feisty fourteen-year-old Ruthie yells at Nicky and Randy for saying ugly (sexist) things about her girlfriend. Nicky's still pissed that Randy got the girl. Nicky tells Ruthie, "You know he just used your friend." Ruthie will not back down. "So, you would have too," she answers, now livid.

Heather is crying. Ruthie has had it, she punches Nicky. Randy and Joe are laughing. But Nicky is drunk, he has a bad temper, he's had a rough night, she could get hurt. I try to calm her down, to defuse the situation, praising her as the pride of feminist womanhood. We dream of daughters like this. Wistful, I say, "Ruthie, your mother would be proud!" Oh no! Panic! Ruthie remembers her midnight curfew—it's almost 1:00 A.M. Oh shit. She blew it. It will take us twenty minutes to get to the car. And then it's out of gas.

Ruthie and Joe walk arm in arm to find a gas station. She's wearing his leather jacket. He's got on her earring. I try to convince Nicky to go with me for coffee at Dunkin' Donuts. Sober up. But Nicky really is too messed up to go out in public. "Uh, no. You're not going anywhere." Randy is emphatic. Nicky's friends hold him back. "Look, you're nineteen years old and you're drunk on your ass. If a cop sees you . . ."

So Nicky and Mingo stay behind at the Building. Back with gas, the couples are making out. Ruthie is truly worried about betraying her mother's trust. "I'm her good girl. I don't want to blow that. I'm her darling." Not a note of sarcasm in her. She's really worried, this is serious.

The couples make out for one more set and then Joe drives us to my car. We figure since they're late and possibly in trouble, it's better for me to take the girls back. Ruthie is in love but *mom looms.* Heather worries about whether they will get in trouble, it's really late. I am asked to wait five minutes until a suspicious mom can come outside to see if the story is true.

Ruthie runs down the plot line. Oh God, no way, I say, can I ever pull this off—posing as a Bergen County mom driving the girls home from a lovely teen party at my house. "It's too sick, I won't be able to do it! She'll know . . ." But I have to!!! Ruthie is panic city. But she'll compromise.

Okay, I don't have to talk to her mom, just wave. "Okay." They go upstairs. Frantic, I clear the neon dinosaurs off my dash, yank the 23rd Psalm and the black velvet dice from my rearview mirror. Turn off the music, brush my hair back neatly, and wait. I'm going for a Teaneck look here. I'm banking on the Honda and the hair to make me look normal.

The mom comes down in her nightgown with a raincoat over it. She's in her bedroom slippers, walking a toy poodle. She's my age. She looks like someone I'd enjoy having a cup of coffee with. It's the critical moment. She scrutinizes me. We wave. A salute to one another acknowledging *the girls are home safely.* I pull away slowly, but peel out for hell after I make the turn. I take a deep breath and a numbing blast of Metallica's "Welcome Home (Sanitarium)."

Two days later I was back in town looking for Joe to see if he'd in fact found True Love. This could make a big difference in his life. Ruthie was much too young for him, but she was smart and very strong. She would be good for him, and he would treat her like gold, I could tell. I wanted to locate the guys but they were no place to be found.

I circled around town a few times but still, nobody at all was out. Joan and her boyfriend were up by the 7-Eleven. She was really high, talking about some job she was getting as a receptionist in a doctor's office. She was looking to drop out of school. She had too many truancies and she just didn't want to be bothered anymore. I mentioned looking for Joe and Randy but said nothing about the other night because of Susie—she was Joan's friend.

Joan was hard to talk to. She was quiet to begin with, on top of that a serious pothead, and then always afraid I'd mention her name.

I might get her in trouble. For what, always remained unclear. I started asking her about dropping out of school but she didn't want to get into it. I almost never saw Joan anywhere, but she and her boyfriend eventually showed up on TV, one of the specials that aired some months after the suicides, a program about youth in crisis—teen pregnancy, crime, suicide. TV was one thing but this was where she breathed.

I drove back near the Building and saw Joe's car parked in the front. This was highly irregular. He would never be so bold in the middle of the day!? I decided to check out the car. His good Harley jacket was on the front seat and so was the boom box. The windows of the car were wide open, so he must be nearby. I hung around about ten minutes debating what to do. Seeing Joan had raised my anxiety level. Even though I didn't believe the kids were suicidal, I sometimes worried about them. As these fears began to surface, I started to imagine the worst.

What if they committed suicide? Why else would any metalhead just leave his car like that, his beloved leather jacket, and his boom box too? What should I do? I try to figure out whether to go to the Building alone, look for them there. But I shouldn't go in alone. If something's wrong, I should get someone. Maybe go back and find Joan. I decide I am being ridiculous, by now I should show a little faith, not jump to any conclusions.

By now, the word on teenage suicide on the streets of Bergenfield was "stupid." Some people did still employ razor-slash wounds for various purposes—as a distress signal, for drama, or to make a fashion statement. But most understood that the suicide pact had accomplished nothing for anyone except to prove the truth of Neil Young's assertion: "Once you're gone, you can't come back."

A few days later, when I finally did run into Joe, I asked him about the other day. "Yeah, guess what! Someone stole my box! We think we know who it was too, and I tell you, he's gonna fuckin' pay." It seems he and Randy had seen Ruthie and Heather the day after their big night, and then again the day after that. So they were in the Building doing what young lovers do, I guess. I didn't dare tell him about my suicide panic attack. Maybe I was hip, but still, I *was* an adult. Anyway, Joe said Randy was finished with Heather, but he really liked Ruthie.

He was also proud to report that he had finally gotten a job, loading trucks in Hackensack. "Fuck you, asshole, I'm takin' home $425 every two weeks," he would say arrogantly to anyone who now messed with him. Joe was happy, tired, and hungry. He was going home.

In the next few days I just talked to people, said goodbye, exchanged numbers. Time passed, and I figured I'd just see Joe eventually, or call him. It was no big deal. Now that he was working, Joe wasn't around much during the day anymore.

But then one evening I come back to my car and find a note from Joe attached to my windshield. The message was poetic, ominous, about lost hope, love, and death. He said he wanted to talk to me, he asked me to call him.

I call him later that night from home and he is very cryptic about what he wants to talk to me about. He asks me to meet him the next night in Bergenfield.

It sounds serious. "Look, do you want to know about sheer horror, unrelenting, total hell?" He mentions that he broke up with Ruthie but that isn't what is bothering him. He explains he got sick of her, she was a bossy pain in the ass. Actually, it was over after about a week. He had pretty much forgotten about Ruthie, he says. No, it was something else. He had to talk to me.

I meet him the next night. I get in his car and he starts driving up toward Dumont. He says he's training Bobby and Randy, they'll soon be a fighting machine. As usual I am subjected to the Bon Jovi tape *Slippery When Wet*. Whenever the guys were feeling soppy about love they played it—by now I actually knew the words to all the songs. But this time Joe's making a different point; he makes his statement in the lyrics "I'm a cowboy, on a steel horse I ride, and I'm wanted, dead or alive . . ."

Soon after, Joe starts talking about his ex-girlfriend. He saw her the other day and she got really fat. He was glad to see she looked so bad. But it really doesn't matter. "I still love her. I slit my wrists over her once already, and she still doesn't want me." He parks. We're now outside her house, where he begins to tell me how fucked up everything is.

The police are especially relentless tonight and Joe is a little wary to begin with. He had been stopped earlier, thrown on the ground and searched, a case of mistaken identity on a recent burglary. They were always on him.

I realize now that he has taken me along to copilot our biggest kamikaze mission yet. For anyone, idling the car outside the ex-lover's house is nothing short of sheer terror. It always feels like life and death.

I had once told Joe I wasn't leaving Bergenfield until I figured out why he and his friends all had razor-slash marks on their wrists. I remember he laughed—"You'll be here for the rest of your life." Now I understood what he meant. It could take a long time for scars to come to the surface. The "burnouts" weren't hiding theirs anymore. So by now, especially after his note, I expected Joe to talk to me seriously about life. Maybe I could help him put it in perspective. It wasn't really my place, but I wanted to leave him with something. I felt like he was a friend, I wanted to do what I could.

I figured that like everyone, if Joe put the puzzle together, he would see how he had been set up, he would be free, he could live his life for himself. He would separate himself from his family bullshit. He would be angry, not guilty about how badly his teachers had failed him, realize they were incompetent and petty. He would resent them for telling him he was retarded because he looked a little weird and didn't jump their hoops to their beat.

I wanted to show him the long view. Where he had to take responsibility, where he could let go. I was afraid that he was starting to lose his lightheartedness, his sense of humor. Starting to accept their definition of him, to believe that he *was* a loser. And the stupid alcohol just made everything worse.

I hated watching this, knowing every day there would be kids like Joe, coming to manhood or womanhood carrying all this shit. But they would hit a brick wall, there would be fewer and fewer open spaces out there for testing a new improved self. I was basically a positive person, but lately what was giving me the most hope was the kids. They were so decent in the face of so much bullshit. If I couldn't promise Joe a better world, at least I wanted him to be clear about the one he lived in. Purge his demons, know who he was, how he got there and why.

But Joe's world was becoming impossible to comprehend in its totality, and he needed concrete solutions as well as "love" and "hope." He was a local legend, famous for being burnt. Joe was proud to be guilty. But now it was getting to him. It was time to face facts, seize the day, move forward.

Joe seemed to be tired of being alive—not suicidal, just exhausted, too old to be playing this game anymore. He was living for his bands, trying to look cool, partying, day-to-day. I wanted to shake him and tell him to take the world by the throat, to act for himself, not to waste his life on meaningless small-town drama. Yes, much more than courage was needed here.

What did Joe really want out of life? He wanted to be loved. Nicky dreamed of being a great drummer, of having "good hair" like Motley Crue's Nikki Sixx. Randy wanted a car, room to move, and he wanted to play guitar like Randy Rhoads. That was the ceiling of their desires.

What could they actually expect from life? Was there still a place of dignity for Joe and his friends? Something of promise for all the kids across America's teenage wastelands? I wanted to really talk to Joe. I wanted to cry, I wanted to go and shoot people.

But I'm off the hook because Joe doesn't talk about any of this tonight. He just goes on and on about the girlfriend. Why did she dump him when he still loved her? How can he live without her? She was his last hope. He wants to cry.

Then he snaps around and pulls me by my shirt, pulls me up close, right in my face he snarls, "Look, I know where you live, I know where you work. If you tell anybody who I am, if you fuck me up, man, I'll find you, I'll . . ."

This *really* pisses me off. "Fuck you! You think you're this big fuckin' psycho . . ." I start babbling something about having an arsenal of guns, razor blades in my hair, killing him with my bare hands—but we just start laughing. This is as close as we can get. We have sealed it in blood.

Of course, at any moment either one of us can still slip out the back door, brush it off, make believe it was all just a joke, a scam. Intimacy comes in ruptures and fissures. Through the cracks of postures and pretenses: from a Hallmark card to a streetside confession, the truth never happens where we say it does. We don't mean what we say and can't say what we mean.

Eventually I stopped going to Bergenfield. I lost touch with Bobby and then with Nicky. But I called Joe a few times after my business there was done. He'd tell me what was new, who was hanging out. It was nostalgic, sentimental. Supposedly, Nicky had instigated a big fight at the Paramus mall. Everyone hated him now. Bobby was long gone, and soon after that, Joe got sick of Randy too. "Nobody hangs around anymore, there's a whole new scene, really cool, you gotta come out here and check it out!" He figured I'd have a good time, hang out like I used to. After a while, I lost touch with Joe too.

I think for Joe, my time in Bergenfield was part of whatever scene was happening for him at that time. Maybe we were friends, maybe it was just a good street hustle. Either way, it didn't really matter. For a while, I saw myself in Joe and I think he saw himself in me. Then life simply moved on.

The End

You made your children what they are...These children
that come at you with knives, they are your children.
You taught them. I didn't teach them. I just tried to
help them stand up.
—Charles Manson

Shortly after the suicide pact, this was how one Bergenfield resident, a middle-aged man, described the kids who hung around the streets of his town: "Those kids, the look in their eyes, their eyes are somewhere else, they're empty, like they weren't going anywhere. Their idea of the future was next week. They have given up on life." It wasn't the first time I'd heard American teenagers described as psychic dead boys and girls. Why were some American kids giving up on life before it even got started? What had chilled their young spirits and wiped out their hopes and dreams?

My neighbor Scott explains that growing up these days, kids feel every adult is out to "get them." He points out that whatever kids do these days, they can't win. Whatever they try to do gets twisted around and turned against them.

Today's fifteen-to-twenty-four-year-olds were born between 1965 and 1974 when birth rates were dropping. Because of this drop, those 37 million people are referred to as the baby bust. In contrast, because of high birth rates between the end of World War II and 1964, the 75 million people born during that period are called the baby boom. Birth rates alone account for the formal identification of these two groups as distinct generations. So the baby bust generation has grown up in the shadow of the baby boom. We had the numbers, and we enjoyed a more affluent economy too. By the 1980s, the United States had suffered severe economic setbacks and high employment. Divorce rates rose, and the patriarchal structure of the American nuclear family eroded. The eighties kids feel cheated—they think that our parents loved us more, that schools were better, that life was easier.

Post-Vietnam, post-Watergate, at the twilight of the American century, the baby bust is now coming of age. Throughout the eighties, times looked lean and mean. The importance youth once held in the social order declined and their civil rights have eroded with it.

My generation grew up being "old enough to kill, but not to vote" —a right we did eventually win. But the contradictions faced by

Scott's generation are even more overwhelming—for example, the issue of reproductive rights versus the rights of the unborn. The baby bust is the last generation conceived *before* abortion became legal. In effect, Scott and his peers grew up understanding that one generation now had the legitimate right to annihilate another, up-front.

Yet as challenges to the *Roe v. Wade* decision mount, and more specifically, as abortion rights for minors come under attack, Scott's generation finds itself fighting to retain rights they have always taken for granted. As studies indicate, the terror of an unplanned pregnancy can be a contributing factor in female adolescent suicide.

Meanwhile, in recent years the national pregnancy rates for teenage girls have soared: about a quarter-million births to unwed mothers between twelve and nineteen occur each year. Women with dependent children now dominate America's underclass.

Adults have always been confused about how much protection kids need and how much punishment they should receive. In recent years kids have seen the drinking age go up and the age of eligibility for the death penalty go down. We consistently doubt kids' ability to make important decisions, but we will punish them for what they decide just the same.

Ushered into history with little fuss and fanfare, Scott's generation fears for its survival: the bomb, AIDS, street crime, acid rain, abusive parents, bad drugs. Some kids just laugh it off, and say they are the Armageddon generation. Some hold fast to adult rules, obey, try to be perfect. Others stay oblivious, living day-to-day. The ones who are most likely to make news run wild, live hard and fast. They seem convinced there's no point in trying, that maybe *this* is all there is. So they get high, they party on, tattoo and pierce their bodies in a celebration of the moment. They try one last time to stand out in the crowd, hoping to be heard once before it's all over.

At first it was the kids' declining test scores that alarmed adults —"Oh how we Americans must appear to the world with our incompetent labor and our ignorant youth." Then it was the "utter lack" of morals. Experts pondered how adults might deal with "kids without a conscience." Young people became "savages," "animals."

The 1980s was the decade when teenage suicide was discovered by the media. There were other media forays into teenage pregnancy, gangs, crack, parricide, homicide, racially and sexually motivated violence . . . it went on and on.

"Youth crime" replaced "juvenile delinquency" as gangs of kids openly raped, robbed, and murdered adults, oblivious to adult laws. Girls were getting more violent too, breaking away from the shadow of boys. They went out on their own, for themselves. Mixing female spheres of domesticity and male street styles, they were having babies, and joining girl gangs too. In the Reagan decade, while adults were away, American kids made their own rules. They fell back on their own resources.

Over the last twenty years kids kept losing ground as an autonomous power block. By the 1980s, they had virtually no voice. And without an effective national policy for youth, kids fell through the cracks in droves. It took a while for adults to figure out that each new youth atrocity added up to a somewhat larger picture of societal neglect. By the end of the eighties, adults were willing to acknowledge that they had really fucked up, that American kids were going down the tubes.

America's young people did their best to survive in a climate that was openly punitive toward the vulnerable. Yet they were consistently viewed as a generation of barbarians and losers, stupid, apathetic.

It was bad enough that young people's numbers had declined, and that when we "grew up" and became adults, we forgot. Life has gotten harder for kids in the last twenty years. Now in their "descendency," youth experience a lower status than members of this transitory age caste have known since the post–World War II years. They have inflated expectations with diminishing opportunities, across the board. Young people are still the only minority without formal self-representation. They don't vote, and few pay taxes of any significance. As consumers, they do have some power, but that remains a dormant organizing motive. At best, adults advocate *on behalf of children*.

As the "minority of minorities," young people get the lowest pay, have fewer rights, and suffer more absolute structural regulation than anyone. Under control, they are encouraged and coerced to defer to adult authority. Kids are taught to mistrust their own instincts as "immature" and "inexperienced." Yet in recent years, many have had few resources beyond themselves. The larger societal system seems set up to strip young people of their desire for self-determination.

The rich social history of young people here and in Europe shows that many are quite capable of self-rule. As John Gillis has shown in his book *Youth and History*, they had guilds, and their own autonomous cultural traditions, preindustrial rituals that expressed strong intragenerational fraternity. At times, even now, parents have had to rely upon their offspring for support, reversing the order of generational dependency. It is only through structural arrangements made by adults that young people are emancipated or kept in a state of normative irresponsibility.

When and if the economic order requires the labor of young people, our thinking about them will quickly change. In effect, we will create new ideologies to encourage their autonomy. Social constructions such as "teenager," "adolescent," or "youth" can be dismantled as readily as they were invented. Much in the way the "cult of true womanhood" urged women to return to domesticity after World War II so factory jobs would be free for male workers, kids can be manipulated into submission or emancipated to suit the economic organizational "needs" of society, as determined by the adult power structure.

Although nineteenth-century reformers and industrialists had very different agendas, their combined efforts ultimately transformed young people into a powerless age caste. For over a century, laws regulating the autonomy of young people worked to erode their autonomy. First, the child-labor laws took working-class kids out of the factories. Now made superfluous in the economic order, they were gradually locked away in public schools under the banner of mandatory schooling. To "protect" them further, their misbehavior was regulated by the invention of a "juvenile court" *(parens patriae)*. Finally, through the notion of "adolescence" as a preparatory stage for adulthood, young people of all classes were reduced to complete psychological and economic dependency upon adults. With the hyper-credentialing of an increasingly postindustrial economy, this dependency can be extended indefinitely; "adulthood," a euphemism for economic independence and personal autonomy, takes longer and longer to achieve.

Now, during the 1950s and 1960s this infantilization wasn't so bad. The nation was "child-centered" and resources for families flourished. Money poured into schools. Low interest rates on mortgages and cheap housing made family life easy. Postwar suburbia was designed for breeding; it was the womb of the republic. In those days it was safe for kids to depend upon adults.

At that time young people were identified and targeted as consumers. In turn, they had more disposable income, and with their newfound consumer power they were able to carve out a considerable degree of autonomy in the culture industry; whole markets developed around their interests, needs, and desires. This industry has flourished, to the delight of young people.

But many social institutions that were developed around the needs of those same young people still operate on the idea of the pampered, privileged middle-class American child of the 1950s and 1960s. Unfortunately, the world has changed drastically.

Legislation on behalf of the family has not worked to benefit the family for quite some time. Our families, schools, and towns watched American children fail as programs were cut and budgets bled. If Bergenfield High School had to carefully allocate its limited resources for its more promising students, it was not unlike the social welfare agency that "creams the client population," concentrating its efforts on those "cases" who seem most likely to succeed. Schools look good, programs look effective, and hard cases are ignored. But funds continue to trickle in during dry, mean seasons. This selection process was the gruesome choice forced on many dedicated caretakers during the 1980s.

Of course, social problems aren't social problems until they begin to visibly erode white communities. Minority youth were the first to fall—in higher infant-mortality rates, lower life expectancies, harsher punishments for crime, and a numbing feeling of despair. Community efforts by churches and concerned parents were activated and showed success throughout the decade. These efforts often went unrecognized, as did the myriad needs of the children they served.

In the 1980s, working-class kids fell closer to the bottom, and middle-class kids scrambled to do their very best with whatever scraps remained. By the end of the decade the United States of

America had produced an unusually high number of abused, exploited, and badly neglected children. In our scramble to regain our national self-image as a wealthy world power, we allowed this to happen as much by design as by default.

As a social worker, my field of service had been child welfare. I spent some time working in the area of child abuse and neglect. It seemed that more and more young people in America were showing symptoms of maltreatment, acting like kids who are exploited and punished. American kids felt ignored, unloved. Some were sad and some were angry. And parents have admitted feeling helpless, incapable of providing for or protecting their children.

So have educators. At the top, good students are anxiety-ridden about keeping up with the kids in Japan. There are fewer legitimate tickets up and out, even for kids with the advantage of stable, comfortable homes. For many middle-class kids, college and career appear out of reach as the cost of higher education escalates and loans and grants become less available. School has become so competitive that grades are now life-and-death. You could become a total failure, washed up at sixteen, if you failed chemistry!

In the middle, kids just try to get by. At the bottom, they're often shuffled around the school system haphazardly, like nondisposable Styrofoam. Even without family contacts to situate them, or college, some diligent working-class kids can move up, to lower managerial positions at food chains and supermarkets. Or they can move down, filling the jails, becoming part of the underclass. Or they can bail out: sometimes the only control over life kids feel they have is starting it (pregnancy) or ending it (homicide, suicide).

Face-to-face, young people in Bergenfield as elsewhere appear rather sober about life, less inflated by ideals, less encouraged to dream. They work hard for anything they've got—money, dignity, serenity, morality. Racial and ethnic lines of difference keep them apart. The variety of youth subcults reflects and reinforces this distance. Turf wars in neighborhoods, at shows, and in schools divide them, and the future seems grim: no jobs, no security, no world, no future. Generally, they ask for very little. Often, they try to do their best. Usually, their positive actions go unrecognized.

Until the Great Crack Epidemic stimulated our interest in autonomous youth subcultures, American kids were virtually invisible.

They were ignored, or worse, narrowly viewed as atomized social actors, represented in one-dimensional clinical, psychiatric, scientific terms. This medical-model approach to the activities of young people has blinded us, making it almost impossible for American adults to conceptualize young people in broader historical, political, or social terms.

Our national preoccupation with psychotherapy and the "inner life" of the individual has blinded us to other ways of seeing. The collective, the sociological, has been conspicuously absent from the narrative. But most Americans have been distracted from the larger questions by breakdown-of-the-family mythologies. Parents report feeling guilty and resentful as it becomes increasingly harder to interact with or relate to their children. They look to "experts" for knowledge that was once within the familial domain. With each new authoritative set of directives, parents appear more inadequate and incompetent. The "experts" tell them how to talk to their child, how to juggle work and family, how to tell if the child is suicidal, on drugs, or having sex. This undermines and disempowers people as parents and as citizens.

At the same time, social welfare in the Reagan years became a low national priority. In many families, both parents had to go to work, yet the country still was not providing adequate or affordable day care. Child care has been arranged privately, illegally, or informally, by dumping kids in libraries or giving them self-rule via latchkeys. Yet parents, increasingly hard-hit by the economic pressures of divorce, unemployment, and the high cost of living, are continuously bombarded by the government's rhetoric about "the family."

Social critics are dismissed as whining liberals, and social disintegration is blamed on "permissiveness." Nobody on any side offers solid answers. Liberals advocate more programs, bigger budgets, and more resources. Conservatives cry out for law and order— stiffer penalties for youths, and more censorship to "protect" them.

Meanwhile, on "social issues"–oriented television talk shows, experts lecture parents on how to overcome the multiplicity of stresses they face. This obscures the broader social origins of their problems. Decisions made at higher levels of government are taken for granted, viewed as given, irreversible truths. Because the societal processes involved are not considered, parents are made to feel personally responsible for the unraveling of the social fabric. This is politically convenient, for once people blame themselves, they stop asking questions.

II

When the cultural practices of contemporary American youth are not ignored, they are interpreted as nihilistic and self-destructive. Adults remain ignorant and confused about what kids do and think. This makes them hostile and mistrustful.

Joe and his friends had insisted that I "see Bergenfield from a kids' point of view." For the most part, they felt that if I wanted to get a handle on the burnouts, talking to adults would be a waste of my time. For that, I could just read the papers or watch television. Likewise, my neighbor Scott has urged me to "make sure my book gets into all those isolated little towns, places where the adults control everything."

There are some exceptions, but the general feeling among young people is that parents, educators, employers, the media, the police, and psychologists will always assume the worst about kids. For example, unsolicited, the storekeepers in my neighborhood regularly trash local kids as either "psychopaths" or "lazy parasites." There is no respect for anything the kids do or say. They hold young people in contempt and actually seem repulsed by them. "They'd just as soon kill you as look at you," one employer told me.

The kids, in turn, have little respect for adults. Echoing a chronic complaint among his peers, Scott says he especially hates the way his generation has been portrayed in the media in recent years; they're always made to look bad. He's right. During the eighties, American youth rarely appeared to us as anything more than troubled, troublesome reminders of social decay. During that decade, public discussions of Americans under the age of twenty-one were framed largely in the discourse of "social problems." Dramatized in a rhetoric of despair, each new youth atrocity was sensationalized, then addressed in a bureaucratic spirit of "concern." When American youth were not viewed as our victims, we were viewed as theirs.

By the 1990s, there were some vigorous attempts to reverse this trend, to portray kids as winners. The truth is, "today's youth" were actually getting high less, going to school, making plans, and fighting for their beliefs. They weren't sociopathic monsters after all. They had values.

But throughout the 1980s, with few exceptions, newspapers and television news reports portrayed youth as amoral, sadistic thugs in gangs. News headlines were terrifying and titillating. The social climate surrounding the event in Bergenfield offered adults a sensationalized, lurid view of kids—especially boys. On a New York City subway, four black "thugs" menace white, middle-aged Bernie Goetz with screwdrivers. In Howard beach a "lynch mob" of white youth terrorize black, twenty-four-year-old Michael Griffith to his death. That was just the beginning of the youth race wars. People cried out against the hate and brutality, communities were condemned, defended themselves against accusations of "racism." But coast-to-coast, we were afraid to ask the bigger questions about what was going on with the kids, and rarely did we give them the opportunity to explain it, to speak for themselves on their own terms.

Somewhere during the 1980s, our social contract with our youth became null and void. Adults lost their legitimacy as trustworthy authority figures.

So, convinced that they weren't going to be getting any help from adults, that nobody would listen, young people often tried to solve their problems themselves. On Long Island, as a last resort, sixteen-year-old cheerleader Cheryl Pierson arranged to pay a classmate, also sixteen, to assassinate her sexually abusive father. In Florida, seventeen-year-old Tina Mancini committed suicide after several months of being forced by her mother to dance nude at a strip joint and then fork over the cash.

In Jefferson Township, New Jersey, fourteen-year-old Thomas Sullivan, Jr., a Boy Scout with good grades and a paper route, brutally stabbed his strict, devoutly Catholic mother to death and then committed suicide, allegedly after fortifying himself with satanic lore and listening to Ozzy Osborne, Twisted Sister, and Motley Crue. Actually, Tommy Sullivan, Jr., first got interested in Satan while researching a term paper on the subject, in his eighth grade at Catholic school. Basically Tommy decided he didn't want to go to Catholic high school. His mother insisted. Tommy found a way out. This was just one of several cases of parricide in suburbia, with or without the help of Satan.

Other kids empowered themselves differently: from New York City's Chinatown to the streets of Los Angeles, we read how youth gang vendettas claimed teenage lives. How some kids owned guns before they even became teens—in 1986, 365 Detroit children under the age of seventeen were wounded by gunfire, 43 of them fatally. By 1990, New York City newspapers were reporting daily on "the drug war's youngest victims," children killed by random gunfire in urban street gang wars. Yet in the last decade drugs and prostitution have constituted the inner-city youth's best shot at "upward mobility."

In the state of Washington, kids organized protest rallies as their friends were institutionalized for "the purpose of brainwashing them into conformity," as one youth explained. "Many parents have become [so] sick of the punk attitude, appearance, music, and way of life that they are institutionalizing their children in order to supposedly help them."

Cops and kids. In Los Angeles, cops were allegedly dragging punks and skinheads out of clubs and off streets, taking them up into the hills to beat the shit out of them. Police violence against minority youth was also reported. Michael Stewart was a black graffiti artist who was "fatally restrained" by a gang of white transit cops in New York City in 1983. His death is generally acknowledged as racially motivated. But was this also a crime against young people? His age was reported as twenty-five, but from all accounts he looked much younger.

With the exception of child abuse, which is also on the rise, generationally motivated violence isn't recorded anywhere but on the street. After Kent State, we don't think about it. It doesn't even exist formally, as a statistical category.

At heavy-metal, hardcore, and rap shows coast-to-coast, the kids are roaring with energy. Violence is expected, bouncers come down hard on kids, and door policies normally include a weapons body search, on males and females. Even as valued consumers, kids get treated like second-class citizens. Bouncers often provoke kids, they push them around, talk to them rudely, order them about. In turn, the kids dish it out. Ironically, as gang members, kids finally do get the respect of adults, or at least their fear.

Through the 1980s, whenever they weren't pictured as cold-blooded perpetrators, American kids came into view as helpless, hapless, hopeless victims. Drug- and alcohol-dependent dropouts, some became urban nomads who dealt drugs and flesh to survive. A rainbow coalition of homeless runaway and throwaway youth enjoyed employment in America's sexploitation industries—pornography and prostitution.

Many such youths report that they left homes where they were abused. Each year about 40,000 kids are injured badly enough by their parents or primary caretakers to require hospital treatment. Some scars don't show: emotional abuse of a child is nearly impossible to prove in court. But the public is less than sympathetic. On the streets, teenage runaways are just more homeless people begging spare change. In Queens, New York, a foster-care group home for infants is firebombed by angry neighborhood residents. Meanwhile other low-income children, mostly nonwhite, fend off pushers in welfare hotel corridors, or play musical beds in New York City's foster-care game.

The average American child has a first drink of alcohol by the age of twelve. The National Institute on Alcohol Abuse and Alcoholism reports over one million cases of kids between twelve and seventeen with serious drinking problems. Frequently, marijuana, cocaine, crack, and dust supplement the booze, and it is not unusual to encounter a nineteen-year-old with a personal history that includes a few years in a drug or alcohol treatment program.

Then there is teenage suicide. I watched as experts trivialized this phenomenon, neatly packaging teenage suicide as another social problem, one more "crisis" to perk up afternoon talk shows. Teen suicide soon became new grist for the mills of professional helping industries. It meant new jobs and contracts. Special task forces, research projects, seminars, programs, and pamphlets. Yet under the law, and in the public eye, kids remained powerless and voiceless.

As I have said, kids are now coming of age when "doing it" means suicide, not premarital sex. Nobody has ever been able to understand suicide, especially among teenagers. Being young is associated with being happy and carefree. You go to high school, you socialize with friends, you get a part-time job. How bad can life be? Why give it up before you start? Why is suicide so appealing?

Historically, we have been ambivalent about suicide; sometimes it was expected as an expression of loyalty. In India and Japan such "altruistic" suicides were deeply embedded in cultural assumptions about the roles of the widow and the warrior, respectively. Under Jewish law, suicide is forbidden. Yet in the history of the persecution of the Jews, there is a reverence for suicide, the preferred alternative to slavery, rape, or forced conversion. The mass suicide at Masada in A.D. 73 has always been viewed as heroic, a victory of the defiant human spirit—the will to freedom in the face of inevitable Roman enslavement. The image of martyr-as-hero is deeply embedded in our culture: from religion to pop, from Jesus Christ to John Lennon.

The Roman Catholic Church once refused burial rites to suicides. Suicide was seen as a profound renunciation of spiritual belief. In modern times the church has come to view the person who commits suicide as not in his or her "right mind." The suicide victim cannot be held accountable for the act.

In the scientific imagination, suicide is viewed as a disease—like drug addiction or depression.

But when people talk about teenage suicide, the word "romance" is often invoked. Supposedly, suicide is not real to young people. They are anesthetized to life and desensitized to death. They don't understand that it is final, irreversible. The poetics of suicide appeal to those most vulnerable to influences, and the young lack the resources needed to buffer the violence of an emergent self.

It is also believed that young people kill themselves to get attention or revenge. Suicide is now hip, dangerous, the final resistance to adult authority, a last stand against conformity. To some kids, suicide is death before dishonor, heroism over defeat. Because attempts so greatly outnumber actual suicides, suicide is as much a statement of the desire to control life as it is to end it.

Death has taken on new meaning in the last twenty years. To the postmodern imagination, suicide is titillating. It is the last great taboo. Having exhausted sex, death—by suicide or homicide—becomes the final frontier of sensate experience. New pleasures. People disagree on whether the taboo on suicide should be strengthened or deconstructed. Are we better able to suppress the urge by making it unthinkable or by thinking it through?

Sometimes our fascination with these forms of final obliteration appears to reflect a collective death wish. Esoteric knowledge is invoked to help explain these things. Astrologers point to Pluto in Scorpio or its position relative to Uranus. The final death gasp of the Piscean age. We talk to God, we read the scriptures, the prophecy of Armageddon. We consider the predictions of Nostradamus.

Rates of recklessness among young people have increased in the last twenty years. Not only are there more suicides, but more homicides and fatal car crashes too. To understand this, we may give up God and metaphysics and turn to Marx. We ponder the final stages of capitalism. We blame it on bureaucracy, on the problems of waste and surplus absorption, social inequality, bourgeois decadence, the welfare state, the religious right, political repression. Or else the decline of the patriarchal family, peer group pressure, designer drugs, violence in films, television, and music.

We condemn ourselves for our capitalist economy predicated on consumption and waste, our desire for spectacle and pleasure. Yet now, the international electronic eye of TV broadcasts disaffected post-glasnost Soviet youth into our living rooms—cynical, alienated, dressed in Iron Maiden and Ozzy T-shirts, hanging out, partying in vacant lots, alcoholic. They too fear they have "no future." Restless, wasted youth now appear as an international malaise among the industrialized nations. These kids, too, want the truth. They want adults to keep their promises, or else fess up to the false ones. Until then, they too will refuse the game.

For young people, suicide promises comfort. It is a violent seductive release, a means to an end, a soothing and delicious deep sleep. In the context of young lives lived like rapid fire, but focused nowhere, suicide seems thrilling, intoxicating, contagious. Death and suicide become eroticized, as terror and rapture, self-loathing and self-gratification.

We shift gears from truth to fiction, from left to right, moving in and out from the personal to the nuclear, without a clue.

In the past twenty years, new forms, expressing the cultural poetics of death, have emerged. Nihilism and negation are produced and reproduced in each lurid tale of self-destruction. We speak theoretically of death in culture, of culture in death. We note the aesthetics of decay everywhere—in skulls and crossbones, razor-blade jewelry, sharp instruments, the symbols of past regimes of terror.

In fashion we invoke an iconography of decline, celebrating life in the "kingdom of death." We gorge on post-apocalyptic art; we see ourselves as dissipated road warriors on an exhausted, depleted emotional landscape. Armageddon, doom and gloom, death and destruction—these themes are localized, internalized. We play it out in everyday life, this simulation of The End—in music, in painting, in film, in new forms created explicitly to contain our emergent psychosis. It makes for compelling art product. Millenarian rock.

III

In real life, real people do it for real reasons. In the Midwest the farmers did it as they watched their farms fold, in the industrial North suicides increase as towns disappear with plant closings. Smithereens. You're disconnected, dislocated, with no future and no exit. Things happen too quickly. You've lost your place, your sense of direction. You have no power, no voice. Anomic, egoistic. Altruistic, fatalistic. Too many choices or too few? Too close to the body social or too distant? Any way you cut it you can't avoid it; life is with people and so is death.

When he gave the eulogy at his godson's funeral, Tommy Olton's uncle Richard was quoted as saying, "When I held you in my arms at your baptism, I wanted it to be a fresh start, for you to be more complete than we had ever been ourselves, but I wonder if we expected too much. In thinking only of ourselves, maybe we passed down too great a burden."

Trans-historically, cross-culturally, humans have placed enormous burdens on their young. Sometimes these burdens have been primarily economic: the child contributes to the economy of the family or the tribe. Sometimes the burden has been social—the child is a contribution to the immortality of our creed. Be fruitful and multiply.

But the spiritual burden we pass on to the child may be the most difficult to bear. We do expect them to fulfill an incompleteness in ourselves, in our world. Our children are our vehicle for the realization of unfulfilled human dreams; our class aspirations, our visions of social justice and world peace, of a better life on earth.

Faith in the child, in the next generation, helps get us through this life. Without this hope in the future *through the child* we could not endure slavery, torture, war, genocide, or even the ordinary, everyday grind of a "bad life." The child-as-myth is an empty slate upon which we carve our highest ideals. For human beings, the child is God, utopia, and the future incarnate. The Bergenfield suicide pact ruptured the sacred trust between the generations. It was a negation.

After I had been to Bergenfield people asked me, "Why did they do it?" People want to know in twenty-five words or less. But it's more complicated than that. I usually just say, "They had bad lives," and try to explain why these lives ended where, when, and how they did. But I still wonder, at what point are people pushed over the line?

On the surface the ending of the four kids' bad lives can be explained away by the "case history" approach. Three of the four had suicidal or self-destructive adult role models: the suicide of Tommy Olton's father, the drug-related death of the Burress sisters' father. Tommy Rizzo, along with his three friends, had experienced the recent loss of a beloved friend, Joe Major. Before Joe, the death of three other local "burnouts." Then there was the chronic drug and alcohol abuse, an acknowledged contributing factor in suicide. Families ruptured by divorce, death, estrangement. Failure at school.

But these explanations alone would not add up to a suicide pact among four kids. If they did, the teenage suicide rate would be much, much higher. The personal problems experienced by the four kids were severe, painful, but by the 1980s, they were no longer remarkable.

For a while I wondered if the excessive labeling process in Bergenfield was killing off the "burnouts." Essentially, their role, their collective identity in their town was that of the "nigger" or "Jew." Us and Them, the One and the Other. And once they were constituted as "burnouts" by the town's hegemonic order, the kids played out their assigned role as self-styled outcasts with irony, style, and verve.

Yes, Bergenfield was guilty of blaming the victim. But only slightly more guilty than any other town. Labeling, blaming the victim, and conferring rewards on more cooperative kids was cruel, but also not remarkable in the eighties.

As I felt from the beginning, the unusually cloying geography of Bergenfield seemed somehow implicated in the suicide pact. The landscape appeared even more circumscribed because of the "burnouts' " lack of legitimate space in the town: they were too old for the Rink, and the Building was available for criminal trespass only. Outcast, socially and spatially, for years the "burnouts" had been chased from corner to parking lot, and finally, to the garage bays of Foster Village. They were nomads, refugees in the town of their birth. *There was no place for them.* They felt unloved, unwanted, devalued, disregarded, and discarded.

But this little town, not even two miles long from north to south, was just a dot on a much larger map. It wasn't the whole world. Hip adults I know, friends who grew up feeling like outcasts in their hometown, were very sympathetic to the plight of the "burnouts." Yet even they often held out one last question, sometimes contemptuously: "Why didn't they *just leave*?" As if the four kids had failed even as outcasts. My friends found this confusing. "No matter how worthless the people who make the rules say you are, you don't have to play their game. You can always walk and not look back," they would argue. People who feel abject and weird in their hometown simply move away.

But that has always been a class privilege. The townies are the poor kids, the wounded street warriors who stay behind. And besides, escape was easier for everyone twenty years ago. American society had safety nets then that don't exist now—it's just not the same anymore.

During the eighties, dead-end kids—kids with personal problems and unspectacular talents living in punitive or indifferent towns with a sense of futility about life—became more common. There were lots of kids with bad lives. They didn't all commit suicide. But I believe that in another decade, Tommy Rizzo, Cheryl Burress, Tommy Olton, and Lisa Burress would not have "done it." They might have had more choices, or choices that really meant something to them. Teenage suicide won't go away until kids' bad lives do. Until there are other ways of moving out of bad lives, suicide will remain attractive.

In a now famous footnote in *Suicide*, written almost a hundred years ago, the French sociologist Emile Durkheim described fatalistic suicide as "the suicide deriving from excessive regulation, that of persons with futures pitilessly blocked and passions violently choked by oppressive discipline." Where there is overregulation, explains Durkheim, "rule against which there is no appeal, we might call it fatalistic suicide."

Sometimes people commit suicide because they have lost the ability to dream. Having lost transcendent vision, they feel fated, doomed. I think this is what happened in Bergenfield; there was a determination among four persons, bound closely together in a shared existential predicament, to *get out*. But they couldn't. As Joe explained to me, "They were beaten down as far as they could go." Lacking confidence in themselves and the world "out there," they felt trapped. Without a sense of truly meaningful choices, the only way out *was suicide*.

But as far as young people are concerned, fatalistic suicide is not the whole story. True, young people are among the most regulated in our society. With the exception of people in total institutions, only the lives of animals are more controlled. Yet most experts attribute youth suicide to anomie—the opposite of fatalistic suicide in Durkheim's thinking.

In an anomic suicide, the individual isn't connected to the society —the glue that holds the person to the group isn't strong enough; social bonds are loose, weak, or absent. To be anomic is to feel disengaged, adrift, alienated. Like you don't fit in anywhere, there is no place for you: in your family, your school, your town—in the social order.

Where fatalistic suicide may result from overregulation, anomic suicide is attributed to nonintegration. Young people are in the peculiar position of being overregulated by adults, yet alienated from them. Many are integrated only into the world shared with their peers—some may be overly integrated into that world, as in gangs or subcults. Young people are always somewhere on a continuum between overregulation and nonintegration. In the eighties, both ends of this continuum grew to extremes.

IV

In recent years many American kids have had their dreams taken from them. Their vision has been blocked, unable to move beyond next week, because the world outside is simply too much. Suicide is known as the disease of hope. Helplessness and hopelessness.

Hopeless because you see no choices. Helpless because you feel that nothing you can do will ever make a difference. You feel powerless and trapped. This makes you feel worthless; you can't defend yourself.

Because of some of the pressures that families have faced, many kids have not been adequately prepared for life by their parents. Because of misplaced priorities and scarcities, few have been readied for work by their schooling. So between the ages of, say, thirteen and twenty-one, when they may be competent enough to make many of their own choices, they are not formally permitted to do so. Circumstances may have them overly dependent upon adults, even though this dependency is an artifact of a social order that has changed drastically. Because of transformations in the nature of the family and in the global economy, the concept of adolescence as a preparatory stage for adulthood is essentially obsolete.

It is also destructive: "adolescence" continues to serve as a psychic holding pen for superfluous young people, stuck in economic and social limbo, in between childhood dependency and adult autonomy. In killing time in teenage wasteland, some kids end up killing themselves too.

The highest suicide rates in the country are among elderly males. Deemed socially useless, these people are farmed out of the labor force, with no sense of future, afraid, vulnerable, waiting to die. Of all age groups, males aged fifteen to nineteen have experienced the most rapid increase in suicide rates since 1970. For these kids, trapped in the purgatory of teenage wasteland with no great expectations, suicide almost becomes an act of collective self-genocide.

But most kids are not committing suicide. In writing this book, I was as much concerned with why they weren't doing it as I was with why they were. I knew that kids fought back symbolically; articulating their dissent culturally, in their clothes, language, music, and attitudes. They looked for the truth in unorthodox knowledge, created autonomous spaces for self-expression, carved out a place for themselves on their own terms, and they survived.

The kids' role in directing my research was crucial, since the discourse of suicide as it pertains to young people has totally overlooked the social context they live in. While I could never "speak for them," I could translate. Since young people's experience of the world around them is largely discontinuous from that experienced by adults, the kids were my informants, consultants, decoders of cultural signs and symbols. Young people move within social enclaves, just like everybody else. The autonomous history of each new generation operates a lot like an ethnicity. Kids are a priori marginal. They live in a historically specific moment of their own, making sense of the world in new ways, different from the parental generation.

While kids are members of families and participate in other institutions organized and regulated by adults, they are also members of an emergent generation. They take their cues from their peers, they enjoy proximity to the newest knowledge. Kids select from and rely upon long-standing traditions learned and borrowed from the autonomous social history of youth. These histories are modified and mediated by class, nation, sex, and race, and are relative to economic organization.

As the kids in the 1990s move into the world, they will carry youth-generated "cultural capital" with them, tools and resources that can be useful for negotiating in the adult world—ideas, values, and assumptions that are gathered from prior generations, handed down through music, from elder siblings and cousins, television and movies and rock magazines. The 1970s and early 1980s are part of the collective experience of kids in the 1990s. There will be redefinition, reclaiming of past traditions.

By the beginning of the 1990s, young people began to demand some recognition as a social category, to present themselves as a self-identified collectivity, aware of their many differences, but bound together by one thing: age. Like every other minority, kids now call for more responsible media representation any chance they get.

Today's young people are not only trying to control media misrepresentation and adult misinterpretation of their activities and goals, they are fighting back. Many are engaged as activists—as fascists, anarchists, separatists, nationalists, feminists, and Greens. Some now struggle for their civil rights as homosexuals or petition for their reproductive rights, and also for the rights of the unborn.

While the world was enthralled by the spirit of young people in Beijing, China, some American kids also emerged as heroic. During the latter part of the 1980s, the nonhearing kids at Gallaudet University were American kids who spoke out in a hearing world that was not listening. Other American kids work to protect the environment or on behalf of homeless citizens, and for a livable wage. Some young people protest against cruelty to animals in cosmetics testing, in the fur trade, and in the animal Auschwitz of corporate meat and chicken farms.

It is true that many of the kids in America are alienated and apathetic. Often, just getting through the day may be heroic. And it is also true that like all Americans, kids bear divergent class agendas. They come in all shapes and colors, from different regions, with varied cultural histories and religious orientations.

There is much to keep them apart, to prevent the "baby bust" from uniting as a generation on substantive, not merely statistical grounds. Yet by the beginning of the 1990s, they were coming together. United against censorship, many are concerned about the erosion of civil liberties: their music, their right to free assembly. At the beginning of 1990, efforts to implement laws against "cruising" in some states and further restrictions on the accessibility of cigarette vending machines were added to the list of mounting constraints on young people's freedoms. There is increasingly much to draw them together on their own behalf. The eighties subcults that often segregated kids by race and class were also finding common ground by the 1990s. At least they did for a few days at a "gathering of the tribes" concert in California. Rap, metal, thrash, hardcore, and other assorted rocker kids came together.

At the Democratic National Convention in 1988, Jesse Jackson's son stood on the podium with his siblings and his parents and declared "My generation is coming." As we enter the 1990s, they have arrived. The time has come to welcome them.

V

It has become our habit to view the 1980s as a retread of the 1950s, and to equate the 1990s with the turbulent 1960s. This is a mistake analytically as well as socially. We cannot answer nineties problems if we frame them in sixties images.

Margaret Mead once described our culture as "prefigurative" because she believed that it was the child—not the parent or grandparent—that represented what was to come. In such a culture, one's peers must predominate because they are the only carriers of new understandings of the world.

It is the end of the century. Our world is changing rapidly, and in some ways, the kids do understand it *better* than adults. It is often the kids of the 1990s who carry the news. We have failed to acknowledge that. Many adult educators and "progressives," intellectuals who came of age in the sixties, find contemporary American kids disappointing. These "political correctness police" want the working class according to Bruce Springsteen, not Axl Rose; they love "the masses" theoretically while abhorring them socially and culturally. Believing some cultural practices are better than others, this self-appointed orthodoxy regularly dismisses and condemns American kids—"They never read."

But these same adults will marvel at the kids' prowess with video games, innovating style and sound, and computer technology. Everyone knows that if you want to know how something works, ask a kid. Often their manual dexterity and visual accuracy far exceed ours.

There will be no Marcuse to enlighten this generation. Often college kids don't read books except to cram for tests. Many young people do read, in or out of school, but books are now only one form in our country's vast knowledge-production network. To many, "electronic text" is as valid as static text (books, magazines). Videos, television, and film can no longer be dismissed as antiintellectual "low" culture. Mentalities are changing. We have to recognize this if we are to move forward.

But in the midst of all these massive transformations, kids still do need our help. In living everyday life, they need adults as allies. Talking about her relationship to adults, one eighteen-year-old from Selden, Long Island, remarked, "We'll be the ones running this country someday. You'd think they'd try and help us out." So far we haven't, but I think we can.

For baby-boom knowledge workers such as myself, it may be more useful to offer technical assistance to young people than grand explanations, to focus on local and concrete goals. As highly educated, credentialed adults, many baby boomers often have the power of knowledge and the knowledge of power. Wherever we may be situated, we can share that with kids today. Most adults only see young people in positions of subservience and submission: as their children, students, patients, clients, or else in menial service-sector jobs. We can offer young people something beyond domination, condescension, empty sloganeering, and "programs."

I always figured I would go back to Bergenfield someday. I wanted to see what went up in place of the Building, to show off my new tattoo. I missed the kids and wanted to know how their lives were turning out. But as I got more involved with young people in the town I live in, I realized my place was here, where I am known and trusted as a neighbor and a friend. By now, they are permanently part of my life.

It takes more than love to motivate people out of teenage wasteland. As adults, we control the resources and we make the rules. We can do things to help young people get ahead while we also help them to fight for better economic and legal participation. Wherever we are, we can offer support—at the workplace, in the schools, the community, and on the streets. Regardless of our own ideological convictions, we can help to empower young people.

At the local level, for example, some teenage girls may need prenatal care, some may need abortions. Young couples may need information about contraception. We can help them to locate the proper agencies, offer moral and material support. Another constructive activity is developing sponsorship networks with local employers. We can send letters of reference, groom kids for interviews, give them pep talks, follow up, and encourage their growth on the job.

Our children in our country are no less viable than young people anywhere else. They, too, must prepare for the global transformations facing us. We can enable young people, help them to develop their inner strengths as early as possible. By encouraging self-reliance, "peer interdependency" becomes a cooperative, productive activity, one that is creative, with positive outlets, not internecine effects.

We can empower kids by validating their perceptions of the world instead of dismissing or trivializing them. By creating arenas for kids to speak on their own terms, for themselves, we help foster their self-confidence.

At the political level, we can also fight to change the laws and practices that keep kids down. We have to question our assumptions about young people's unreadiness to participate in the world, to recognize and value their demonstrated competence. We can no longer assume that most kids will go on to college, or that our vocational programs are preparing them adequately for jobs. We can no longer expect American youth to subsist on below-minimum-wage "training salaries" because we can no longer take for granted that parental support is supplementing this income.

The kids' wasted years are based on the obsolete assumption that these years are preparation for adulthood. Often, they aren't being prepared for anything. At twenty-four, many kids still have the jobs they held in high school. They get married, start families, and are stuck in jobs that do not offer any growth or security.

We especially have to rethink the wasted years from seventeen to twenty-one, between high school and the traditional age of majority. We can find a more efficient economic organization to absorb our superfluous young people—those not effectively absorbed by the schools we created at the turn of the century for that purpose. In cities and in suburbs, American youth are being wasted, getting wasted, subsisting, marking time as troublesome artifacts. We speak of them as redundant. They have no place to fit in; by seventeen, many are stranded, dead-end kids, all dressed up for the future with no place to go.

In the information age, kids need real education, not banal, custodial schooling. In an ideal world, adults would provide "minors" with knowledge, skills, love, support, security, and care until they could go out into the world on their own. Parents can no longer bear this burden alone. It is a societal responsibility.

But we can't have it both ways. If we fail in our societal responsibility to our young, we have no reason to "protect" them with infantilizing rules and regulations. In a worst-case scenario, adults would recognize and admit that they are ignoring the needs of young people. Young people would be fully emancipated at, say, sixteen. The social organization of young people's time would revert back to what it was prior to the reforms that took place a century ago (labor laws, mandatory schooling). Young people could earn livable wages, vote, fight wars, drink, and be legitimately responsible for themselves. Many already are de facto, and some are de jure.

But if we renewed our social contract with young people, had a robust national policy for them, if American education and family life actually did prepare kids for autonomous living instead of warehousing and infantilizing them, the somewhat cynical suggestions above would not have to be articulated.

This is a book mainly about some white boys and girls who live in the nonaffluent suburbs of New York and New Jersey. Had my own life experiences and social location brought me into contact with kids in other geographic regions, with different social and cultural histories, I would still be looking at American kids engaged in a long, hard, sometimes futile struggle for dignity and recognition.

In writing this book, I wanted to say something to young people about the world they live in. I wanted to present a longer, broader view of the world in which the Bergenfield suicide pact was objectively possible.

But this book is mainly intended as a dialogue with other baby boomers, with my generation. Many of us are now making the laws. We are setting agendas for the kids at home, in school, at work. We have the power, and the choice to use it for positive motion. Some of us have lost loved ones to teenage wasteland; some of us have survived it ourselves. We know what is at stake here.

As "adults" we must also recognize that strategies now used by us to regulate young people are rooted in class struggle as well as intergenerational conflict. Rules were made to control people during large-scale societal transformations. Populations were moving around and the nature of production was changing. To some extent, this is happening again. We have to rethink where young people fit into this, and how we can integrate them, not alienate them.

Margaret Mead once said, "In the past there were always some elders who knew more than any children in terms of their experience of having grown up within a cultural system. Today there are none. It is not only that parents are no longer guides, but that there are no guides, whether one seeks them in one's own country or abroad. There are no elders who know what those who have been reared within the last twenty years know about the world into which they were born." She said that in 1969. It's still news.

For some time now, kids have been able to create their own meanings, to make sense of the ruptures of the social order. Despite the media porn, and the teen casualties, many contemporary American youth have gone a lot further with a lot less than others before them. They are stronger and braver for it. More than ever, kids now coming of age deserve our respect. They earn it every day. Remember, it is much harder to live up to ideals, to strive for excellence, to be moral, loving, and strong during decline than in ascendancy.

The twenty-first century promises a harmonic convergence in the resolution of cold war ideologies, racial conflict, and social inequalities. It also threatens war, disaster, and despair. This is what living in the world means. As we move forward, we are exploring new forms of economic organization, experimenting in new modes of production. We are rethinking the nature of the nuclear family, organized religion, the world order, and the fate of our most powerful technologies.

We don't know what's coming next: the most glorious or most hideous of human possibilities. Afraid to imagine the new, we hold fast to the old. Often we don't even know who or what we can believe in. Sometimes the world seems like a fragmented whirling mass, reeling out of control. We feel scared, angry, sad. We give up, we say we don't care, but we do. So we stand together, as human beings before us have done, and we survive, we get by.

"Life Ain't So Bad"

—anonymous graffiti
Garage door #74
Foster Village
March 1987

Afterword

Slamming Towards the Millennium

Youth in the 1990s

f they had survived, the four kids who died in the Bergenfield suicide pact on March 11, 1987, would now be between twenty-five and twenty-nine years old. They would have aged out of the statistical category of youth (fourteen to twenty-four). Ten years after the suicide pact devastated the small New Jersey town, Bergenfield has changed. The community has grown more ethnically diverse. The Building where the burnouts partied was demolished; a Pathmark Superstore replaced it. Foster Village Shopping Center got a makeover for the '90s, Have-A-Pizza closed, and ethnic food stores have cropped up along the Ave. Cooper's Pond was renovated, becoming more popular than ever, with police patrolling on a nightly basis. The 7-Eleven still offers kids a suburban rite of passage. The children of ZOSO, the burnouts I befriended hanging out, have grown up and aged out of street life. They got jobs, got married, had kids, and moved on.

By now, in Bergenfield as elsewhere, '80s thrashers and headbangers have been replaced by a new cohort of suburban kids inspired by hip hop, goth, rave, and alternative subcults. Marilyn Manson replaced Ozzy Osbourne and Judas Priest as adults' favorite scapegoat. New youth subcults emerged, incurring the wrath of adults, including some aging turnpike road warriors. On Long Island, white guys in their late twenties, "working men," still embrace their metal music, Harleys, tight jeans, concert T-shirts, and "old school" work ethics. Retired from headbanging, they show up at Motorhead and Iron Maiden shows with short hair and wives. The metal orthodoxy are appalled by "kids today," abhor the wiggers—white kids who wannabe black, "bad" and "down" in the "hood" with their "homies," riding in their jeeps blasting rap music, wearing baggy clothes, simulating ghetto slang. "These kids have no racial pride," the old guard will complain. Maybe it's just another trend. Or maybe it's something more—by adopting an underclass worldview, these suburban kids are slumming with the future in mind, embracing inevitable downward mobility before it embraces them. Borrowing "gangsta" styles from a segment of their own age cohort that has gained some adult recognition and fear, if not respect.

Today, as young adults, the baby bust is carving out a tenuous place in the social order. The 1990s slammed the middle strata hard. Corporate downsizing hit white-collar workers and professionals with the same ruthlessness as the exportation of jobs and local plant closings that devastated the working class in the 1980s. Parents became jobless or else overextended in eighty-hour work weeks. Family life was reduced to split shifts. The future of the professional-managerial class did not look promising. In the early 1990s, slackers emerged, a white, educated, overqualified, smug, cynical, undermotivated middle-class youth subculture, smirking at the prospect of no future, stunned into inertia. Slacker youths now seem determined not to be used and spit out as their parents were. The politics of refusal has taken a whimsical turn. Like the wiggers, slackers are trying on the clothes of the economic decline, a dress rehearsal.

As always, America's young people command the greatest share of adult interest and respect in their function as consumers. According to Rocking the Ages, the 1996 Yankelovich report on generational marketing, today's youths have $125 billion ready to spend on goods and services. The report describes today's "twentysomethings" as "the new pragmatists," hedging bets against a questionable future. Bound together, as all generations are, by the experiences of their formative years, "Xers are the most peer-focused generation ever." Whether in gangs or in dorms, in corporations or convenience stores, it is friends who matter most. The '80s latchkey kids have learned to look to each other for cues, not to adults. As Margaret Mead argued a generation ago, it is now the child, not the parent or grandparent, who represents what is to come. By default (parents are absent) and out of anthropological necessity (adults are clueless), the peer group emerges as the primary agent of socialization for the young—at school, on the street, in gangs, and on the Internet. The prefigurative, peer-based style of cultural transmission Margaret Mead observed in the late 1960s and I noted in the late 1980s appears to be accelerating.

Adults report feeling alienated from, and contemptuous of, young people. In *Kids These Days*, a 1997 survey conducted by

Public Agenda, adult respondents dismiss teens as lacking proper moral and ethical values. They view teens as "rude," "undisciplined," "wild," "disrespectful," and "unfriendly." The problem, though, isn't viewed as rooted in economic or even social conditions, but as an intrinsic flaw, a priori, something missing in the values and moral fiber of teens themselves. American adults view children as "spoiled," "out of control," "unhelpful," "unfriendly"—and they feel this way about rich and poor kids alike. After they finish blaming the young, most Americans lay the blame on parents. The majority do not think kids will make America a better place when they grow up. Adults do acknowledge that schools, media, sex, violence, and drugs are mitigating circumstances, but still, we blame the victim.

Young people continue to seek recognition, hoping to become visible and viable in the social landscape. In the 1980s, adults noticed youths as their suicide rates began to alarm us. By the 1990s, homicide replaced suicide as the second leading killer of young people, after accidents. Homicide rates, juvenile crime, and gang activity upstaged suicide as the focus of adult concern. In the early 1980s, 50 percent of the forty-four largest US cities reported gang problems. By 1992, the figure had grown to 91 percent, and the next thirty-five largest cities also reported gang problems.

Gangs are also spreading to nonurban youth populations, appearing in suburbs and small towns, even on Indian lands—remote, rural, impoverished. Nationwide studies indicate the number of Native American gangs has more than doubled since 1994. The Bureau of Indian Affairs estimates there are 375 gangs with 4,650 members, up from 181 gangs in 1994. The overall homicide rate on Indian lands has soared 87 percent in the past five years even as it has declined nationwide by 22 percent. Life on the reservation can be brutally isolating; some families are destitute, without hope. The alcoholism death rate for Native American youths aged fifteen to twenty-four is 5.2 per 100,000 population, compared to 0.3 for non-Native Americans. The accident rate, too, is higher for Native American youths. Their suicide rate is 2.3 times the corresponding rate for white populations, and their homicide rate, while about 9 percent lower than for all races combined, is almost twice the rate for white kids.

The Navajos are the largest Indian nation in North America, with 110,000 members living on 26,000 square miles extending into Arizona, Utah, and New Mexico. The Navajo Nation has fifty-five gangs with 900 members, who outnumber and outgun the police. Navajo youths identify with and idealize Latino gangs. Not only are the Latinos defiant pop culture icons, they are an hispanicized Indian people with visibility and street authority. Navajo kids are proud to be "down with the brown." Gang membership offers recognition, community, economic opportunity, and relief from the relentlessly remote geography of reservation life. Gang membership may temporarily lower suicide rates by focusing inward rage outward, but gangs are a suicide pact of another sort, a collective death wish, a peer-regulated willingness to die for the greater glory of colors and turf.

During the 1990s the media have continued to wallow in the social pornography of the day, generating images of young people committing heartless, heinous crimes. "A new generation of callous criminals?" asks *People* magazine. There's "Prom Mom," the eighteen-year-old from Jersey who delivered her son in the ladies' room on prom night, dumped him in the trash, then went back to dance. Even younger and more ruthless, privileged fifteen-year-old wiggers Christopher Vasquez and Daphne Abdela are accused of stabbing their forty-four-year-old drinking buddy to death in Central Park—thirty times—before dumping the body into the lake. Then there's the tragic twelve-year-old Malcolm Shabazz, troubled grandson of Malcolm X, who torched grandmother Betty Shabazz to death.

America has plans for its unruly youngsters. Uncooperative children of privilege are becoming the new growth market for psychiatric drugs—Ritalin, Prozac, Paxil, and Zoloft. In *Talking Back to Ritalin*, activist and psychiatrist Peter Breggin says, "Psychiatric drugs are the 'solution' of the 90's for dealing with kids in distress. From preschool to adolescence, children are being pushed to take psychiatric drugs—by school, by pediatricians and family practitioners, by psychiatrists certainly, and often by parents who are also overwhelmed by life and dazzled by experts." Breggin argues that "telling children they have ADHD [Attention Deficit Hyperactivity Disorder] and treating them with Ritalin is not only bad for their bodies and brains but for their morale and self-confidence." As we have seen, while middle- and upper-income kids get dumped into psychiatric hospitals, out-of-control prole kids and poor kids suffer a different fate.

While communities are hard-pressed to find resources needed to build teen centers, juvenile detention facilities are a '90s boom industry. This will bring jobs—from government contracts and a bureaucratic apparatus of administrators, child-savers, experts, and researchers who will document the whole thing. The Juvenile Justice and Delinquency Act of 1974 was designed to remove juveniles from adult jails. The idea of "kids in jail" had been declared a national disgrace. Youth advocates report children in adult institutions are 500 percent more likely to be sexually assaulted and 200 percent more likely to be beaten by staff than kids placed in juvenile centers. They are also more likely to be attacked with a weapon. While the 1974 act, originally scheduled to expire in September of 1997, has been extended, its future remains uncertain. In its place, the Juvenile Crime Control Act is proposed. It calls for mandatory prosecution of fourteen-year-olds who commit a serious violent felony or a specified drug offense including conspiracy or attempts to commit a crime. These cases must be tried in adult court. At the prosecutors' discretion, thirteen-year-olds may also be tried as adults.

Since the late 1970s a majority of states have already changed their laws to make it easier to try juveniles in adult courts. As the stresses of poverty are visited most heavily upon children of minority races, so will the punishment be. We now legislate kids into poverty, then legislate them into prison. A 1996 University of Florida study actually found that youths who are tried as adults commit new crimes at higher rates than their counterparts who stay in juvenile courts. Crimes are committed more quickly and are more serious. Adults monitor juvenile crime today much in the way we watched suicide rates in the 1980s. Suicide rates among young people never approached the magnitude of adults' rates, but there did seem to be a proportional increase in kids' rates, raising the possibility of an emerging trend. High-profile cases like the Bergenfield suicide pact and a series of clusters in the 1980s prompted adult concern. Similarly, in the 1990s, though more kids are killed by adults than by other kids, the proportion of kids killing kids has risen slightly. Alarm over this blip in kid-on-kid homicide rates legitimizes new regimes of social control.

The office of Juvenile Justice and Delinquency Prevention reports that from 1980 to 1994, 9 percent of people murdered in the United States were under eighteen. The number of juveniles murdered in 1994 was 47 percent greater than in 1980. Yet most kids were killed by adults, not peers—30 percent were under six, most beaten to death by parents or adult caretakers. Child protective service agencies received two million reports of child maltreatment in 1993; four in five perpetrators were parents. In 1993, 1,028 children were known to have died as a result of abuse or neglect. A recent Gallop Poll showed that only 13 percent of violent crimes are committed by juveniles. Other studies have shown that preventive programs can help lower recidivism rates among young offenders—after-school programs, teen courts, mentorship programs, cooperative partnerships, and community service. But there's no money for that, no provision in the new "get tough" laws to divert kids, to pick up the slack from bad schools, welfare "reform," and a national policy of neglect. Basically, this unspoken policy assumes that young people are responsible for raising, educating, and caring for themselves, and when they blow it, well, that's too bad, no second chance.

Suicide rates among young people have risen very slightly from 1985 to 1992, a statistic possibly more reflective of better reporting methods and greater public awareness than an actual rise. But the rate among black males aged fifteen to nineteen has shown an increase from 8.2 to 14.8 deaths per 100,000 population, bringing it much closer to the rate for white boys (18.4 per 100,000 in 1992). One explanation for this increase may be social mobility—suicide is a disease of anomie. Movement to a suburb or to college or a change in economic or social status could do it. If a middle-class black kid lives in the suburbs, he is more likely to commit suicide than a white kid who lives in an urban ghetto. In sociological terms, race as a variable is more likely to wash out when region and class are held constant. Researchers are now beginning to examine female methods of destruction. Suicide and homicide remain predominately male practices. Boys are more visibly slammed at home and on the street, into prison and toward death. But teen pregnancy, incest, rape, sexual abuse, psychiatric exploitation, and eating disorders are the constituent elements of female teenage wasteland. During the 1990s, the girlworld experience of psychic pain has moved from the private and invisible to the public and measurable.

While we adults hold young people responsible as if they were fully empowered, emancipated adults, when it comes to civil liberties we conveniently view young people as "children" needing our protection, guidance, and support. In recent years we have seen the rise of constitutionally shaky legislation affecting young people that would seek to impose curfews, force drug testings, enable search and seizure, block access to shopping malls, prevent cruising, limit the right to assemble, limit access to abortions and birth control, deny welfare benefits, and tighten up access to tobacco or alcohol. At the same time, public schools are overcrowded, safety nets are fraying, and the resources to nurture young people and protect them from homelessness, hunger, parental abuse, and poor health are getting slashed and burned.

The 1990s brought a psychic blow to the baby bust—the deaths of respective rock heroes. Kurt Cobain died of white boy disease (suicide), and Tupac Shakur of black boy disease (homicide). Yet the resilience and goodness of young people prevail. Most labor on in faith, holding fast to some remnant of the American Dream. They love and support their parents even as the labor force pulls families apart and the nation fails to support family life in any meaningful way. In terms of intergenerational politics, adults have no time or money for kids. The logical outcome of this disregard and disrespect should be violent rage against the machine. Instead, kids blame themselves, suffer sadness privately, show signs of widespread clinical depression. They act out the emptiness we have given them, hoping to fill the moral and spiritual vacuum with sex, drugs, booze, and commodity fetishes. Of course some American kids appear morally bankrupt—look who their role models are.

In the years after the Bergenfield suicide pact, alloy nation faded into the underground, great thrash metal bands got dropped from labels, and the popcult zeitgeist changed. Clothing styles, values, and scenes were transformed as the flannel hordes emerged from Seattle and grunge inherited the earth. Kurt Cobain was an alienated stoner kid who grew up in a trailer park in a small town outside Aberdeen, Washington. The product of a broken home, this lumpenprole hero not only made it out of teenage wasteland alive, he soared to the highest ground. Cobain was the Great White Hope for kids trapped in bad lives across America's nonurban wastelands. His triumph gave them hope, faith that you could be yourself, be human, and not get totally destroyed. In Nirvana, Cobain transformed a kid's private hell into a generation's collective howl. He wasn't supposed to blow his brains out at twenty-seven. But his inner agony won out over his band, his wife, and his child. Cobain's suicide anointed him as the baby bust's first celebrity martyr.

Young people fought back with style and grace. The 1990s brought exhilarating subcultural innovation, particularly among middle-class youths. Girls made forays into male-dominated genres of hip hop, hardcore, and metal. College-based "alternative" youth culture came above ground with grunge music. Slackers and bohemians congregated at coffeehouses and online at Internet cafes. Designer drugs, smart drugs, heroin, and alcohol continued to mediate lived experience. Despite adults' dismissing them as apathetic and self-centered, young people actively supported social causes, entered politics, and donated to freedom struggles across the world. Baby bust journalists Natasha Stovall, Evelyn McDonnell, Ann Powers, and Lorraine Ali gave rock criticism a fresh new voice. Kevin Smith, Harmony Korine, and Paul Thomas Anderson gave independent filmmaking new vision. Myths about a generation of slackers were eventually exploded as young people showed themselves to be pioneering, industrious, and bold in the marketplace. After years blaming underemployed, underutilized youths for their lack of motivation, adults saw that given some real opportunity, young people were eager to learn and earn.

In the 1990s, bands such as Hole, L7, and Bikini Kill brought new life to feminism, as journalists and scholars pondered "Women in Rock." Riot Grrrl fanzines and activities brought girls a new cultural authority. If females spent the '80s holding the boyfriend's leather jacket or watching band practice, rooting from the sidelines, by the 1990s they were doing it for themselves. With an agenda that let it bleed from the inside out, they articulated every female torment from anorexia to incest. Post-punk queercore music scenes set the stage for lesbian and gay kids to come out loud and strong. They found heroes in Ru Paul, Sleater-Kinney, Melissa Ethridge, Tribe 8, Pansy Division, Wayne/Jayne County, kd lang, and Ellen DeGeneres.

Like lesbian and gay kids, Native American youths suffer suicide rates two to three times higher than other kids. Blackfire is a Navajo punk band that walks in two worlds. Their music mixes traces of ska and hardcore with more traditional Indian sounds. A sibling trio, their father is a medicine man. As the Jones Benally Family, Blackfire and their father tour the world performing twenty-seven traditional and intertribal Native American dances in the hope of linking people back to their culture. The family dances in traditional hand-sewn garb, with eagle feathers passed down over generations. Born in the heart of "Big Mountain" Arizona, on the reservation, Blackfire rarely plays in bars; the group opposes the alcohol abuse that has devastated reservation life, land depletion from strip-mining of coal, and oppression and relocation of Natives. Concerned over suicide rates, gang-related violence, and alcoholism, Blackfire hopes to steer kids away from death culture and towards proud Native traditions.

Blackfire's lead guitarist Klee Benally says, "Our generation has a whole lot of anger. We can try to turn negative into positive, be productive. We can make the world a better place. It's all about respect. Respect is a big word in all disputes—you dissin' me? We all come from an indigenous culture, we all have spirituality. Who you are is passed down. All cultures have a basis in respect. We have to think for our children's world, how we want them to grow. Maybe we can teach our children." He believes schools today fail because they want to teach kids "what" they are, not "who" they are. "What they are in American society is consumers."

Young people hunger for meaning and connection as well as material things. The baby bust generation has been described as "the most socially pluralistic ever," multicultural, diverse, flexible. Actually, you can see this in America's '90s version of rave culture, where lines of gender, race, and class wash out to a sea of body-modified (bomo) androgynous celebrants. In a do-it-yourself scene that flourishes underground, peer orchestrated, here today and gone tomorrow, the fragmentation of postmodernity becomes creative expression. Dancing alone, together, on the grimy warehouse floor, to the pulsating bass-drum beat, on drugs that simulate ecstatic, holy communion, individuality within collectivity is realized. The connectivity and technological omniscience promised in the Aquarian age has arrived, not in us, as we suspected in the 1960s, but in them, now.

Worldwide, the baby bust is ascending. Like all rising generations, they carry the news, news that will ultimately render prior mentalities and technologies obsolete. As they accumulate resources and gain power and recognition, they are transforming the planet. With their technologically astute sensibilities, rapid-fire media savvy, global mentality, openness to adventure, and focus on the here and now, the first generation of the Millennium offers a glimpse of a glorious unseen future. A world of splendid possibility that we adults can barely imagine.